PLANNING IN THE
SOVIET UNION

PLANNING IN THE SOVIET UNION

BY
PHILIPPE J. BERNARD

TRANSLATED BY
I. NOVE

PERGAMON PRESS

OXFORD · LONDON · EDINBURGH · NEW YORK
TORONTO · PARIS · BRAUNSCHWEIG

Pergamon Press Ltd., Headington Hill Hall, Oxford
4 & 5 Fitzroy Square, London W.1
Pergamon Press (Scotland) Ltd., 2 & 3 Teviot Place, Edinburgh 1
Pergamon Press Inc., 44–01 21st Street, Long Island City, New York 11101
Pergamon of Canada, Ltd., 6 Adelaide Street East, Toronto, Ontario
Pergamon Press S.A.R.L., 24 rue des Écoles, Paris 5e
Vieweg & Sohn GmbH, Burgplatz 1, Braunschweig,

First English edition 1966

This is a translation of the original French *Destin de
la planification soviétique* published by les Éditions
Ouvrières, Paris in 1963

Library of Congress Catalog Card No. 66-14654

2523/66

CONTENTS

PREFACE TO THE ENGLISH EDITION ix

PRREFACE TO THE FRENCH EDITION xiii

LIST OF STANDARD ABBREVIATIONS xix

INTRODUCTION xxi

CHAPTER I. BACKGROUND 1

External Aspects of Economic Life 2
Setting for an Exchange of Views 12

CHAPTER II. CHARACTERISTICS OF THE SOVIET SYSTEM 20

A Collective Economy 21
Money and Commodity Concepts and their Role 27
Political and Administrative Organization 28
Territorial Divisions 30
The Party 36
Other Special Features of the Economic Structure 41

CHAPTER III. IDEOLOGY AND PLANNING 46

Meaning of Ideology 46
The Influence of Ideology 50
The Origins of Planning 55
The "Laws" of Socialism 57
The Transition to Communism 61

v

CHAPTER IV. THE PROCESS OF PLANNING 63

General Characteristics of Soviet Planning 63
Planning Procedures: Current Plans 67
Long-term Plans 77
Content of Plans and Product Classifications 79
Regional Planning 83

CHAPTER V. CO-ORDINATION OF PLANS AND DETERMINATION OF
OBJECTIVES 89

Co-ordination of Plans 89
Choice of Main Objectives 95
The Instruments of Planning: Norms, Balances and National
Accounting 101

CHAPTER VI. ECONOMIC ORGANIZATION AND ECONOMIC
HIERARCHY 108

The Sovnarkhoz Experiment: The Reform of 1957 108
The Sovnarkhozy: Organization and Functions 113
Consequences of the Creation of the Sovnarkhozy 118
Administration of other Sectors of Production 125
The 1962–3 Reforms and the Present Organization of the
Economy 131

CHAPTER VII. PROBLEMS OF ECONOMIC ADMINISTRATION 137

Problems of Distribution 137
Implementation of Investment Plans 143
The Need for Specialization and for "Co-operation" by Enter-
prises 146
"Success Indicators" 159

CHAPTER VIII. REGIONAL ECONOMIC POLICY   172

Basic Principles: Utilization of Local Resources   173
The Building Up of Regional Complexes   179
The Importance of Demographic Factors in Regional Policy   186
The Balance between Town and Country: Example of the
    Ukraine   189
Changes in the Geographical Distribution of Industry   195
Attempts at Decentralization   201
The Soviet Road to Development: The Example of Central Asia   204

CHAPTER IX. ECONOMIC EQUILIBRIUM AND THE SEARCH FOR
OPTIMIZATION   220

The Dynamics of Growth in a Socialist Economy   221
Growth Mechanism: The Effects of Technical Progress   224
The Problem of Efficiency in the Soviet Economy: Utilization of
    Resources   233
The Inadequacies of Enterprise Accounting   236
The Problem of Value and Prices   241
Calculations of Rate of Return and Investment Choices   247
The Use of Mathematical Methods and the Search for the
    Optimization   253
The Overall Efficiency of the Economy   260

CONCLUSION   264

Will the USSR overtake the West?   264
Attitudes *vis-à-vis* the Soviet Experience and Lessons of the
    Latter   279

POSTSCRIPT   292

BIBLIOGRAPHY   301

INDEX   304

PREFACE TO THE ENGLISH EDITION

THIS study, conceived as a result of a two-month visit to the USSR in 1961 for the purpose of investigating regional planning on behalf of the French Government Planning Office, is a broad and all-embracing account by a Frenchman of the observations which he had the occasion to make both in his discussions with Soviet scientists and his travels across the Soviet Union. As a guest of the Institute of Economics of the Academy of Sciences of the USSR he had the benefit of direct contact with prominent economists of the USSR and of their views on the many organizational and economic planning problems. Some forty-one interviews of a total duration of approximately 120 hours gave M. Bernard a good insight into the trends of economic thought and the objectives pursued by the government and its executive organs in planning policy. These discussions coupled with visits to various scientific institutes, factories, in addition to the casual encounters with the ordinary citizen, enabled him to gather impressions which bear the imprint of authenticity.

M. Bernard, before publishing his account on the termination of his mission, embarked on a thorough study of the Soviet daily and periodical press, the economic and political literature in Russian as well as in French and English published on the subject and the reports of missions which have preceded him. It is therefore the results of these studies, enriched by his personal investigations on the spot in 1961, that the reader will find in this book. As the author states himself, this book is intended for the average informed reader, and it may be added that it unquestionably furnishes a broad outline of the many economic and social problems which form the essence of Soviet thinking and planning.

The chapters dealing with the Soviet planning apparatus, its organization and administration together with the reforms which have been at work since 1957 will give the reader a very clear picture of the complexity of the problems involved. He will realize that these problems have not yet found a final solution and that the government is still battling with the concepts of centralization and decentralization, and in industry between a vertical and horizontal structure. In the author's view, the planning apparatus although admirable is still organizationally rudimentary. His recital of the many failures, bottlenecks, misconceptions and various other shortcomings in planning, although true, and cited before him by such eminent Soviet economists as L. V. Kantorovich, at times assume such proportions that they seem to mar the more fundamental aspects of government activity and the progress achieved.

The sections discussing economic growth, investment, location of industry, transport, manpower, use of available local resources, migration, etc., deal only in broad outline with the magnitude of these problems. Efficiency of investments, the choice of criteria, the problem of priorities, productivity in highly integrated units, rationalization, specialization and co-operation are all touched upon. The experience of regional planning in Central Asia is discussed at some length. But the author's views are that so far Soviet planning has not succeeded in establishing a balanced economy, although in its dynamics it undoubtedly presents a more balanced picture than any of the Western economies. This is true both as regards geographical location of industry, the policy of priorities which is perhaps one of the major factors of disequilibrium in the pattern of development and allocation of resources. Emphasis on heavy industry and the neglect of construction, agriculture and consumer industries, so marked up to recently, accounts for yet another form of disequilibrium, namely between income and consumption. However, in this respect, there appears to have been a shift of emphasis in recent times.

The author ascribes many of the weaknesses of the Soviet economic system to the difficulty of achieving a working "command economy", the failings of the incentives system, i.e. of the "success indicators" and the lack of an adequate prices system related to production costs at enterprise level. He does, however, admit that he looks at and analyses these problems from the angle of a Western economist whose approach and values are not those of the Soviet planners.

There are, nevertheless, indications of a new turn in Soviet economic thinking. Mathematical techniques and econometrics are finding followers with the increasing use of computers and problems of cost and yield as well as profitability in production and agriculture are receiving greater attention.

M. Bernard, looking at the USSR as an outside observer, does not think that the country gives the impression of a modern industrial power. Nor does he think that its standard of living has caught up with the West, not to mention the USA. Although unquestionable superiority may be recorded in the field of education, social services and even in certain branches of technology, the balance of achievements in comparison with the West is still modest.

Whatever the views of the reader, he will find in M. Bernard's book much to ponder about. Coming from someone with a large experience in the field of planning in his own country, M. Bernard's account and criticisms should prove particularly valuable to those who are or may in the near future be administering the planning apparatus of this country.

P. F. KNIGHTSFIELD (Dr. Econ.)

PREFACE TO THE FRENCH EDITION[1]

IN THE pages which follow, Philippe J. Bernard brings us the observations and reflections which are the fruit of a two-month visit to the Soviet Union: in the course of his stay, which took place in 1961, he was able to make contact with various teams of economists, both theoretical and practical. By virtue of his professional experience in the Organization for European Economic Co-operation, the International Bank and, of recent years, the General Commission for Planning, the author is well placed to make an informed judgement. We are grateful to him for his report, based in large part on direct evidence, concerning the state of Soviet economic planning as it was at the period covered by his visit.

In a very real sense, he has enabled us to take our bearings. Indeed, the methodology of Soviet economic administration is in a constant state of evolution, and the stage which it can be said to have reached at any given moment is never more than a transitory phase, so that any assessment which is made must involve some set of assumptions about later developments in the process.

At the time when M. Bernard visited the Soviet Union, Soviet planning was open to a number of very serious criticisms which, so far as we can judge, are still pertinent. The advantages of a centralized planning system, in other words adequate co-ordination of long-term economic decisions, accompanied by control over the hazards of trade fluctuations, are not disputed. On the other hand, overall productivity is undoubtedly much lower than it could be, owing to the indeterminate nature of economic criteria and also to the fact that the Soviet system still has no substitute for the various market mechanisms which operate in Western economies to provide the information on which production policy is based. These defects become increasingly

[1] The text of this edition has been brought up to date to the middle of 1964. A few footnotes have been added to take account of information received since.

apparent with the gradual improvement in technical progress and living standards, as production becomes more diversified, and must meet demands which are increasingly complex, and increasingly difficult to assess and to forecast in statistical terms.

These are problems of crucial importance for the future, and the Soviet régime will not be able to overcome them until it has at its disposal two essential instruments:

Firstly, a price system which correctly reflects the costs of production and trade, and on which economic calculations may therefore be based;

And secondly, a system of information which goes into the amount of detail necessary to serve as criteria for current decision-making, in the full detail of product assortment required by commercial practice.

It is obvious that all this is beyond the scope of traditional planning methods. In particular the details of the product mix which is required for current transactions are far too diversified in the work of planning and in the necessarily aggregated information flows issuing from the planning authorities. This is why the latter deal well—much better than in Western economies — with the major investment and production decisions which are big enough to be readily identifiable amid the aggregations, but there remain numerous inconsistencies and irrationalities in the details of economic life, particularly in respect of the satisfaction of consumer demand.

The working out of a price system compatible with proper economic calculations implies—if inconsistencies are to be avoided—that price interdependencies be simultaneously established. The result achieved automatically in a market economy —no doubt with many imperfections—may only be obtained in a centralized economy by the resolution of extremely complex econometric models. One must use a model in which there appear explicitly, if not all the price-linked interdependencies, at least the principal relationships between prices of the main categories of goods and services. Such models must be flexible, since the prices would have to be adjusted at frequent intervals to take into account technical progress and the resultant changes in the interdependencies.

The mere listing of problems to be solved in the process of setting up a system of centralized planning, at the present stage of its evolution, shows the importance of modern techniques of information processing. There is a good deal of evidence, much of it, unfortunately, rather vague, to suggest that the Soviet authorities are at present engaged in a strenuous effort to reshape their planning techniques to take account of the means of economic calculation which are now available, to them, and whose effectiveness has been so abundantly demonstrated in other fields. But all those who have attempted to use electronic computers as an aid to extending the area of economic information are aware that this kind of revolution involves a great deal of trouble and much preliminary experimentation. Such difficulties are encountered in the West, even when the problem is only one of gradually extending the bases of relatively small-scale econometric models. They may well be far more formidable in the case of the Soviet Union, where the task is one of setting up econometric models for the global study of an economy of huge dimensions. It is not surprising, therefore, that the results of their efforts are not yet apparent.

None the less, until this work has been completed, it is clear that the many imperfections and inconsistencies which M. Bernard describes must persist. In particular, until a reliable price mechanism is operating, it will be virtually impossible to extend the scope of economic calculation and, in a country as vast as the USSR, Soviet achievements will have to go very much beyond Western practice in this particular domain if an optimal solution to the problem of industrial location, and the related problem of transport is to be found.

In the light of these considerations, it is not hard to understand why the image of Soviet planning, as conveyed through the facts which are to be found in the following pages, is still so full of shadows. Will the shadows lift? It is obviously much too soon to say so, for we should be anticipating the conclusion of a creative project which is barely begun, and which is subject to all the uncertainties which are attendant upon any creative work. Any attempt at long-term comparisons with the West would also be premature. But since it is difficult to resist the very understandable temptation to make some comparison, however tentative, it might be said that, in a major confrontation between the methods of economic administration practised by the East and the West, the Western economies, although undoubtedly less beset by immediate difficulties of the kind which M. Bernard describes than their rivals in the East, are on the other hand prey to a fundamental weakness in that they are at present ill-equipped to make macro-economic decisions. By adopting the dangerous policy of giving priority to the elaboration of overall economic objectives, the Soviet planners obviously ran the risk of innumerable failures in their individual objectives. But by allowing the responsibility for solving problems in each market unit to rest with multiple centres of decision-making, the Western economies run the risk of creating inconsistencies of a macro-economic character, which there would be no means of correcting in the short term, even though decentralized decision-making operates under conditions superior to those in the East. In other words, the distance separating the two rivals is still too great for any prophecy to be made about the outcome of their rivalry. But the contest is on, and the West for its part will require, if it is to stay in the running, an immense creative effort which, so far, it has barely begun.

M. Bernard's lucid analysis is extremely thought-provoking, and should make a substantial contribution to the East–West dialogue.

CLAUDE GRUSON
Director-general of the
National Institute of Statistics and
Economic Research, Paris

"Si on considère l'URSS avec le regard ingénu que l'anthropologue porte sur les sociétés précapitalistes, on ne sera pas loin d'en parler équitablement, et c'est avec plaisir qu'on rendra justice à ce qu'il renferme de travail, d'héroïsme, de progrès . . . . On peut dire sans paradoxe que l'acommunisme est la condition, non seulement de toute connaissance de l'URSS, mais de toute critique moderne du capitalisme."

M. MERLEAU-PONTY
Les Aventures de la dialectique, Gallimard, 1955.

LIST OF STANDARD ABBREVIATIONS

Plan. Khoz.	*Planovoe Khozyaistvo* (Planned Economy)
Vopr. Ekon.	*Voprosy Ekonomiki* (Economic Problems)
Nar. Khoz. 19 . . .	*Narodnoe Khozyaistvo* 19 . . . (National Economy 19 . . . : Statistical Yearbook)
SSSR. v. tsyffrakh	(The USSR in figures: Annual Statistical Digest)
ISEA, G, No. . . .	*Cahiers de l'Institut de Science économique appliquée*, série G, No. . . .

INTRODUCTION

THE subject of Soviet planning is undoubtedly a fascinating one. Indeed, there is no present-day problem of greater importance than that of the economic rivalry between "East" and "West", between the socialist or planned system as exemplified by the USSR, and the capitalist or market economy system, or what might better be described, in view of the variations from country to country, as the non-socialist system.

Study of the Soviet economy, this system which has been developed over some forty-five years, after what is claimed to be an almost total break with the past, has now emerged from its "metaphysical" phase, when events could only be judged in terms of black or white, and an almost total and absolute condemnation or approval were the only attitudes possible.

This extremism has nowadays given way to a more balanced conception which recognizes the universal nature of economic science, and encourages the belief that study of one country's experiences may be of value to another. Particularly at a time when countries in the West are concerned with establishing, or perfecting, a system of economic planning known as "supple", "indicative" or "active" or again "concerted economy", or some system with similar aims but no particular designation, it is not only useful, but indeed indispensable, to know what to think of planning in its most extreme form up to date.

The debate is of interest not only to economically developed countries on one side or the other. In the drive for economic progress, countries the world over go through what are often difficult periods of experiment in their search for original formulae. Whatever one's attitude towards the Soviet experience, whether one seeks to draw inspiration from it, to safeguard against it, or to find an answer to it, one can no longer ignore it.

Far indeed from being more or less settled, the Soviet economic system is at present in a state of constant evolution. In recent years, certain far-reaching reforms have been carried out. These have not all been in the same direction, so much so that one sometimes has the impression that the Soviet authorities take a perverse pleasure in undoing today what they only barely finished doing yesterday. The reform in industrial administration and the creation of the "sovnarkhozy" in 1957, changes in planning procedure and the relative increase in enterprise autonomy, then the creation of the large economic regions, the sweeping changes in agricultural administration, and finally, in 1962–3, the reform in Party organization and fresh reforms in economic administration —all these changes show that Soviet planning is in a period of transition, and is still seeking its true direction.

The majority of these reforms are connected with the problem of centralization. It can justifiably be argued that the economic system of the USSR was for a long time the most highly centralized in the world. State-controlled enterprises and administrations could not, in principle, make any decisions outside the area of competence strictly laid down for them. The economy had to function in conformity with plans devised and elaborated at the summit, and transmitted through the economic body to the various branches or sectors concerned. In this way, the Soviet economy resembled a gigantic army, but one without any proper echelons or intermediate levels of command: the various lines of communication converged only at the summit, with the supreme command.

Under pressure of circumstances, this system has tended to undergo some modification. There has been, as it were, a dual tendency to decentralization or deconcentration, both on a geographical basis, and on the basis of units of production. But these changes have created as many problems as they have solved, if not more. Whether it was that the authorities sought to carry these reforms to their logical conclusions, or whether, on the other hand, having once begun they had to go further, a whole series of adjustments, reversals of policy, and new reforms were found necessary, none of which certainly ever reached full term. While it is true to say that, owing to the progress made in statistics and computing, contemporary economic trends lead to a "simultaneous emphasis both on centralization of decision-making and decentralization in execution"[1] and that the Soviet authorities are begin-

[1] Prospectus of the congress of TIMS (The Institute of Management Sciences) Paris, September 1959.

ning to be conscious of the need for this, yet it must be admitted
that the Soviet economy is still a long way from having achieved
this difficult synthesis. If only for this reason, a study of recent
Soviet experience must surely be instructive.

The present work is the result of a two-month visit to the Economics Institute of the Academy of Sciences of the USSR in
Moscow, which took place in 1961, and included journeys to
Kiev, Kharkov and Leningrad. The object of the mission en-
trusted to me as a member of the French planning office was to
study the regional aspects of Soviet planning. These terms of
reference, together with the problems of centralization already
mentioned, led naturally to an effort to assess the techniques and
the originality of the "Soviet development model". The forty-one
main interviews granted to me by one or two Soviet specialists,
often accompanied by their assistants, took me, in fact, far beyond
the original subject. I might say that each of these interviews lasted on an average about 3 hours: their length is partly explained
by the great courtesy of the people concerned, who never allowed
the visitor to feel that the interview was over, partly by the un-
certainty of the programme and the impossibility of knowing
whether, once an interview had been broken off, another one
would be authorized, and, last but not least, by the somewhat
erratic Soviet meal hours.

The material thus acquired was supplemented by study of some
of the numerous written sources available. In particular my research included several months' systematic examination of the
daily press; this is full of concrete examples of the principal economic problems and offers numerous instances of shortcomings
in the economy and its administration: these sometimes evoke
criticism from Soviet readers who are fearful of foreign reactions,
as witness the letter appearing in *Pravda* of the 30th March 1962
under the title "Must one wash one's dirty linen in public?"
Close attention was also paid, over a longer period, to the main
economic journals. My study of source materials was facilitated
by the very numerous translations or analyses now available
either in French or in English.[2]

This study does not claim to present a complete and detailed
analysis of all the problems facing Soviet economists or planners

---

[2] See attached bibliography.

at the present time: its aim is rather to offer to the average informed reader a balanced overall view of these problems. Certain
questions have perforce been omitted, or only briefly touched
upon, as, for example, the planning of external trade, of financing, of agriculture, wages and labour.

That the present work has been done in good faith I should like
to make clear to those Soviet officials whom I met, and whom I
wish to thank here for the patience and kindness with which they
answered my questions. I have particularly in mind one official
who, on the day of my arrival at the Institute of Economics, expressed the hope that any report which I might write would not
resemble the study produced by a Western economist, whom he
named and critized. Doubtless it will reflect, though how far I
cannot quite say, the principles, values, modes of thought of an
economist trained in Western methods. But is not this relativity of
judgement a general phenomenon, whatever the time or place?
At this present juncture, when so many efforts are being made on
all sides to reach a better understanding of what is being done
elsewhere, the economic systems of East and West are not only
very different, but are to a great extent designedly so. Despite
certain indications that it may some day change, present-day
doctrine in the USSR holds that co-existence of States is admis-
sible but not co-existence of ideologies. Failing any true *rapproche-
ment*, or other sweeping changes, if—as seems likely enough—a
greater degree of mutual tolerance were to occur, then a deeper
knowledge and understanding of the opposing system would become essential. It is hoped that the present work will contribute
towards such an understanding.

Among the people who received me in Moscow, some of them
on several occasions, I should especially like to thank Academician Nemchinov, corresponding members of the Academy Khachaturov and Nekrassov, professors or economists Feigin, Gatovski,
Luri, Maslov, Mstislavski, Notkin, Tokarev. I should also like
to thank E. I. Beliakova and G. M. Popov for their kindness.

In the course of my research, I have had assistance from many
quarters. I should like particularly to mention the benefits I have
reaped from teamwork with those groups engaged in studying
the Soviet economy in Paris, at the School for Advanced Studies
at the Sorbonne, or the Institute of Applied Economics. My
thanks are due especially to F. de Liencourt, E. Zaleski, B. Ker-

blay and H. Chambre, the two last-mentioned being research directors at the School for Advanced Studies, and M. Ferro and C. Makhrov, who were kind enough to read and comment on this work at various stages in its preparation. Similarly, I wish to thank Ch. Salzmann and Professors Piatier and Bettelheim for the interest which they have taken in my work. I should also like to mention the advantages gained from my many contacts with specialists or members of research missions, both French and foreign, who preceded me or followed me in the USSR. And, finally, I owe thanks to Mlle Z. Flipo and Mme T. Assanovitch for their help in analysing material and revising the manuscript. Responsibility for the opinions expressed in this book is, of course, entirely mine.

CHAPTER 1

BACKGROUND

THE vast territories united over the past few centuries under the power of the Tsars of Russia, which today make up the USSR, are distinguished by the great uniformity of their physical features. Their situation in latitudes where the Eurasian continent reaches its greatest extent from east to west, and their isolation from the temperate influences of the Atlantic explain their marked continental characteristics; the absence of any barrier to the north and, on the other hand, the existence of mountain ranges in the south further accentuate the rigours of the climate. Obviously, there are variations both in the nature of the soil and of the vegetation, which from north to south goes all the way from frozen tundra to steppeland by way of the various forest belts, and also in the climate, whose features are low winter temperatures and a level of precipitation which diminishes from west to east. But with the exception of certain fringes, such as the Black Sea coast, the Caucasus and the high mountain ranges, the uniformity is very marked; a journey in the interior of the country, in any direction, will reveal variations in climate and other physical conditions which on the whole are far less marked than those encountered, for example, in western Europe.

The uniformity of the landscape, which goes on repeating itself for hundreds and thousands of miles, and the very size of the country—a total area of more than 8 million square miles, and nearly 7000 miles between its two farthest points—lend it its peculiar features. As with the North American continent, there is a constant impression of distance and vastness. An illustration is provided by the night trains leaving Moscow for various parts: no sooner have these left the town than men are strolling along the corridors in pyjamas, all the passengers are chatting and getting to know each other, games are being organized; everyone is settling in for a journey which at best will last the entire night, but may well take several days, given the sedate pace of Soviet railways. At daybreak there is a grey glimmer of nondescript woodland interspersed with fields, marshland and villages of scattered wooden houses separated from each other by broad muddy paths; crossing the plains of Central Russia, one has the impression of a slightly more undulating countryside, with small woods not quite so regularly dotted over the landscape, and now and again ponds on which, even in winter, a fisherman may be seen seated on a stool fishing through a hole in the ice; in the Ukraine, particularly in the south-east, there are almost no trees, but very flat steppe, with large villages which, although still scattered and muddy, are rather more attractive. The railway line runs on a section about 100 yards wide cut through the surrounding woods or fields, for there is no shortage of land here, and the authorities need not use it sparingly.

EXTERNAL ASPECTS OF ECONOMIC LIFE

The outward aspects of economic life do not display the same degree of uniformity. This is a point which cannot fail to strike observers who are anxious to uncover the secrets of an experiment which has been going on for over forty years, and who have been prepared for the vision of a new world. However, the features which they find noteworthy are not peculiar to the system which has developed since 1917, but are also very largely a reflection of the earlier period, or in fact of sociocultural patterns peculiar to the peoples inhabiting the Soviet Union.

On the whole, the USSR does not convey the impression of a *modern* country, in the sense in which, under the influence of American civilization no doubt, the term is usually employed elsewhere. There is, of course, ample indication that the USSR is a great industrial power—to begin with, there are the rows of modern aircraft lined up at the airport—and nothing that one may observe while on the spot in any way belies the very real successes of Soviet science and technology, with its sputniks, its large factories and its giant dams. And yet, most of one's impressions are the other way round. In the outskirts of the big cities, there are to be seen a great number of low houses, mostly wooden, which could often be made to look attractive, except that the Soviet authorities usually seem to be ashamed of them, and they are for the most part in a very tumbledown state. There is considerable untidiness in general layout. On certain routes, whole areas of new buildings may be seen, while on others there is relatively little. The centre of Moscow and other big cities does not seem to have changed very much in the last forty years, except for the widening and rebuilding of a certain number of squares and avenues, and the overcrowded housing, though the latter is not immediately apparent.

The overcrowding is terrible—a total living space of 9·5 square yards per head of the population in the towns at the beginning of the seven-year plan, according to the statistics. Speaking with people one meets, one learns what this means in terms of real discomfort. In one old Moscow apartment (which consisted of four large rooms) one room was requisitioned from the family living there for a young couple with a child; the family (three generations, including a young couple and a friend) are now crowded into the other rooms, the total in the flat being over ten people; and yet this situation is a relatively favourable one. It is only fair to point out that since 1955–6 the rate of new building has speeded up considerably, and is at present very high.[1] But the growth in the urban population is such that housing conditions do not seem to have been noticeably eased, and in certain rapidly developing areas in the east (western Siberia, Kazakhstan) delays in building seem to be causing a deterioration in housing conditions in a situation where present living standards (average size of dwellings, volume of retail trade) are, despite higher wages, already 10–30% lower than the average for the Union as a whole.[2]

There is a striking sameness and lack of architectural interest in the new buildings, even bearing in mind the shortcomings of other countries in this respect. It is illuminating to note reactions on this score from Latin-American tourists or political refugees, who are surprised at not finding in the USSR a "new"

---

[1] Cf. on this subject, Conclusion.
[2] KORZINKIN, I. MATROZOVA, and N. SHISHKIN, On the redistribution of manpower, and its allocation to permanent work in the newly-developed areas, *Sotsialisticheski Trud*, No. 6, 1961.

country which, like their own, is eager to foster modern developments in architecture or the pictorial arts. Inside and outside, quality often seems poor; one sometimes sees portions of balcony, or other external decorations, missing from buildings which are only a few years old. Yet it must be admitted that, compared with countries such as France, more perhaps than with some of France's neighbours, the absence of private property and speculation probably makes for an easier solution of town planning problems; the new blocks lining the highways are regularly laid out, and empty spaces are set aside for recreation grounds and children's playgrounds. One notes, too, that the heavy, pseudoclassical style that was in fashion in Stalin's time is now on the way out; the models followed in some of the new buildings are now being discarded in favour of the more challenging forms accepted elsewhere, and in some of the architectural reviews a new spirit can be detected.[3]

Road surfaces often leave much to be desired. Private cars are few; there are scarcely any heavy lorries either, and the swarms of light lorries to be seen on the outskirts of cities are often loaded with a most disparate assortment of goods. The factories, which are situated fairly far apart in the outlying districts of Moscow, or massed in a dense concentration in the south-east and southwestern suburbs of Leningrad, or again more widely spaced along the roads leading east of Kharkov, do not resemble the modern factories in other countries, and there are indeed some extraordinary old factories to be seen in the very heart of the big cities, especially Moscow. Inside, these factories are not distinguished either for their modernity or rational layout, or even —insofar as one can judge from a brief visit—for their productivity, whatever the size or amount or power of their equipment. The many foreign engineers or technicians or scholars whom one meets in the course of one's travels, some of whom have had to spend long periods in the USSR, are a source of much corroborative information on this subject, in their respective fields. Likewise, the reports of French technical missions which have visited the USSR in recent years, while drawing attention to

---

[3] See A. BESANÇON, Isskustvo i arkhitektura SSSR: Deux lignes divergentes, *Cahiers du Monde Russe et Soviétique*, No. 4, 1961.

techniques or methods which they have found interesting, have been full of similar comments.[4]

This impression of a relative lack of modernity is even stronger when one observes the people. Nowadays we are all aware that one of the greatest achievements of the USSR, probably in fact the outstanding one, is in the field of education and science. The figures published tend to show that the numbers completing engineering or other advanced training courses, and the numbers of technicians specialized in various fields, are probably greater proportionately than those qualifying anywhere else, and that the number of people in production who have such a training already represents a very large proportion of the population.[5]

Certainly, from what one can observe in the USSR, there is no reason to doubt the accuracy of these figures. And yet, once again, immediate impressions all seem to point in the opposite direction. One's first vision of the Russian people is of crowds of men and women walking endlessly in the streets, the women in woollen headscarves, and almost none of them, men or women, with any trace of elegance in their attire. Motley crowds, often composed of families laden with bundles and seemingly prepared for a wait of several days, fill the station waiting-rooms and approaches, where all the diverse nationalities of the Soviet Union rub shoulders. However, only in a minority of cases are these migrants in transit. In Moscow incursions from the pro-

[4] See particularly the observations of the missions from the French Coal Industry, May 1958, published in *Annales des Mines* (pp. 677, 762, 1959) on chemicals (December 1959), on machine tools (December 1960), etc.

[5] In 1959 the total number of degrees granted in higher education in the USSR (191,000) was far in excess of that recorded in the USA (88,000); in particular, the USSR was ahead—sometimes by three or five times— in all the scientific disciplines, with the exception of mathematics, physics and biology (36,000 degrees in the USA as against 21,000 in the USSR). However, degrees seem to be granted more easily in the USSR, and the number of students is still lower than in the USA: only 12% of those of university age were actually in Soviet universities and institutes of higher education (only 6% if one counts full-time students alone) as compared with 25% in the United States. At the same period, the proportion of the total population aged over 15 which had received higher education was 2·5% in the USSR, compared with 6·8% in the United States, the latter comparison, of course, reflecting previous Soviet backwardness in this respect. (N. DE WITT, *Education and Professional Employment in the USSR*, pp. 341 and 440, National Science Foundation, US Government Printing Office, 1961.)

vinces are often explained by the existence of the so-called kolkhoz markets, to which members of collective farms come to sell their produce at prices higher than those paid by the State. The other reason is the priority in supplies of foodstuffs enjoyed by shops in the capital, plus the fact that it is forbidden to send parcels weighing more than 5 kilograms (at least so far as provisions are concerned) out of the city; therefore, there are numbers of people who come to the capital to shop as, for example, the man who had travelled to Moscow because his wife had been unable to find a coat for their small boy in the town where the family lived.

When travelling by train, one often sees large gangs working on the track, with women very much in the majority: even a rapid glimpse is enough to convince one that here are no specialists, or people of a very high standard of education. When I asked about this, a great effort was made to convince me that there was no longer, strictly speaking, any unskilled peasant labour in the USSR. Once, however, someone did admit that what I had seen illustrated a situation which still exists in the European part of the USSR; these were kolkhoz members who, during one of the many slack periods on the farm, were engaged in seasonal work, for fairly low wages and often a long way from their homes, on road construction or railway maintenance.[6] I was told that beyond the Urals this no longer happened, since wages were higher in Siberia and the labour force, which was scarcer, was made up mostly of young people. I was also assured that within two years, seasonal work by farm-workers, which was at that time still on quite a large scale, would disappear entirely.

From the point of view of the tourist, whose opinions are largely based on his experience of shops, restaurants or cafés, and the various entertainments available to him, there is a consensus of opinion that, theatres and concerts apart, Soviet cities, and Moscow in particular, have few attractions, and life there on the whole seems drab and difficult. The "parks of culture and rest" in which the "culture" basically consists of propaganda

---

[6] The average number of conventional work-days *(trudodni)* earned by kolkhoz members in recent years was only 210 per annum, which represents an even lower number of actual work-days.

hoardings with photographs and figures showing the country's latest achievements (even a child would ask his parents: "Where is the culture?") certainly provide an ever-welcome source of greenery, but are not very different from parks anywhere else. Anything in the way of service is generally slow and inefficient. Retail outlets are few in number, and the attention paid to customers almost non-existent, although staff are usually plentiful; queues are frequent, and the selection of goods inadequate.

It could be argued, of course, that in the Soviet Union work in production, and in industry particularly, is rated much more highly than work in commerce and the service industries, and therefore attracts the better elements. Certainly the level of wages in industry, and the prospects for further training and promotion seem to be much better than in the other sectors; in commerce and the service industries, they do appear to be very poor. Thus, the situation seems to be the opposite of that existing in the West, where in practice commerce, services and maintenance usually offer higher wages, and also better prospects of obtaining promotion or achieving much-desired independence. However, the present unfavourable situation of the service industries may very well improve, and the suggestion made to the young people of the Komsomol (the Communist Youth Organization) that they should take up hotel work, which was described as being just as interesting as any other, may soon produce results. On the other hand, it could be that the shop assistants' lack of politeness merely reflects the greater independence of the workers and may well conceal more positive human qualities.

Nevertheless, this is only a partial explanation. In reality the absence of politeness must be seen less as a result of the independent status of the worker than as the consequence of a lack of interest, an almost complete indifference to the job in hand. The reason is fairly obvious and is frequently condemned in the Soviet press. For instance, in the issue of *Ogonyok*, the leading illustrated paper, dated 3rd June 1962, one of the secretaries of the Moscow Communist Party tried to discover why inefficiency and even rudeness on the part of those serving the public were such a widespread phenomenon in the USSR; she came to the conclusion that the cause must be the absence in wage calculations of anything reflecting a personal interest in sales. The same is true in many other sectors, notably agriculture, and if industry seems to be an exception—although, as will be seen later, it still has its problems—the reason is precisely that since the time of the first five-year plans, piece rates and other payments by results have been widely used, to a much greater extent than in the West.

The fact that the USSR has not yet reached a stage where the private profit motive has been eliminated is clearly shown by the undeniable importance of the part played by dealings "on the side" and the "spekulanty", whom the tourist may encounter any evening in and around the centre of Moscow. In restaurants and other public places tips also play an important part, more so than in many "capitalist" countries.

Thus, many of one's impressions of every day life leave one unconvinced that a superior state of civilization is in any way imminent. Admittedly, quantitative changes may one day become qualitative changes, this being one of the principles of Marxist dialectics, but in the meantime it must be noted that Soviet claims about the evolution of "real" man, a new kind of individual, are far removed from the realities of life there. From what one can judge of the status of women, they seem to divide their energies between their domestic responsibilities and outside employment, and there is no indication that a happy compromise is more easily or more frequently achieved in Russia than it is anywhere else. If masculine egoism in the relations between the sexes is a thing to be condemned, it seems no less common here than elsewhere (this is a frequently recurring theme in propaganda). The proportion of women in paid employment is much higher than in most other countries, but this equality in the matter of work very often means that women are engaged in heavy tasks which they would not be expected to carry out elsewhere: a fall of snow will afford the spectacle of men specialists working the few machines which load the snow into the lorries, while an army of women are shovelling snow into the gutter. Many women do, of course, manage to fill highly qualified posts; they are largely predominant in medicine (80% of doctors are women) and in the teaching profession. But heads of departments are still in the majority of cases men, and certain professions, for example the diplomatic service or responsible posts in politics or economic administration, still appear either to be closed to women, or less open than elsewhere.

Despite the foregoing observations, there is no question of suggesting that the USSR, in its immediately visible achievements, presents a uniformly backward appearance. They have had many most notable successes. In the technical field, mention should be made of the quality and cheapness of the telephone service, the considerable spread of television, the excellent underground and suburban train services, the high level of sports facilities, pre-fabricated building techniques, and some achievements in the field of public works.[7]

On the social human level there are many more "positive" features in evidence. One of the most striking is the appetite for knowledge about everything scientific, as witness the number of bookshops and bookstalls, even in outlying districts, and the enormous amount of serious reading, which is particularly noticeable in the underground and other public places. *"Knigi* (books), *Knigi"* is a sign one sees almost everywhere. Queues for new books are a most striking proof of this appetite for reading. There was, for example, the queue which formed when the complete edition of the works of Dostoevsky came out in 1956 (there had been no edition for a very long time); it began early in the morning, and did not stop until the edition had been completely sold out a day or two later. Few works are available in the bookshops for more than a few weeks, or months, and this includes scientific works, despite the fact that they run into large editions. (Prices of course are also very low.) Enthusiasm for the theatre and other manifestations of "culture"—a word of fairly wide connotation, it would seem—is perhaps not quite so great as is sometimes reported, but is nevertheless striking. There is also, despite the still appreciable differences in living standards and in status among the various sections of the population, a considerable degree of ease in social intercourse among people of different backgrounds, and a relative standardization—levelling downwards, some might say—in manners, clothes and speech; all signs of a degree of social mobility which is undoubtedly very much greater than in western Europe.

And yet, alongside this ease in social relationships which undeniably exists in certain spheres, the factory in particular, there

---

[7] A French engineer did, however, remark to me that although the quality of Soviet steel is excellent, their concrete often leaves much to be desired.

is also a very strong sense of hierarchy. There is a big gap between "them", the bosses (the *nachalstvo*), and "us", the ordinary people; as a rule, a superior will use the familiar "thou" to his subordinate, who does not, however, reciprocate. Also, there is one problem which we should not omit to mention, since it is becoming one of the most acute in Soviet life today, although it cannot be described as the problem of a backward country; this is the problem of entry into institutes of higher education, which has arisen with the spread of education and the progressive raising of standards in studies, and in the examinations and competitions which determine fitness for such studies. Ideologically, intellectual and manual work are held to be of equal worth; it is further stated, as indeed the point was made to me during my visit to the Leningrad Institute of Economic Science, that degrees granted by all the schools, institutes or faculties which in principle follow the same programme, are of equal standing and afford their holders identical career opportunities; this is manifestly the very reverse of true. All the members of the Soviet intelligentsia try to ensure that their children will get places at the best institutes, or, at a pinch, any institute at all, so as to preserve them as far as possible from work in "production" and to keep them in Moscow or Leningrad, thus severely straining the principle of equality of opportunity for all.[8]

This very rapid review of some of the features of Soviet life would not be complete without at least a brief reference to certain behaviour patterns which might be regarded as characteristic of the Russian people. On this rather complex question, I shall confine myself to just two examples.

The first is a limited propensity to order and good organization. In this respect, the attitudes which one notes in the Soviet Union at present are very different from those of the Anglo-Saxon and Germanic peoples, or even of the Latin peoples, of whom it has

---

[8] This problem runs like a thread through a great deal of contemporary Soviet literature, often in the form of a contrast between the decent provincials who try to find a place in the institutes by going through the proper channels and, if they fail, go back to work in production, and the children of influential parents, for whom strings are pulled. See particularly the comedy "Good luck" (Dobry chas) by V. Rozov (*Teatr*, No. 3, 1955). See also A. Kuznetsov, *L'étoile dans le brouillard* (Zvezda v tumani), French translation (subject to controversy) by P. Chaleil (ed. Vitte), Lyons, 1958.

traditionally been said that their talent for improvisation goes some way towards excusing their disinclination for discipline.

Far be it from me to deny that great efforts are made in the USSR to keep promises, to meet deadlines, to apply rational methods, to see that the population observes some sort of discipline in matters of hygiene and social ethics, or that these efforts are now meeting with some degree of success: the whole of "socialist construction" may be regarded as being directed towards this end; many of the "tough" features of Leninism might be explained as a struggle against *oblomovshchina* (from Oblomov, the hero of Goncharov's novel of the same name who spent all his time in bed). Nor is it suggested that discipline is repugnant to the Russians, or the other peoples of the Soviet Union, since one of the constant, dominant elements in their behaviour pattern seems in fact to be a desire to conform, to be well-integrated into the social group, to be united as a people and to apply themselves single-mindedly to the tasks assigned to them.

Left to himself, however, the individual seems to have a natural propensity for ignoring the rules, letting things slide and acting, not entirely without reflection, but without very much practical forethought or organization. Furthermore, the desire to conform by no means embraces all aspects of social life. There is at present among the young a very strong anti-conformist trend which is not confined to the *stilyagi* or to pure intellectuals. The diversity and originality of human types in the Soviet Union appears, moreover, to be very great. If on the whole this is a help when it comes to the almost mystical belief in the limitless possibilities of science and organized human effort, it is nevertheless something of a hindrance in everyday life.[8a]

The second peculiarity is the relative indifference of the population to material possessions. Here again, there is, of course, no suggestion that the inhabitants of the Soviet Union are not interested in the conditions of their daily existence, or that various ways of life or consumer goods that are available in the USSR or elsewhere do not hold out their attractions. Nevertheless, perhaps because of the lesser degree of security in their possessions, there does not seem to be such a strong sense of attachment to

[8a] cf. K. MEHNERT, *The Anatomy of Soviet Man* (Der Sowjetmensch), Weidenfeld & Nicholson, London, 1961.

them as can be observed among other peoples; or again, it may be that there is a greater interest in making or acquiring goods than in the actual enjoyment of them. No doubt this is not so much a feature of the régime as a trait of the Russian character, perhaps that "sense of eternity" of which Dostoevsky speaks.[9] In fact it is very possible that individualism, which is regarded as a "survival of capitalism" may tend to increase rather than diminish with the gradual building of communism.

SETTING FOR AN EXCHANGE OF VIEWS

The USSR does not exist in a vacuum. However, although it has many points of contact not only with the countries of the socialist "bloc", but also with the rest of the world, the differences which separate it from the latter are none the less striking. What then are the relationships between representatives of both blocs and, since we are concerned with economics, between Soviet and Western economists, and in what direction should these relationships develop? I should like to offer some observations drawn from my experiences during my visit in 1961; I do not claim any particular originality for them, but offer them simply as facts which came to my notice.

An economist, and especially an economist on his own, may come up against a certain reserve (this is natural, given the subject in question; is it not still described, particularly in the USSR, as "political economy"?) but he is none the less received with courtesy, and contacts with Soviet colleagues can be relaxed and pleasant, since the interest taken in his visit is certainly very great. But it frequently happens in the course of a conversation that a word uttered quite innocently, or some retort made by one side or the other to what has previously been said may, without necessarily endangering these cordial relationships, touch on a side issue, and suddenly reveal the extent to which the parties differ over interpretations of facts as well as of economic systems. In most cases the visitor has little doubt but that these differences are mainly due to inaccurate information or lack of information on

---

[9] In an essay which appeared in the review *Vremya* (Time) in 1861.

the part of the officials he is interviewing. It may, however, be worthwhile to reflect on some of these divergences.

On the basis of the "positive" and "negative" features noted above, it ought to be possible to conduct an exchange of views in a fairly detached manner, but experience shows how difficult such exchanges can be. One of the first things one notices, in interviews with Soviet citizens, especially if the person in question is not in a very senior position, is the existence of a sort of double defence mechanism when it comes to comparing the two systems, or even simply to discussing the achievements of the Soviet Union. By open, or implied, criticisms of capitalist economies, or simply in his way of presenting the achievements of the socialist economy, the other party to the discussion may sometimes appear to by asserting the *de facto* superiority of socialism. But since, at the same time, he usually makes no bones about admitting that there is still a very marked superiority in living standards in the Western world, or that the Soviet economy has at present many imperfections—this has been admitted at the highest level since the death of Stalin—one sometimes finds him taking a different line: that the Soviet society is better because its principles, its ideals—sometimes represented simply as those of a society where there are no longer rich and poor—are better. Conversely, there can be no kind of future for a society characterized by the "anarchy" of unplanned production, or a principle as revolting as that of "profit", to say nothing of the "law of pauperization" which may be quoted at the visitor in very official quarters. Or again, the argument sometimes runs, Soviet society is better simply because it wills itself to be so. If present achievements do not seem to bear this out, one is referred to planned objectives. By means of a syllogism, whose first two terms are that the socialist economy is a superior form of economy, and that the Soviet economy is a socialist economy, the superiority of the Soviet economy over all other economic systems is thus proved. Naturally, this shift from direct observation to rhetoric which, even among the most sincere, often seems to be quite unconscious can, when it happens, make an exchange of views very difficult, if not impossible.

This sort of attitude impels the Western economist, whatever his personal standpoint, to formulate a whole series of questions. Generally he does not put these openly, for fear of becoming involved in endless debates, or giving needless offence, experience having taught him how difficult it is to ensure that even his intentions will be correctly interpreted. But his discussions do give him grounds for surmising what the replies would be. The striking thing is that the questions that follow do not seem to occur to Soviet minds. Does there not still exist a great discrepancy between the country's avowed ambitions, or those successes which have already been achieved in the form in which they have been claimed, and the realities which every citizen can see for himself? Tangible though they undoubtedly are, have these successes not been bought in some cases far too dearly or, to put it another way, do the inadequacies and weaknesses of the system not tend to outweigh these successes? The answers to these questions need not necessarily be in the affirmative, but one should at least, I would think, be able to raise them.

Furthermore, in a country which admits its imperfections, openly avowing them both in the press and in statements from the most official sources, why is there such vehement criticism of what is done in other countries whose methods are different? How is it possible to quote some method or achievement of the capitalist countries as a standard, or a model to be copied, and then the very next day to denounce these same countries for being irrevocably wedded to crises and decadence? How can they not see that it is illogical to insist on attributing every achievement of the Soviet economy to the existence of a socialist system while simultaneously envying the achievements of Western economies and denying that these are in any way due to the economic system in force there, or asserting, as I have heard it asserted, that such economies have nothing to teach and cannot serve as an example except at a purely practical level? Why the insistence on catching up with the United States, the very model of supercapitalism, which cannot by definition be regarded as an ideal? Has the United States, which is the home of capitalism in its most dynamic form, ever troubled in the past about overtaking and outstripping those old European societies which were the symbol of a former feudalism? How, too, can men who suffered so much from the last war and who seem so sincere in their desire to prevent the outbreak of another one, not realize what dangers and provocation are inherent in this attitude of total condemnation, when what they describe as "peaceful competition" is in fact aimed at the actual elimination of the opposing system? Not one of these questions would seem even to have crossed the minds of most of the Soviet specialists whom I was able to meet, judging at least from what they said.

Nor does the average Soviet economist appear to be in any way concerned with questions having a bearing on the universal validity of the Soviet model. It is not unreasonable to reflect that, given the backwardness of Tsarist Russia, and the socio-cultural characteristics of the Soviet peoples, the political and economic régime which was established has answered a real need and has yielded results which can be described as remarkable, but that the degree of success which would attend transplantation of this model to another environment is quite another question. Because merchants have never been very popular in Russia, and the mass of the people never very much given to thriftiness, foresight and calculated initiative, does this justify making it a universal rule that no individual or group of individuals should run an economic undertaking or, through the exercise of free will on the market or in the political arena, exert any influence on the evolution of society? It could also be argued, as supporters of the market economy often claim, that the Soviet method of economic development is only a cruder version of methods which have been perfected elsewhere, that it can at a certain stage produce rapid results but that these will tend to become less effective with the passage of time, unless the method itself undergoes fairly radical changes.

However, Western economists, whose personal viewpoints may, as we have said, vary widely and who may, on certain issues, be severely critical of their own country's performance, find not only that such questions are not asked, but that even the standards on which they would base their judgements are rejected. These standards, which more or less broadly reflect the trends of Western development, could be said to include, firstly, the level of material achievement, as shown by the national income and individual living standards, and its improvement. Secondly, there is a certain idea of social justice, exemplified by a relative equality of opportunity and conditions, and the absence of too sharply defined class barriers, or even their disappearance. Finally, there is the proposition that only the individual himself can determine what is for him the ultimate good, which means that the desires of the individual in terms of consumption or self-fulfilment are the real criteria: everyone must be free to choose the way of life which suits him, to join the opposition, to strike, etc., without thereby ceasing to be a part of organized society.

Whereas the third of these three principles has no place in the Soviet model, the first two seem to be common both to the Soviet and the Western models. For this reason, the visitor from the West feels that he has been transplanted to an environment which, for all its alien features, is not radically different from his own, but in which he may trace the logical outcome of many traditions and endeavours which have been common to Europe in the course of the past few centuries.

Helped by these principles, he will note, as one of the positive features of the system, the opportunities for obtaining higher education and managerial posts which are afforded to persons of all conditions. But he will also note that living standards are still lower than elsewhere, that freedom of choice for the citizen or the consumer is almost non-existent and that there is still a very great inequality in living conditions, in spite of the narrowing of wage and salary differentials which has taken place in recent years. Nevertheless, when engaged in discussions with Soviet officials, he will be disconcerted to discover that his criteria, which he considered universal, may not only be disputed on some point or other, but simply rejected outright. "Judge the Soviet régime for what it is, or would like to be," the argument may run; "this is how we should proceed if we found ourselves in a similar situation, having to pass judgement on a Western society," they may add, though the logic of this argument is not immediately clear. "I am freer than you", he may sometimes even be told, this being a reference to the bourgeois idea of liberty which, from the Marxist standpoint, can only be understood as a screen for the power wielded by a minority. Thus, if one can judge from its spokesmen, the Soviet régime seems anxious for approval, but at the same time unwilling to recognize any criteria other than its own. The visitor who has been prepared to accept a situation *à la Pirandello* in which everyone has his own conception of truth will find that, while he himself is prepared to make allowances for the other man's point of view, there is little likelihood that he will be repaid in the same coin.

How is one to interpret these attitudes? First of all, they can be explained simply as a ritual gesture, lip-service paid to a lesson which, after all, all Soviet citizens learn at school, and must go on repeating for the rest of their lives. Many visitors from the West, who have succeeded in establishing close relationships with Soviet citizens with whom they have been in contact over a long period, have found that there may come a moment when all pretence at maintaining this façade is dropped; even in the course of journeys, or even briefer contacts, it is possible to experience one of those "moments of truth" when, either overtly or implicitly, one's companion suddenly adopts an attitude or makes a statement which could not be more unorthodox. The tendency to accept such an interpretation may be all the stronger because Soviet ideology, since the events of 1956, has lost much of the attraction which it long held for many Western Europeans, and it is tempting to suppose that before long it may be little more than an empty formality in the Soviet Union also.

There would seem to be little doubt that the USSR has a ritual language which, although somewhat esoteric, nevertheless has some significance, and that problems of ritual occupy an important place in Soviet life, as did certain traditions in the old Russia.[10] But it does not necessarily follow that the attitudes we have been describing are entirely artificial, or bear no relation to the real feelings of those who adopt them.

In practice these attitudes are no doubt indicative of the great self-confidence of a people who know they are powerful and believe that they are good and, at the same time, of their great sensitivity to criticism; or again, they may be an example of this dissociation of attitudes which has long been noted by certain students of Russian affairs. They may likewise be regarded as a manifestation of the tendency to extremes which is supposed to be typical of the Russian character. But perhaps the simplest explanation is that they stem from the inadequacy and the deliberately misleading nature of the information available to the general mass of the people, and also from a deep mistrust of

---

[10] See F. DE LIENCOURT, Les intellectuels soviétiques, du stalinisme au khrouchtchevisme, La Nef, January–March 1962. Ritual manifestations of this sort often appear as a kind of exorcism of some characteristic usually attributed to the "bourgeois" world and its appendages, hence the term *protivism* (from protiv=against) to describe them, suggested by Lewis S. Feuer, in his article "Meeting the Philosophers" (*Survey*, April 1964).

outside opinions. This may be justified to some extent, in view of the attitude of relieved conscience which seems to be the most usual one among Western visitors to the Soviet Union, once their period of acclimatization is over, such an attitude being itself, of course, provoked by the smugness and intolerance of Soviet judgements, public and private, about other countries, much more than by actual experience of Soviet life.

One man in a very senior position with whom I talked—a most courteous individual—tried to justify this mistrust, which he admitted did exist, by the dishonesty or ill-will of a certain number of Westerners with whom Russia, or the USSR, had had dealings. When pressed to give an example he quoted M. de Talleyrand, an odd example to say the least, for history scarcely seems to bear out that this gentleman did any harm to Tsar Alexander's interests. Of all the examples which came to mind, I was strongly tempted to quote back at him that of a certain secretary-general of the Communist Party and Marshal of the Soviet Union: there may be Soviet citizens who regard the posthumous condemnation of Stalin as an act of courage, but there are very few indeed who will admit that it does lend some justification to past or present attitudes, judgements, or actions by foreigners, when it comes to criticizing or opposing the Soviet Union on some issue. Blood is thicker than water, and many Soviet citizens thus find themselves waging war on two fronts.

These then are, broadly speaking, the conditions in which an exchange of views may have to be carried on. Naturally, progress in mutual knowledge and understanding must inevitably be slow and difficult, but it is undoubtedly being made bit by bit. The foregoing remarks should not be taken as implying that no interesting exchanges are possible from one side or the other. A visitor like myself, going to Russia under the auspices of a body such as the French planning organization—that is, an organization whose very existence is some proof that it is possible to stabilize and stimulate one's economy while still retaining the most obvious advantages of a market economy—is certainly in a good position to confirm the possibility of such exchanges, judging at least from the curiosity aroused by my visit, and the number and range of the questions which I in my turn had to answer. I might add that Soviet officials sometimes appear disconcerted when they meet with a degree of conviction as strong as their own, and that they become more amenable to discussion when it seems to them to be based on rationality and a long-term view, to which they themselves seem to attach such very great importance.

CHAPTER II

CHARACTERISTICS OF THE SOVIET SYSTEM

SINCE the political and juridical system of the Soviet Union differs widely from that of most other countries, it is important to recall first some of the general features of this system as they are at present; we shall pay particular attention to those aspects which have the greatest bearing on economic organization.

The preamble to the principles of civil legislation of the USSR and the Union Republics adopted by the Supreme Soviet in December 1961[1] defines the present Soviet economy in the following terms:

> During the period of the building of socialism, the economy is based on socialist ownership of the means of production in the shape of State (public) property and collective ownership of co-operative farms. The latter will gradually draw closer to State ownership until a unified form of communist public ownership of the means of production has been achieved.
>
> Personal property derives from social property, and is one of the means of satisfying the needs of citizens. With the advent of communism, citizens' personal needs will to an ever-increasing extent be satisfied from public resources.
>
> In the building of communism, full use is made of the concepts of money and marketing, in conformity with their new role in a planned socialist economy, and major instruments of economic development, such as accounting, money, prices, cost, profit, trade, credit and finance, are utilized. The building of communism is founded on the principle of the material incentive of citizens, enterprises, collective farms, and other organizations.
>
> The Soviet State exercises planned control over the development of the national economy of the USSR, in accordance with the Leninist principle of democratic centralism. This is accompanied by further reinforcement and development of the independence and initiative of enterprises and other economic organizations in respect of management and ownership, and extention of their power within the framework of a single national economic plan."

[1] Text from *Izvestia*, 10th December 1961.

A COLLECTIVE ECONOMY

The chief characteristic of the Soviet economy is public ownership of the means of production. Private ownership of the means
of production is, according to Marxist theory, the principal characteristic of the system known as "capitalism", and it is this feature
of capitalism which was so widely condemned in Marxist analysis.
Nationalization of the means of production, although it often
took the form of emergency measures, goes back to the very
first days of the October revolution of 1917.[2]

In industry, implementation of this principle is now almost
universal. To maintain it, however, constant vigilance is required.
For example, *Izvestia* of the 2nd December 1961 reported the
discovery, in the cellar of a Moscow house, of a well-fitted workshop equipped with machines for the manufacture of lipsticks.
The "industrialist" in question, with the assistance of three
members of his family, had managed to buy cases from a factory
in Riga (at least 59,000 for the year 1960) and was making,
assembling and reselling the lipsticks; needless to say, the various
participants in this venture all ended up in prison.

In the handicrafts industries, there is still an individual sector
legally operating, though it is in fact very small. Until recently,
there was also a fairly sizeable co-operative sector, the *artels*,
where there are, in principle, no employees. In 1960 these artels
were abolished. For example, in the Leningrad *oblast* (province),
as I learned when I visited its executive committee *(oblispolkom)*
there were some 300 co-operative enterprises which had at that
time been made into State enterprises. The reason given for this
step was the difficulty of finding a proper place for the artels in
the plans for the distribution of raw materials, for the artels in
fact mostly used industrial scrap and waste materials, which
left them at a disadvantage; membership of a State enterprise
would, I was told, ensure them a better supply. There does however appear to be some effort to encourage certain forms of
craftsmanship (art handicrafts). The weakness of the artisan

---

[2] Confiscation of large estates on the 26th October (8th November) 1917,
nationalization of the land on 25th January (7th February) 1918, overall
nationalization of large-scale industry on the 28th June 1918. For the various
stages, see E. ZALESKI, *Planification de la croissance et fluctuations économiques en URSS*, ch. 1, vol. I, 1918–32. (ed. SEDES), Paris, 1962.

sector probably goes a long way toward explaining the scarcity or poor quality of the most ordinary goods and services which one encounters in the USSR.

In agriculture, implementation of the principle of public ownership is still much less complete. The land is collectively owned, but it may be farmed either by State farms, the sovkhozy, whose staff are wage-earners, or by the collective sector, the kolkhozy, which covers most farms, and whose members' pay depends both on the income of the kolkhoz and on their own work. In addition kolkhoz members also work individually on the private plots attached to their homes. Each kolkhoz family is entitled to work a piece of land of from 0·25 to 0·50 hectares, according to the region, and to own a few cows and other domestic animals (whose number also varies according to the region). Sovkhoz workers also own livestock, and until recently some three million town dwellers were likewise engaged in livestock raising.

Dairy cows and small livestock (fowl, pigs and sheep) account for most of the private ownership. The huddle of small wooden izbas with a small shed for the cow at the back of the house, is a familiar feature of the Soviet countryside. On the outskirts of towns, especially Moscow, where there is no room for cattle, one may often see poultry kept in small enclosures. In 1959, on 4% of the total area of land cultivated, private owners possessed 41% of the cattle, 57% of the cows, 36% of the pigs; they accounted for half the milk and meat production, and 54% of the total cultivation of potatoes and vegetables. Allowing for purchases of grain and fodder by the peasants, it is generally estimated that in 1955 the value of production from the private plots was 30% of total agricultural production.[3]

In agriculture the struggle to keep the public sector uppermost is a particularly difficult one. "Depredation" of communal resources by kolkhoz members bent on private production has repeatedly been denounced in recent years by N. S. Khrushchev. A report on agriculture in the Kemerovo oblast (western Siberia) contained a remark to the effect that "kolkhoz sheep die, but

[3] *Comparisons of United States and Soviet economics* (Economic Committee of the US Congress) Part I, November 1959, p. 206; J. CHOMBART DE LAUWE, *Les Paysans soviétiques* (ed. da Seuïl), p. 142, Paris, 1961. It is also noted that roughly 80% of eggs are produced on the private plots.

the private ones do not even sneeze", and denounced the methods used by an assistant brigade leader to increase the number of his private livestock in what was apparently a perfectly legal manner: he had divided his house — and his family — in two, thus providing the unusual spectacle of ten pigs feeding at the same trough, and four cows in the same shed.[4]

For some years now, a fresh offensive has been going on against private agricultural production by Soviet citizens, which is condemned as a "contradiction" within the collective farm, or in the relationship between the collective farm and the State, and which should therefore be abolished.[5] A decree of 1st October 1959, as a first step, forbade livestock raising in the towns. In addition an effort was made to effect the transfer of dairy cows from private ownership to the collective. The result was that, whereas from 1956 to 1959, the number of cows had increased almost as much in private holdings (3·6 million) as in the collectives (4·5 million), from 1959 to 1963 the numbers fell sharply in the first category (from 18·5 to 16·1 million) while they continued to rise in the second (from 14·8 to 21·8 million).[6] It was said that this change should not be brought about by force; an effort should be made to ensure that livestock products on the collective farms cover all the needs of the members, so that there would no longer be any economic advantage to be gained from activities in the private sector, and these could, therefore, be given up.[7]

Looked at in this way, the problem is somewhat similar to that of the "worker-peasants" in many parts of western Europe. In the model sovkhoz near Kharkov which I visited in 1961, I was told that the transfer of dairy cows from private to collective ownership was in fact the result not of coercion but of an attempt at persuasion and the use of economic incentives, consisting of a very low price for milk supplied to kolkhoz and sovkhoz members, and an even lower price for milk bought from them. It is not, however, quite clear what is really meant by persuasion. Without taking sides on this issue, it should nevertheless be pointed out that the stepping-up of the policy of collectivization which has been going

[4] *Izvestia*, 24th November 1961.
[5] P. GOLUBKOV, Problems of the development of the kolkhozy on the road to communism, *Vopr. Ekon.*, No. 11, 1961.
[6] *Nar. Khoz.* 1961, 1962—Figures as at 1st January.
[7] GOLUBKOV, *ibid*.

on in recent years has coincided with a new crisis in agriculture, or at least a slowing-up in the rate of progress.[7a]

Another of the aims of agricultural policy is to merge the two kinds of public ownership. It has not been made clear what form this fusion should take or when it will be achieved, and it is sometimes said that it may not be possible before the final move to full communism, which is another way of putting it off indefinitely.[8] It might be effected by the transformation of a certain number of kolkhozy into sovkhozy, as has been done in the past, although this raises financial problems, in view of the very small sums which most collective farms have up till now paid out to their members; or again the model statutes of kolkhoz and sovkhoz might gradually be modified. As far back as 1961, I was told, about 20% of the kolkhozy were paying their members fixed wages, as is the case in the sovkhozy, instead of the form of remuneration known as the *trudoden* (a notional work-day[9] based on the execution of a given piece of work, the value of which is not calculated until the final accounting). It might also be feasible to effect some change in the model statutes of the sovkhozy which would give the directors wider managerial powers, and would afford staff and unions a greater degree of control. However, the reforms in agricultural organization which were undertaken in March 1962 did not seem to be leading in this direction, since their effect was to consolidate the respective positions of the sovkhozy and kolkhozy, and to reinforce the control exercised over the latter.

In principle, both wholesale and retail trade are entirely nationalized[10] including the many street traders to be seen everywhere. However, leaving aside the black or semi-black market, there is one important legal exception, namely the kolkhoz markets which

[7a] After the fall of N. S. Khrushchev, it was reported that concessions had been granted concerning the cultivation of private plots.

[8] In this context, see PASKHOV, Aspects of the fusion of the two forms of socialist ownership, *Vopr. Ekon.*, No. 5, 1960.

[9] Cf. H. WRONSKI, Le Troudoden, *Rémunération et niveau de vie dans les Kolkhoz* (e d. S.E.D.E.S), Paris 1956.

[10] In 1927–8, the public sector (state and co-operative) accounted for 75% of retail trade and 80% of the gross value of industrial production, but only 2% of agricultural production. ZALESKI, *op. cit.*, p. 67. In 1940 this percentage for retail trade had risen to 85·7% and in 1960 to 95·6%. *Nar. Khoz.*, p. 680, 1960.

exist in all towns, and where kolkhoz members come to sell their produce direct. These markets, where prices are generally higher than in the State shops, are estimated to have had a turnover in 1960 not exceeding 4·4% of total retail trade, and 7·4% for food products alone.[11] However, the proportion of certain products, which passed through the kolkhoz markets is said to be much greater: one man to whom I spoke in 1961 mentioned a figure of 30% for milk.

The attitude of the authorities towards kolkhoz markets is ambivalent. These markets are still indispensable, particularly because they provide the towns with a ready source of vegetables and fresh food which State trading, still inefficient, cannot do (there are still queues at the shops from time to time). But it is obvious that many of the journeys made by kolkhoz members make no kind of sense in economic terms, and are only justified by the erratic behaviour of prices and the great variations to be noted from place to place. For example, *Pravda*, 14th January 1962, criticizes a kolkhoz in Alma-Ata whose members went as far afield as Omsk and Chelyabinsk to sell fruit, vegetables and wines in the markets there: the kolkhoz chairman, wrote one of his members to the newspaper, knows only one word: profit. One hears of instances where it pays a kolkhoz worker to take a train to go and sell a sack of apples, or even a plane for a sack of oranges or lemons (which fetch extremely high prices in the towns) all the way from Georgia to Moscow or other large towns.

However, it is not so much this irrational aspect which seems to perturb the authorities (otherwise they would take the necessary steps to establish efficient trading on the basis of the indications provided by relative price levels) as the fear that the private profit motive might creep in and deflect citizens from productive work and the objectives of Soviet society; moreover, illogicality is less obvious in those cases where trading has become regularly established and the sales on the kolkhoz markets of large towns are handled by people receiving their produce from relations or friends back home, as was the case for produce from Georgia which was sold in Moscow by Georgians living in the capital. However, the Georgian Council of Ministers issued an edict forbidding the export, for commercial purposes, of fruit

[11] *Ibid.*

and vegetables from Georgia, in an effort to wage further war on "speculators" who were sending such produce to the great urban centres of the USSR, and also to compel the peasants to give priority to the harvest "and other essential farming work". Georgian peasants were henceforth forbidden to sell the produce from their private plots outside the frontiers of their republic.[12]

There is another sector, though it does not come under the heading of means of production in the strict sense, where public and private ownership exist side by side, namely house building. House building, which had for long been kept at a very slow rate, made spectacular strides some ten years ago. This spurt was the result both of an increase in public building, and, to an even greater extent, in private building; from 1952 to 1960 there was an increase of 175% in the area of floor space in the former category, but in the latter category the increase was no less than 266%, thus accounting for 33% of the total construction of urban dwellings (as compared with 12% under the second five-year plan)[13] without taking into account almost all rural dwellings. Private house building was encouraged by the State (allocation of materials, and land, and State loans at very low interest rates). In those towns where growth has been most rapid, and where enterprises had to use every means to attract the labour force which they needed, private building assumed great importance, as an indispensable adjunct to the inadequate amount of public construction. A document reports this as having been the case at Novosibirsk.[14] These buildings were of uncertain quality, one need hardly add, but had the advantage of quantity.

The government could not, however, be entirely favourable to such a development, not only because of its efforts to combat the "private property instinct", which is an added obstacle to the mobility of the labour force, but also because of the great shortage of land in the big towns. An order by the Central Committee and the government, published in *Pravda*, 7th August 1962, considerably limited the opportunities for private house building, by stopping or cutting down allocations of land and loans to would-be builders of "dachas" in the big towns. On the other hand, the

---

[12] Report from "Zarya Vostoka" reprinted in *Le Monde*, 21st July 1962.

[13] *Nar. Khoz.*, p. 611, 1960.

[14] P. RONDIÈRE, *Démesurée et fabuleuse Sibérie*, p. 99, Hachette, Paris, 1962.

same order attempts to encourage the setting up, side by side with state building enterprises, of co-operative building societies which are supposed to operate under the direction of the local soviets.

Time will show whether this reform, which seems to have been motivated to a large extent by ideological considerations, will produce results, and will not affect the rate of growth, as seems to have been the case with similar measures taken in agriculture.[14a]

MONEY AND COMMODITY CONCEPTS AND THEIR ROLE

In order to justify the use of money and prices within a socialist system, Soviet authors sometimes point out that the relationship of the State with two categories of agents — peasants and consumers — is still based on the exchange of goods; all the concomitants of "market production" — money, value and prices — must therefore exist within the economy as a whole. The programme adopted by the Communist Party of the Soviet Union in October 1961, which, like the legislative principles previously quoted, contains phrases relating to the use, during the period of socialism and the period of transition to communism, of instruments such as accounting, money, prices, cost, profit, etc., also states that "when the transition to a single form of communist public ownership, and a communist system of distribution has been accomplished, the money–commodity relationship will become obsolete and will wither away".[15] Thus conformity is maintained with the description of the consequences attendant upon the abolition of the capitalist regime as laid down in Marxist analysis.

In practice, however, present trends do not suggest that the disappearance of prices and accounting is in any way imminent. Since the adoption of the New Economic Policy (NEP) at the

[14a] It seems that, as in the case of cultivation of individual plots and the sale of their products by kolkhoz members outside of their region, the fall of N. S. Khrushchev will mean a reduction of the pressure imposed on these manifestations of "individualistic spirit".

[15] *Programme*, II, I, 3, text in *Pravda* and *Izvestia*, 2nd November 1961; cf. also on this subject G. GROSSMAN, Soviet Economic Planning: Industrial Prices in the USSR, *American Economic Review*, May 1959.

end of the civil war (1921–2) and the acceptance of the principle of economic accounting *(khozrashchot)*, the trend has rather been in the opposite direction. Especially during the past few years, increased attention has been given to accounting, profit and the fixing of a fair price level, and in this sense it is certainly true to say that there has been some "Westernization" of the economy. For instance, an announcement was made that work undertaken by the various institutes for economic research should in future be chargeable to the users (which requires that appropriate adjustments be made in the latters' budgets).[16] Further on in this same Party programme, from which the above passage was quoted, there is a reference to the need for making wider use of accounting in all possible ways, and of employing the various economic tools to a greater extent.

The fact that references to this point are so frequent at present, as are reminders that the building of communism "is based on the principle of personal material incentive" of citizens and enterprises, indicates that implementation of this principle is still far from perfect, or that it raises very complex problems. In certain sectors, for example in trade as we have clearly seen, use of the personal incentive motive is still very inadequate. In cases where individual or collective bonuses do operate to give workers a material interest in the carrying out of plan objectives, they sometimes have unexpected effects by inspiring individuals to act in a way which may be contrary to the spirit of the official instructions which they have received. Numerous examples of this will be given later.

POLITICAL AND ADMINISTRATIVE ORGANIZATION

A few words must be said on the organization of the government. According to the 1936 Constitution, which is still in force, the highest organ of the State is the Supreme Soviet (Council) of the USSR, which is divided into two chambers: one is the Council of the Union, which is elected by direct suffrage, on the basis of one member per 300,000 inhabitants, and which, after the

---

[16] A. Efimov, Economic Research and Planning, *Ekonomicheskaya Gazeta*, 4th September 1961.

elections on the 18th March 1962, consisted of 791 members, the other is the Council of Nationalities, which is also elected by direct suffrage, and which at the same date consisted of 652 members, namely 25 for each of the republics in the Union, 11 for each of the autonomous republics, 5 for each of the 8 national oblasts (autonomous provinces) and 1 for each of the 10 national territories *(okrug)*, plus 7 members representing the army, who are all at present marshals or vice-marshals.[17] The Supreme Soviet elects a praesidium of some 30 members, and its president fulfils the functions of head of the State. The powers of the Supreme Soviet and its Praesidium appear to be mainly formal.

It should be noted that the Council of Nationalities has an economic commission, which has played a certain part in recent years, particularly in matters concerning the definition of economic objectives relating to the various territories. Executive and administrative authority is vested in the Council of Ministers of the USSR. After the changes made in article 70 of the Constitution,[18] this consisted, during 1962, of about 50 members, plus the chairmen of the councils of ministers of the 15 federal republics, who belong *ex officio*. In addition to the deputy-chairmen of the Council of Ministers, the Council includes ministers, about 15 at present, who control the various ministries (foreign affairs, culture, finance, public health, defence, etc.) of which only a few are of an industrial nature: ministries of power, transport, medium machine building (this is generally interpreted as being the ministry for atomic questions).

The ministers are either federal ministers, or federal-republican ministers. The former exercise all-Union control, either directly or through authorities created by them, over the departments for which they are responsible (for example, communications, geology); the latter exercise this control through the corresponding ministries in the federal republics. They may be directly responsible for the administration of a clearly defined and limited number of enterprises only, listed by the praesidium of the Supreme Soviet of the USSR (for example, cultural affairs, motor transport).

[17] Results of the elections of 18th March 1962, *Pravda*, 21st March 1962. See also M. FAINSOD, *How Russia is Ruled*, Harvard University Press, 1953.
[18] *Pravda*, 9th December 1961.

In addition, the Council of Ministers also includes the chairmen (and even in the case of *Gosplan* some deputy-chairmen and a director) of some twenty State committees of the Council of Ministers (as of April, 1962); these State committees, which really fulfil the function of economic ministries (committees on planning or Gosplan, on work and wages, co-ordination of work on scientific research, professional technical training, automation, committees concerned with various branches of industry, building, external economic relations, external cultural relations, etc.) had, in principle, no administrative powers in the period between 1957 and 1962.

Lastly, the Council of Ministers also includes the presidents of some seven major departments, notably the State bank *(Gosbank)* and the construction bank, the statistical office and until its abolition the State scientific and economic council *(Gosekonomsoviet)*.

TERRITORIAL DIVISIONS

The principal administrative subdivisions of the USSR are based on the principle of national autonomy; these units are the "republics of the Union", which at present number 15. Prior to July 1956, they were 16 in number, but at that date the Finno-Karelian Republic was "at its own request"[19] reduced to the rank of autonomous republic. These Union republics vary very much in size: the Federated Soviet Socialist Republic of Russia (RSFSR) alone covers four-fifths of the area, and includes almost three-fifths of the population; the Ukraine, with an area of some 232,000 square miles, and some 42 million inhabitants in 1959, is roughly comparable to France; the three republics of Byelorussia, Uzbekistan and Kazakhstan — the latter covering an area of at least 1 million square miles — have close to 10 million inhabitants; lastly, the ten other republics have a population of less than 3 million each.

The republics, whose economic powers have grown steadily during recent years, have a complete administrative organization modelled on that of the Union. They have a Supreme Council and a Council of Ministers. The latter, like the Council of Minis-

---

[19] The Soviet Union in facts and figures, *Soviet News*, p. 7, London, 1958.

ters of the USSR, consists of the heads of two types of department: federal republican ministers who are the counterparts of similar administrations in Moscow and supervise all the enterprises or administrative divisions of that ministry which exist within the republic, and republican ministries, which have no counterpart at Union level, and vary in number with each republic, but generally comprise at least education, social security, local industry, the communal economy and, since the abolition of the corresponding federal ministry, the ministry of trade. There are also republican State Committees, in particular one for planning (the republican Gosplan). Most of the republics also have their own Academy of Sciences, subdivided into various institutes, with the exception of the RSFSR, whose Academy is merged with the Academy of Sciences of the USSR.

The next lowest administrative division is known as the oblast (province) or the *krai*. When the oblast corresponds to a national unit, it may have the status of an Autonomous Soviet Socialist Republic (ASSR). According to the following table,[20] the USSR would appear to have comprised 144 of these secondary units in 1960. Within the oblast, or krai, or ASSR, there also exist subdivisions corresponding to those of a national unit with a certain degree of autonomy, but less than that of the ASSR (and *a fortiori* less than the Union republics): these are the autonomous oblasts and the national territories *(natsionalni okrug)*. The term *krai*, mentioned above, which only exists in the RSFSR, relates to very extensive areas containing autonomous oblasts. This summarizes the position. It should be noted that the autonomous regions or territories also seem to have their own planning organization.

Changes in these administrative divisions are frequent.[21] With regions which do not correspond to any ethnic group, the principle is to make them relate to an economic unit; in many regions the creation of new industrial belts, changes in the agricultural pattern and the opening up of communications, have brought about marked economic changes. In European Russia and the

---

[20] See Table I.
[21] On the problems of territorial division of the USSR, see particularly H. CHAMBRE, *L'Aménagement du territoire en URSS*, Mouton, The Hague, Paris, 1959. Cf. also T. SHABAD, *Geography of the URSS, A Regional Survey*, ch. II, Columbia University Press, New York, 1951.

TABLE I

Territorial Divisions of the USSR as at 1st January 1960

Republics	Oblast	Krai	Autono-mous republics (ASSR)	Total oblast, krai and ASSR*	Autono-mous oblasts	National territories	Economic administ-rative regions sovnarkhoz
RSFSR	49	6	15	70	6	10	68
Ukraine	25			25			11
Kazakhstan	15			15			9
Uzbekistan	7		1	8			5
Byelorussia	6			6			1
Turkmenistan	2			4			1
Georgia			2	3	1		1
Tadzhikistan	1			3	1		1
Azerbaidzhan			1	2	1		1
Kirgizia	2			3			1
Armenia				1			1
Estonia				1			1
Latvia				1			1
Lithuania				1			1
Moldavia				1			1
Total	107	6	19	144	9	10	104

* Including "regions directly subordinated to the republics" (raiony respublikanskovo podchineniya).

SOURCES: SSSR Administrativno — territorialnoe delenie soyuznykh respublik, *Izvestia* Editions, Moscow, 1960. For the economic administrative regions (as at 1st January 1958), V. M. KOSTENNIKOV, *The Economic Regions of the USSR*, Geografiz, 1958.

Ukraine, however, the oblasts, which fairly closely correspond to the provinces *(gubernii)* of Tsarist times, although they are usually slightly smaller, have at present more or less fixed limits. With units which correspond to ethnic groupings, these changes usually consist in promoting a national territory to the rank of an autonomous oblast or republic (the last promotion of this kind took place at the beginning of 1962) or even to a Union republic: in exceptional circumstances it may be a change in the other direction (it is known that several ethnic groups lost their autonomy at the end of the war). The next, or tertiary, territorial division is the *raion*, which may be translated as district, and which takes the place of the divisions of Tsarist Russia known as *uyezd*, *stan* and *volost*. There are about 3500 raions. The Leningrad oblast, which stretches some 190 miles, consists of 26, while the whole of the Ukraine has 786.

Finally, below the raions, there are the villages *(seleniya)* and the towns, the latter being organized as municipalities *(gorsoviet)*. Settlements having the status of towns are relatively few. The big towns are divided into wards (which are also called raions).

Republics, oblasts (or their equivalents) and raions make up the traditional or common pattern of territorial division, each with its own powers and functions. There are, however, several other divisions which have been defined, or redefined in recent years, and which relate to a specific economic function. These will be studied in greater detail later on, and are only mentioned briefly here. They are:

(a) *the economic administrative regions* in which there operates, to use a former designation, a "Council for the national economy" *(Soviet Narodnovo Khozyaistva,* shortened to *sovnarkhoz)* and which were created by a decree of 10th May 1957 which came into force on the 1st July 1957.[22] The sovnarkhozy[23] are today the principal organ of control over heavy industry. At the time of the 1957 reform, there were 105 sovnarkhozy. At that time, some 80 of the economic administrative regions were made up of one single oblast, krai or ASSR. The others consisted of regroupings of several of these units. The administrative region of Leningrad, for example, comprised 3 oblasts (Leningrad, Novgorod and Pskov), and the same was true of Kiev. The republic of Kirgizia, which had 3 oblasts or their equivalent, or Byelorussia, which comprised 10 oblasts, each made up one economic administrative region only. On the other hand, the Moscow oblast was divided into two such regions, Moscow Town and Moscow Oblast. The principle seems to have been to amalgamate those oblasts which were not in themselves sufficiently important to constitute a distinct economic region, and to attach to the big towns those areas which were economically dependent on them.

[22] See above, Table I.
[23] See, for example, the list in KOSTENNIKOV, *op. cit,* or P. M. ALAMPIEV, *Ekonomicheskoe raionirovanie SSSR,* Gosplanizdat, 1959.

TABLE II
Large Economic Regions of the USSR

Large economic regions	Principal towns*
1. North–west	Leningrad
2. Centre	Moscow
3. Volga–Vyatka	Gorki
4. Central Black Earth Region	Voronezh
5. Volga	Kazan, Kuibishev
6. North Caucasus	Rostov on Don
7. Urals	Sverdlovsk, Chelyabinsk
8. Western Siberia	Novosibirsk
9. Eastern Siberia	Irkutsk, Krasnoyarsk
10. Far eastern region	Khabarovsk
11. Donetz and Dnieper region	Kharkov
12. South-west	Kiev
13. South	Odessa
14. West (Baltic)	Riga, Vilnius
15. Transcaucasia	Tbilisi
16. Central Asia	Tashkent
17. Kazakhstan	Alma-Ata
Economic and administrative regions	
(a) Byelorussia	Minsk
(b) Moldavia	Kichinev

* The principal towns listed here are those in which the "Co-ordinating Councils" envisaged by the 1961–2 reforms will generally meet. The list of these towns has not been published, and the above list is, therefore, not an official one.

After 1957 a certain number of small sovnarkhozy were abolished, particularly in the European part of Russia; conversely, a new one was created in Uzbekistan, which originally had only 4, and 3 new ones in the Ukraine, which had thus, at the end of 1962, 14 sovnarkhozy as against 11 in 1957. The Poltava oblast, which was originally merged with the Sumi oblast and that of Kharkov to make up the Kharkov economic administrative region, was separated from the latter and given its own sovharkhoz. Later on, in July 1960, the 5 sovnarkhozy of Uzbekistan were replaced by one single sovnarkhoz for the whole republic. In 1960 there were in all 102 sovnarkhozy, of which 67 were in the RSFSR, 14 in the Ukraine, 9 in Kazakhstan, and 1 each in the other republics.[24] According to the officials with whom I spoke

[24] M. S. URINSON, *Organizatsia planirovania narodnovo khozyaistva v soyuznykh respublikakh*, p. 9, Gosplanizdat, 1960.

at the Institute of Economics, the usual tendency was to elevate regions to the rank of economic administrative regions as their rate of industrialization gradually improved; although it looked as if the trend had been in the opposite direction, since the number of sovnarkhozy had declined in four years.

The reform of November 1962 reduced the number of sovnarkhozy from 192 to 47. The list was published in *Ekonomicheskaya Gazeta* on 16th February 1963 and again on 11th January 1964. On average, the new sovnarkhozy are twice as large as the old ones. The Ukraine and Kazakhstan have now only 7 sovnarkhozy each. For the first time, 1 sovnarkhoz may include several republics: thus, the 4 Central Asian republics, closely inter-related geographically, now comprise only 1 sovnarkhoz. The Urals have now only 3 (Perm, Sverdlovsk and Chelyabinsk), and western Siberia 2 (western Siberia and Kuznetsk). In three instances (Volga–Vyatka, the Black Sea region, and Central Asia) the economic administrative regions coincide with the large economic regions, to which we now turn.

(b) Another kind of territorial division in the USSR are *the large economic regions (krupny ekonomicheski raion)*. These regions, which are in fact groups of several small republics, have up to the present been essentially statistical divisions, used by Gosplan in its planning work. Since the 1961–2 reforms, they have become increasingly important as models for economic analysis and points of comparison in the making of decisions, and each of them is at present the seat of a "co-ordinating council".

Between 1939 and 1960, there were 13 of these large regions.[25] By a decision of Gosplan, dated 22nd February 1960, the number of large economic regions "which must be taken into consideration in the working out of general questions relating to the prospects of national development in the USSR" was raised to 16.

In the course of 1961, this division was once again modified. As compared with the earlier pattern, the changes consisted of joining the north region (Arkhangelsk) to the north-west (Leningrad) and dividing the Ukraine into three regions centred respectively on Kiev, Kharkov and Odessa.

Following these changes, there are now, therefore, 17 of these large economic regions, with a more even distribution of popu-

[25] See the list in CHAMBRE, *op. cit.*

lation than previously. In addition, within the large regions of the west and south-west, the 2 republics of Byelorussia and Moldavia figure separately, thus bringing the number up to 19 instead of 17.[26]

The first 10 large regions are divisions of the republic of Russia (of which 6 are in European Russia, if one excludes the Urals). The next 3 are divisions of the Ukraine, while the following three in fact comprise several small republics, namely the 3 Baltic republics (west), the 3 republics of Transcaucasia, and the 4 Central Asian republics. Finally, there is Kazakhstan, which itself constitutes one large region.

(c) Lastly, a brief mention should be made of the new *agricultural administrative divisions* which were announced in March 1962. There were set up administrative councils covering several districts or raions, at the rate of one for every four or five raions, i.e. for example 382 for the RSFSR.[27]

THE PARTY

The foregoing brief sketch of the political and administrative organization would not be complete or realistic without mention of the role of the Communist Party. The question which concerns us here is the extent and nature of the Party's intervention in the making of decisions in the economic field, and the principles on which such intervention operates. This is certainly one of the matters on which we are least informed. Nevertheless, some indications may be given. For example, in his report on the revised Party statutes, which were presented to the XXIInd Congress on the 28th October 1961, Frol Kozlov, one of the secretaries of the central Committee, referred to the circumstances surrounding the appointment of a director of a building-materials factory in Kuibishev, who later turned out to have been a bad choice.

[26] TOKAREV and ALAMPIEV, Problems of the improvement of territorial organization and economic regionalization, *Plan. Khoz.*, No. 7, 1961 (with map); P. ALAMPIEV, The new network of large economic regions of the USSR, *Ekonomicheskaya Gazeta*, 28th May 1961. See also P. LOMAKO, The coordinating and planning councils have begun to work, *Pravda*, 23rd February 1962.
[27] See later, Chapter VI.

As will be seen later on, the appointment of factory directors is one of the functions of the sovnarkhoz. F. R. Kozlov[28] goes on to tell us how, when the appointment was to be made, the sovnarkhoz telephoned to the oblast Party Committee, and it was decided, without examining the question carefully, to appoint comrade X. Obviously, the sovnarkhoz made no decision without first clearing it with the Party. In certain cases, Party intervention in current economic administration is even more overt; thus, under the earlier arrangements, control over the kolkhozy seems to have been mainly in the hands of the secretaries of the district Party committees, who had a say at all times and on all questions. When it comes to important decisions, these all seem to come from inside the Party. This was particularly so, I was told at the Institute of Economics of the Academy of Sciences, in the case of the reform in industrial administration in 1957. Important decisions are often announced in the form of resolutions under the joint signature of the Party Central Committee and the Council of Ministers of the USSR.

According to its constitution, the Communist Party is "the highest form of socio-political organization, the controlling force which guides Soviet society". The Party is organized on a "production and territorial basis", which means that the primary Party organizations are created at the place of work, and are grouped with other similar organizations according to territory. (The Party committees functioning at province, district and town level are usually designated as Obkom, Raikom, Gorkom.) Although the 300,000 primary Party organizations "do not take the place of councils, unions, co-operatives and other public organizations, and must not permit any confusion between the functions of the Party and those of other administrations, or needless reduplication of their work" (article 42) yet they do have the right of supervision over all such activities. Article 59 even expressly permits the primary Party organizations to "supervise the work" of the enterprises, kolkhozy, sovkhozy, research institutes, etc., within which they operate, although this right does not extend to the Party organizations within ministries, State committees, sovnarkhozy, etc.; it is important, according to F. Kozlov, that

[28] Speech by F. R. KOZLOV, *Pravda* and *Izvestia*, 29th October, 1961, Party Statutes: *Pravda*, 3rd November 1961.

State administrations and economic administrations should be free from "petty supervision".

At the apex of Party organization are the Congresses: they must meet at least once every four years. Between Congresses, the Central Committee takes over control of the Party; it elects a praesidium and a secretariat; it must meet in plenary session at least once every six months.

The Party is subject to the Leninist principle of "democratic centralism". This means that an iron discipline must prevail, that the minority submits to the majority, that there are no factions, that all Party organs must be elected according to rule.[29] However, the fact that elections are held regularly does not mean that there is any freedom in the choice of those elected except at the lowest levels (primary organizations and possibly to a certain extent in the raion committees). But even at these levels the freedom is only relative, since there are never more candidates than there are posts to fill.

When the projected Party programme was being discussed, a Party member from Kharkov referred to the way in which elections are carried out in the primary organizations. First of all, before the elections, the Party office selects a list of names; at the meeting, the president asks for candidates to be proposed, but first gives the floor to those whom he has asked to read the list which has been prepared in advance; as soon as the list has been read, a motion is put to the vote proposing that the nominations be closed; as the list contains the same number of names as there are posts to fill, the election is then over. While recognizing the usefulness of a list, especially at district, town or province level, where people may not know each other, this comrade was of the opinion that it was necessary that one should be able to discuss the merits of each candidate publicly, and that nominations should not be stopped once the official list had been read out. He thought that the new Party constitution should indicate how elections within the Party were to be conducted.[30] One need hardly add that there

[29] See in particular *Kommunist*, No. 14, November 1955, for comments on the reforms in Party organization which were introduced at that time.

[30] Selection from correspondence: replies, comments and proposals on the draft statute of the Party, letter from I. KOSHCHEYEV, *Kommunist*, No. 14, pp. 91–2, September 1961.

is no trace of such a suggestion in the final version of the constitution.

The existence of a powerfully centralized Party hierarchy acts as a strong counterbalance to the centrifugal tendencies which might arise from the autonomy granted to various ethnic groups. (Autonomy itself is only granted on condition that each local government carries on the struggle against its own bourgeois elements.) Indeed it would be difficult to pretend that the Party is other than an instrument of the dominant Russian group for the control of the other national groups. A survey of the years from 1924 to 1958 reveals that, although holders of the office of first secretary of the Party in the Central Asian republics were usually nationals of these countries, the key post of personnel secretary —which gives control over nominations—has, without any exception, never been held by a native,[31] a point whose importance the reader will not fail to grasp. The amount of real decentralization in the Party appears to be nil. Among recent trends, it is noted that, on the one hand, in the Moslem countries, even Party members take part in religious ceremonies, a thing which would have been impossible twenty years ago, while, on the other hand, denunciation of nationalist deviations among the cadres of the non-Russian communist parties seems to have become fairly frequent of late. (See particularly the speech by F. Kozlov to the XXIInd Congress quoted earlier.)[32]

It is not within our present scope to judge in what direction the balance of power has shifted during recent years. Suffice it to say that, judging from what the observers tell us, there was a development of the "collegial principle", which showed itself for several years not only at the level of political control, but also had its effect on economic organization. An example given was the reform in the procedure for discussion of the budget in the Supreme Soviet, which made it possible for the commissions to be informed before the opening of the session; the creation of an economic commission within the Soviet of Nationalities; strengthening of the "collegial" administration of Gosplan, by giving

---

[31] Information furnished by Mme Hélène Carrère d'Encausse.

[32] See H. CARRÈRE D'ENCAUSSE, La politique soviétique des nationalités, La Nef, January–March 1962, Revue française de Science politique, July–September 1962.

greater authority to heads of departments; the transformation of ministries into State committees (administered by a collective group and not, as in the case of the ministries, by one single man) and the creation of the sovnarkhozy.[33]

In November 1962 it was decided to reorganize the Party structures throughout the entire hierarchy. The *territorial* principle was then superseded by the principle of production. The result of the reform was in effect to divide the entire Party organization into two, one half dealing with industry and other urban activities (construction, transport, education, research, etc.) and the other with agriculture. The real purpose of the reform was in fact agriculture. The district (raion) Party committees were abolished, and replaced by some 1500 committees responsible for the administration of sovkhoz and kolkhoz production. These committees, which cover very much wider areas than the districts, are in control of all Party organizations working on, or assisting, agricultural production.

This reform complemented the reform in agricultural administration which took place in March 1962, and which was mentioned earlier. There was afterwards in each oblast a Party office for agriculture, and one for industry and other activities, the latter being subdivided according to sectors. Only the Union republics still retained a central Party Committee, which was itself divided into two offices, one for industry and the other for agriculture. After these reforms, there was no truly governmental administration of agriculture, except for a technical body *(Selkhoztekhnika)* which handles distribution and sales of plant and products for agriculture, and the Ministry of Agriculture, which itself is now no more than a research organization. Administration of agricultural enterprises had become entirely the responsibility of the Party.

N. S. Khrushchev's speech at the plenum of the Party Central Committee on 14th February 1964[33a] bore witness to the desire to leave the initiative for important economic decisions with the

[33] M. KASER, The reorganization of Soviet industry and its effect on decision making, *Value and Plan* (ed. G. GROSSMAN), University of California Press, 1960.

[33a] *Izvestia*, 15th February 1964. Cf. E. ZALESKI, *Les réformes de la Planification en URSS*, Cahiers de l'Institut de Science économique appliquée, August 1964.

Party. Within the framework of the Praesidium of the Central Committee, bureaux were set up for industry and construction, agriculture, and chemicals and light industry respectively. There also exist, within the Praesidium, bureaux whose powers extend over wide geographical areas (for example, RSFSR, Central Asia, Transcaucasia) and which are themselves subdivided into specialized offices.

It must be added here that, after the fall of N. S. Khrushchev, in October 1964, the division of the Party organization between industry and agriculture was widely criticized and it was announced that the organizational set-up would be re-established as it existed prior to November 1962. Thus, in the Ukraine, it was announced that the obkoms, raikoms and gorkoms would be re-established and the special organizations for agriculture abolished.[33b]

OTHER SPECIAL FEATURES OF THE ECONOMIC STRUCTURE

To round off this description of the Soviet system, we shall summarize briefly some of the main features of the country's economic structure which have not so far been touched upon.[34]

One of the first of these is the still very considerable size of the population engaged in agriculture. According to the census of 15th January 1959, 38·8% of the civil working population which totalled 99·1 million persons (annual workers) were employed in the agricultural sector (compare France, 20% in 1962). Industry and construction, transport and communications accounted for 36·9%, administration and services for the remainder, i.e. just over 24%.

Some allowance must, of course, be made for the fact that the statistics are not strictly comparable: Soviet statisticians do endeavour to point out that the number of people employed in the kolkhozy, and therefore included under agriculture, in fact includes some, who, in the West, would be regarded as being employed in industries serving agriculture or in services or handicrafts. Nevertheless, even allowing for necessary adjustments in

---

[33b] *Pravda*, 22nd November 1964.

[34] Except for some indications on growth. On this subject, see concluding chapter, pp. 264–279.

the figures, there is still a very wide divergence in this respect between the USSR and industrial countries in the West.

Similarly, the urban population (48% of the total in 1959, 52% in 1963) is relatively much smaller than in most developed countries today.

If, therefore, the division of the working population into three main sectors is taken as an indication of economic development, the USSR emerges as a country which is still only partially developed. This structure is, of course, changing very rapidly. From 1939 to 1959 the proportion of the working population engaged in agriculture fell from 50·1 to 38·8%. Similarly, the urban population grew from 18% in 1913 to 33% in 1939 (or 32% within present frontiers) and 52% in 1963. But even allowing for differences in definitions, the position is still far from comparable with that of the highly developed countries. The proportion of agricultural workers in the total population is today scarcely less than what it was in France in 1906 (44%) and is higher than that of England or Germany in the same period. On the other hand, although the total urban population is only of average size, the number of large towns appears to be fairly considerable, there being, again in 1959, 25 towns of more than 500,000 inhabitants, and 148 of more than 100,000, in other words a proportion in relation to population slightly higher than that of France, at least for towns in the first category (even if one is talking in terms of conurbations rather than towns). The number of average- and small-size towns does, however, seem to be comparatively smaller.

The size of the large towns seems to be related to the size of the big industrial enterprises, which in their turn are usually concentrated in the large conurbations. In 1959 61% of industrial workers were employed in enterprises of 1000 workers and over,[35] which would make socialist industry "the most highly concentrated in the world",[36] 38% of the industrial force were employed in factories of more than 3000 workers, whereas in the United States, according to D. Granick, only 20% were employed in factories of more than 2500.[37] Doubtless, Soviet enterprises do not correspond to the Western concept, since they are not spread over

[35] Nar. Khoz, p. 218, 1960.
[36] Les Progrès du pouvoir soviétique depuis quarante ans (French edition, Foreign language editions, p. 56, Moscow, 1957.)
[37] D. GRANICK, The Red Executive, Doubleday, New York, 1960.

several towns or different geographical areas, nor indeed do they quite correspond to our idea of industrial establishments: in the big towns there are, in fact, numerous small factories or workshops, apparently employing only a score or so of people, and which rank not as enterprises but only as workshops subsidiary to large enterprises in the town. Nevertheless, it would seem that concentration of industry in large units was a feature of Russia even in Tsarist times.[38]

Agriculture is also concentrated in large enterprises, and this is becoming more and more the case, since recent amalgamation of kolkhozy has considerably reduced their numbers; one kolkhoz nowadays usually extends over several villages, which themselves are often widely scattered. By the end of 1962 there were in the whole of the USSR only 40,500 kolkhozy and 8600 sovkhozy, to which must be added 50,000 individual peasants.

The large size of industrial establishments does to a certain extent—though not exclusively[39]—reflect the size of industrial equipment. The USSR seems always to have had a taste for the gigantic. Someone recently recalled the words of Stalin, when he asked how much a large steelworks in America would produce and, having been told 2·5 million tons, demanded that a factory be built in the USSR which would produce first 2·5 million tons, and then 4 million tons of steel. Production per blast furnace in 1958 exceeded that of the United States.[40] It must not be

[38] Maurice Dobb writes on this subject: "The proportion of all workers in factories who were employed in enterprises with more than 500 workers reached the surprisingly high figure of 53%, as compared with an American figure of 31%, which represents the proportion of wage-earners in manufacture in 1914 who were in establishments employing more than 500;" and Dobb notes: "Liaschchenko, *Nar. Khoz.* SSSR 559; American Statistical Abstract, 1916, 177. Liashchenko gives a figure of 33% which is apparently a mistake". M. Dobb, *Soviet Economic Development since 1917,* p. 34, Routledge & Kegan Paul, London, 1948. However the statistical yearbook *(Nar. Khoz. SSSR)* p. 218, 1960, shows that in 1913, only 8·4% of workers in large-scale industry worked in factories employing more than 500 workers. This point should be verified. Further on in the same text, Mr. Dobb makes a number of points in support of his argument; for example, production per blast furnace in the Ukraine in 1913 was higher than in Germany or Great Britain for the same period; the number of mechanical horsepower available per worker was higher than in French or German industry.

[39] As will be seen in Chapter VII.

[40] L. Smolinski, The scale of Soviet industrial establishments, *American Economic Review* (Proceedings), pp. 138–48, May 1962.

thought, however, that this striving after size and technical advancement is a universal phenomenon; in many fields, if not indeed most, the USSR is not in advance of what is being done elsewhere; for instance, observations from travellers, particularly on the Trans-Siberian railway, reveal that, despite the size of Soviet rivers, the bridges—which one is forbidden to photograph —are always of a very conventional type, with large numbers of spans.[41] Nor is this predilection for size always based on economic considerations, which explains why there is sometimes criticism of "gigantism" in official pronouncements.[42]

"Yield does not always increase with the size of enterprises," as P. Khromov remarked, emphasizing that enterprises in the USSR are usually larger, and yield smaller, than in the United States.[42a]

One of the characteristics of the economic structure of the USSR is the importance of female labour. Eighty per cent of women of working age (i.e. for the purpose of Soviet statistics from 20 to 55 years old) living in towns are gainfully employed, which is certainly a much higher proportion than elsewhere. There are, of course, many crèches and similar institutions, although the insufficiency of these is a frequent subject of criticism. Nevertheless, the scale of female employment and the cramped conditions in urban dwellings cannot but have an effect on the birth-rate. This was 47 per 1000 in 1913 and 31 per 1000 in 1940, but had fallen to 26 per 1000 in 1955 and 22·4 per 1000 in 1962 (21·3 in 1963), a rate slightly higher than in western Europe, but not in excess of the American rate. This is an average rate, strongly influenced by the size of the rural population; the rate for the large towns is certainly lower; a figure of 13 per 1000 has been reported for Leningrad, which would make it one of the lowest in the world. (It is also known that certain of the "people's democracies" show very low birth rates.)

Another point worthy of a brief mention is the degree of wage inequality. A recent article confirms what was already known, namely that although the extent of this inequality had tended to

---

[41] See remarks in the first chapter, pp. 2 *et seq.*

[42] See for example, N. S. KHRUSHCHEV, Speech of 17th October 1961 (XXIInd Congress).

[42a] P. KHROMOV, Size of industrial enterprises and labour productivity, *Vopr. Ekon.*, No. 1, 1963.

decrease in the period from 1926 to 1930, with the onset of the five-year plans in 1930, it once more began to grow. From 1934 to 1956 "the wages of the lowest paid workers" increased less than those of the average earner (index of 109, taking the increase in low wages as equal to 100) or of the highest paid workers (index 107). The disparity in wages calculated by deciles and quartiles was greater in 1956 than in 1934. None the less, since 1946 there has been a slow reduction of the spread, which continued from 1956 to 1959, though the inequalities of income remained greater than in 1934.[43] Thus, the USSR also seems to be engaged at present in an evening-out of wage inequalities; this movement, although one can never be very dogmatic about such manifestations, appears to be one of the characteristics of the evolution of contemporary society.

[43] M. MOZHINA, Changes in wage distribution among industrial workers, *Trud i Zarabotnaya Plata*, No. 10, 1961.

CHAPTER III

IDEOLOGY AND PLANNING

THE Soviet economic system evolved from a political revolution which in its turn was inspired by an intellectual and doctrinal movement commonly known as Marxism, or Marxism–Leninism. What connection is there today between this system and the ideological or ethical principles of a movement to which, as we have seen, adherence is still claimed in Soviet society? To put it more precisely, the question we have to decide is to what extent the organization and transformation of the Soviet economy are still, in fact, inspired by this ideology, or whether, on the contrary, they are obeying an inner logic of their own, in which ideological considerations in practice play only a secondary role. Before attempting a reply, it may be useful to recall one or two facts, if only in the form of a brief summary.[1]

MEANING OF IDEOLOGY

Perhaps the most striking feature of Marxist–Leninist ideology is its negative character. The new way of life which it seeks to create is, even now, still defined first and foremost as being an opposition to the way of life known as capitalism. It is striking to note that the very first sentence of the new Communist Party programme—only the third document of its kind since the foun-

---

[1] On Soviet ideology, see H. CHAMBRE, *Le Marxisme en Union Soviétique* (ed. DU SEUIL), Paris, 1955; H. MARCUSE, *Soviet Marxism. A Critical Analysis*, Columbia University Press, New York, 1958; G. A. WETTER, *Dialectical Materialism: A Historical and Systematic Survey of Philosophy in the Soviet Union*, Routledge & Kegan Paul, London. The term "ideology" is employed here in its usual sense of a "body of ideas" about social realities. We should note, however, that at the outset of his career, Marx himself, in his criticism of the bourgeois ideology of his time, uses this term only in the pejorative sense of thought detached from reality, or a body of illusions.

dation of the Party at the beginning of the century—describes the present era as that of the downfall of capitalism. The works of the "Masters", Marx, Engels, and Lenin, too—which are still revered and quoted, although the mania for quotations may have abated somewhat since 1956—are, as everyone knows, essentially critical works, with few indications on the organization of a future society.

At the conference of Heads of Departments of the Social Sciences in institutes of higher education, which was held in Moscow at the beginning of 1962, and was one of the many conferences following on the XXIInd Party Congress, M. A. Suslov, one of the secretaries of the Central Committee, following Lenin's example described Marxist–Leninism as falling into three parts: Marxist philosophy, Marxist political economy, and scientific communism; this division itself corresponds to the three parts of Engels's *Anti-Dühring:* philosophy, political economy, socialism. Suslov remarked critically that equal weight was not given to those three parts, and that the third is neglected in institutes of higher education. He demanded that the principles of scientific communism should be taught, and announced that a textbook on this subject was being prepared; he himself did not give very much information about these principles, beyond stating that research and education in the field of social sciences must be intensified in order to carry on the struggle against hostile ideologies.[2] On this point the Communist Party programme begs the question in fine style by stating that the task which the social sciences must set themselves is to "discover the processes leading to the formulation of a law for the advance of humanity towards communism".[3]

Communism itself is presented as a system which will abolish the division of society into social classes and groups "and under which all men will have an equal standing in society, a similar situation in relation to the goods of production, will enjoy equal conditions in work and distribution, and will take an active part in the control of public affairs";[4] alienation which, according to Marx, is a concomitant of the capitalist type of production, will have disappeared, and a new type of man will thus emerge.

[2] *Pravda,* 4th February 1962.
[3] *Op. cit.* II, V-3.
[4] *Programme.*

"Creation of the new man is the general goal of our ideological work, the final criterion of our efforts", stated L. F. Ilyichev, also a secretary of the Central Committee, whose job it was to present the report to the all-Union conference on questions of ideological activity which met in the Great Hall of the Kremlin in December 1961.[5] The speaker emphasized that communist education must be the fruit of preparation, respect and love for arduous toil: "Communism and work are inseparable."

But Marxist–Leninist ideology is more than just a criticism of capitalist society and an affirmation of the aims of communist society. It is also a system of thought and a "signpost for action".[6] It must be divided into three distinct elements:[7]

(a) A *philosophy*, dialectical materialism and historical materialism. If one can hazard an opinion, one might say that, but for its connection with a specific political experiment, this aspect of Marxism would now no longer be the subject of such bitter controversy; for example, historical materialism has nowadays been very largely absorbed into the body of doctrine employed by Western sociologists and economists, and is only questioned insofar as it claims a monopoly of the truth; as for the dialectical method, this is not a philosophy different from all others, at least judging from what Lenin said, for in the conclusion to his great philosophical work he speaks "of philosophical materialism in general, and of the dialectical method of Marx and Engels in particular", and elsewhere he also refers to the "natural-scientific materialism", which would increasingly come to be accepted by the scholars of his time;[8]

(b) the second element is a *political doctrine*, which determines the broad means by which the aforementioned aims should be achieved; these means are, notably, the class struggle and the dictatorship of the proletariat, which, following on the XXIInd Congress has now, as we know, been redefined in the USSR as the "State of all the people";

[5] *Pravda*, 26th December 1961.
[6] *History of the Communist (Bolshevik) Party of the Soviet Union.*
[7] These headings are suggested, notably, by the American scholar D. Comey.
[8] LENIN, *Materialism and Empiriocriticism: Critical comments on a reactionary philosophy* (1908). V. I. LENIN, *Collected Works*, Lawrence & Wishart, London, Foreign Languages Publishing House, Moscow, 1962.

(c) The final element is the *plan of action* which sets forth the strategy and tactics to be used, in other words, the core of the doctrine which is the essential justification for the existence of a monolithic party whose mission it is to define and implement this plan, in accordance with the broad aims of the political doctrine.

It may be argued that the broad aims of communism, and the values of Soviet society, do not differ basically from the aims and values of Western societies. In so far as one can agree on a definition of these in the West, such aims and values must largely be regarded as common to both types of societies, since they spring from the same traditions, in other words the enlightened optimism and the liberal tradition of eighteenth- and nineteenth-century Europe. Communist ideology is original only in its opposition to capitalist economics and capitalist society, which it denounces as being the sole obstacle to achieving those general aims which were mentioned above. When there is any doubt about the line to be taken in a given situation, the simplest solution often seems to be to invoke the example of the opposing system, as a warning to be heeded. Ideology is none the less a powerful instrument, somewhat resembling those religions which start off as heresies, one in opposition to the other, and go on drawing some of their strength from this very opposition, or from combined opposition to an agnostic world.

Communist ideology does, however, contain some undeniably positive elements. One is the call for "close links with the masses... the masses who gave birth to them (the Bolsheviks), suckled them and reared them".[9] This appeal is based on the axiom that the Party is identified with the people. In the economic context it follows that, since the Soviet economy belongs to the people, the people's efforts will ensure its success and victory over hostile forces. This is what Strumilin, the doyen of Soviet economists, meant when he once reminded his colleagues: "Armchair scholars often forget that the collective will of the producers is one of the factors in the economy."[10] This reference to the collective

[9] Sixth and final conclusion of the *History of the Communist (Bolshevik) Party of the Soviet Union*, Foreign Languages Publishing House, Moscow, 1939.

[10] Quoted in the biographical note on Strumilin by R. DAVIES, *Soviet Studies*, pp. 286–96, January 1960.

will—all the more easily invoked since few attempts are ever made to determine where exactly the collective will would lead if left to itself—is an essential element in the determination of Soviet policy and programmes.

Another positive element of this doctrine is its "voluntarist" aspect, the belief in the power of science, in man's ability to transform nature and the society in which he lives. Whether this objective is more susceptible of achievement in the USSR than in countries where there is less speech-making about it is an open question, but it is obvious that Soviet life at all levels is still very much conditioned by this belief, which found expression in the very earliest decrees of the Revolution, when the vision of the future was acclaimed as a sort of "communistic Americanism", in the words of the poet Alexander Blok.[11] Of all the visions of Marxism and socialism, the vision of human society collectively breaking the bonds of necessity and achieving freedom is certainly the one which has most profoundly influenced men's minds in the Soviet Union.

THE INFLUENCE OF IDEOLOGY

We can now return to the earlier question of the role of ideology as a factor in the evolution of the economic system. Firstly it might be argued that ideology has little or no influence. It could be said that certain decisions continue to be inspired by ideological considerations, for example, those relating to the question of ownership which were quoted earlier on, but not the most important decisions. In practice, one might say, the development of the economic system is governed by technical requirements resulting from the search for progress. One can indeed quote examples of some of the important decisions made in the past few years, to support the view that the authorities are now more concerned with practical matters than with adherence to a theory and that when the ideological apparatus is set in motion over some technical question, it is little more than camouflage. What, for example, is "abolition of the difference between manual and intellectual work", which is presented as one of the consequences

---

[11] Quoted by R. BENDIX, "The cultural and political setting of economic rationality in Western and Eastern Europe," in *Value and Plan*, p. 24, *op. cit.*

of the "transition to communism", if not the expression of a spontaneous evolutionary trend resulting from the introduction of automation? In the same way, the "agrotowns" advocated by N. S. Khrushchev from time to time are the expression not of a desire to "proletarianize" agricultural workers, but of the need for further concentration of agricultural units in an effort to reduce the still considerable degree of isolation in the Soviet countryside. As for the formula "work will become the expression of a vital urge", this might be described simply as a reminder that work, in a communist society, will continue to be obligatory.[12] Recourse to ideology could be described simply as a formula for speeding up industrialization.

The progress made by Soviet economic science has in nowise lessened the extent of their present borrowings from "bourgeois" economics. On many points, when faced with ideas or techniques which have long been accepted by Western economists, Soviet economists are today fighting a rearguard action (use of econometric methods, problems of values and prices, use of the concept of amortization, calculation of the rate of return on investments, etc.). They deny this, of course, and attack those Western experts who say so, and prefer the interpretation, which is in any case a perfectly reasonable one, put forward by Professor Maurice Dobb, who holds that the present orientation of the Soviet economy is not the result of copying Western models, but is a natural development of socialist economics.[13] Nevertheless, they find this comparison embarrassing. For instance, in articles concerning the above questions, there are always passages in which the author adopts a rather disdainful attitude towards Western economies, and stresses the superiority of the Soviet economy; but these passages usually occur in such manner as to seem quite foreign to the argument, if not indeed frankly interpolated.[14] Another sidelight on the small part really played by ideology is the lack of attention paid nowadays in the univer-

[12] The above expressions are borrowed from Mr. Nacou.
[13] Y. SUKHOTIN, Foreign economists and Soviet analyses relating to the rate of return on investments, *Vopr. Ekon.* No. 9, 1961.
[14] Without encroaching on what may be said later on about these various questions, we quote the following passages as illustrative of this point of view: "The use of mathematical methods of economic analysis . . . must not be based on econometrics, which is only one of the latest forms of bourgeois

sities to dialecticians who try to give their colleagues guidance on the correct doctrinal approach to problems in their own disciplines, or problems concerning lines of demarcation with allied disciplines.[15]

However, such an interpretation does not appear to be entirely acceptable, for it presupposes the existence of an inescapable necessity bound up with the search for economic rationality and the development of industrial societies, a necessity which Western societies themselves are in the best position to bear witness to. But no society does in fact evolve solely under the pressure of technical contingencies. The aspirations, the beliefs, the idiosyncrasies of members of a society, taken individually or as a group, play a very great part in determining what changes that society will undergo. Nor can the avowed endeavour of Soviet economists and politicians to relate their actions to an overall politico-philo-

apologetics . . . only on the basis of Marxist–Leninist science is it possible to obtain truly scientific results." (A. BOYARSKI, Econometrics and the use of mathematics in economic analysis, *Plan. Khoz.*, No. 7, 1959.)

On value, see STRUMILIN: "As Marx said: . . . Labour is the basis of the value of all goods. In practice, however, this straightforward definition is not the essential point. The value of the product of labour only takes on its full significance when it becomes a factor in social acts, for example exchange. For a long time, the theory of value, the main regulating factor in the relationship between production and prices in a situation where private ownership of the means of production prevailed,[was regarded as an alternative to the economic Plan. But it is not the function of the Plan to become a substitute for the theory of value, but rather to ensure that it operates under new conditions, in the interests of socialism, and to give greater power to this economic law which is important to us." (The theory of value and planning, *Vopr. Ekon.*, No. 7, 1959.) On amortization, see A. EFIMOV who, after speaking of "the unfounded nature of commonly held concepts of bourgeois political economy about the spontaneous growth of capital" writes: "The existence of obsolescence of fixed capital in the socialist system is today generally recognized . . . Some authors, while admitting this fact, maintain that the term obsolescence can only be applied to a capitalist economy. However, there seems little sense in introducing new terms for an already established concept" (*Vopr. Ekon.*, No. 9, 1959). There are numerous instances of this same rearguard action in other fields; the admission that "ground rent" applies in socialist economics (lecture at Moscow University, September 1958, article by P. MALYSHEV in the *Scientific Reports of the Advanced Party School*, Economic Series, No. 3, 1959); references, still tentative, to the law of "supply and demand" in socialist economics, etc.

[15] See G. A. KLINE, Review of the English edition of *Dialectical Materialism in the Soviet Union*, by G. A. WETTER, Soviet Studies. July 1959.

sophical system be entirely without meaning. This preoccupation with the search for an original version or interpretation of their problems, while at the same time thereby discrediting the capitalist system, although they are more than ever indebted to it, is more than just a smoke-screen for transplanting new ideas which can be adapted to the conditions of Soviet society. It takes on an objective value of its own, and becomes one of the factors in development; at the same time, it certainly cannot by itself make the system logical or the economic régime efficient.

After the revelations at the XXth (1956) and, more especially, the XXIInd (1961) Party Congresses, when the "cult of personality" was denounced in relation to the enormity of the crimes of Stalin, the man who, for 29 of the first 36 years of the Soviet Revolution, was the undisputed master of that Revolution, and who today is represented as a bloody tyrant, a falsifier of history, etc., one may well ask whether it is still possible to believe in the existence, or the continuance, as a solid body of doctrine, of what is generally described as Soviet ideology.

This is not really the place to attempt an answer. But the fact remains that official attitudes and pronouncements are still conditioned by communist ideology, perhaps for the simple reason that it has been so thoroughly inculcated. Nevertheless, such pronouncements a e often made with distinct embarrassment, and an example of this is to be found in the proceedings of the general Assembly of the Historical Section of the Academy of Sciences of the USSR, held on the 17–18th November 1961. The greater part of this meeting was devoted to denouncing the evils of the cult of personality, but in the official report this section was preceded by another which rearranged some of the interventions by the various speakers, and expressed the need for "launching a large-scale attack on bourgeois Western historiography," for "discovering the objective laws governing social development" and "making a valid contribution to the great cause of the building of communism", which in a context such as this sounds particularly false.[16]

In the preceding pages we have spoken of the Marxist–Leninist ideology as a coherent and more or less immutable body of doctrine. From this standpoint, the only question which arises is

---

[16] *Voprosy Istorii (Questions of History)*, No. 1, January 1962.

whether this ideology, without actually disappearing, is not in practice destined to become increasingly forgotten, or disregarded, as it were "eroded", to use the term employed by the specialist review *Survey* in one of the questions put to its correspondents.[16a]

There is, however, another question, namely whether the passage of time may instead lead to changes in the content of this ideology, though we are not as yet in a position to assess the importance or the extent of these.

According to a recent study, the end of Soviet isolation and the decision in favour of a policy of co-existence between countries with different economic systems could lead to a transition from a closed to an open society. New legislation inspired to a great extent by considerations of moral principle and a return to the idea of universal rules of conduct, the co-existence between different social strata implied by the move from the proletarian dictatorship to the State of the whole people, the pragmatism which relates truth to success, the disassociation of violence and revolution, and the greater freedom allowed for the expression of different views—all these things are regarded as evidence of this transformation.

However, a transformation of this kind must inevitably raise many problems. The social impetus provided by the new morality is very much less powerful than that provided by the ideology of a particular class bent on achieving power, hence the accusation of revisionism. Societies which are striving for the establishment of communism, and which are "motivated in fact by the knowledge that they are working for what they regard as justice", come to discover that the ending of economic alienation does not of itself bring about political freedom; moreover, under pressure of competition from capitalist societies, they may in their turn be driven towards a sort of "secularized technocracy". In any event, the Utopian ideal, which has up till now been bound up with class structure, will have to be replaced; but it might very well be that this will be done by a nationalist ideology, and not by the idea of the construction of communism, as the leaders would desire.[16b]

[16a] *Survey*, April 1963, see replies by D. BELL, A. EHRLICH and R. PIPES.

[16b] M. ENGELBORGHS-BERTELS, Les mythes dans une société communiste, *Bulletin du Centre d'étude des pays de l'Est*, Université Libre de Bruxelles, No. 3, 1963, No. 4, 1963, and No. 1, 1964.

THE ORIGINS OF PLANNING

It is interesting, however, to study the extent to which planning is really bound up with Marxist doctrine. It has been noted, in this connection, that economic planning did not form part of the programme outlined by Lenin in his famous *April 1917 Theses*[17] any more than it did in the pre-1914 programme of the Russian Social Democrat Party[18] which was the precursor of the Communist Party, but that the principles of planning in a socialist State were set forth in general terms in the works of certain Russian Marxist theoreticians of the time.[19] It should also be noted that although the major Marxist works do not go into detail on this question, the actual words "plan" and "planning" had already been used, notably by F. Engels in his *Anti-Dühring*, where they occur at least seven times, ("planned co-operation", "socially planned regulation of production", "anarchy ... replaced by conscious organization on a planned basis", "social production in accordance with a determined plan", "on the basis of one single, vast, plan", "the useful effects of the various articles of consumption, compared with each other and with the quantity of labour required for their production, will, in the last analysis, determine the plan". "Society ... taking possession of all means of production and using them on a planned basis").[20]

But in the master works of Marxism, the idea of planning or organization of production had actually very little relation to what was subsequently achieved in the USSR, for it still turned on the old socialist idea of the "withering away of the State". "The interference of the State power in social relations becomes superfluous in one sphere after another, and then ceases of itself. The government of persons is replaced by the administration of things and the direction of the processes of production. The

---

[17] E. ZALESKI, *op. cit.*, p. 26.
[18] C. BOBROWSKI, *Formation du Système Soviétique de Planification*, p. 16, Mouton, The Hague, Paris, 1956, quoted by ZALESKI, *op. cit.*
[19] *Ibid.*
[20] F. ENGELS, *Anti-Dühring*, 1878. Lawrence & Wishart, London, 1936. pp. 169, 307, 311, 325, 340, 347. Similar expressions are to be found in other works by Engels *(Dialectics of Nature, Critique of the Erfurt Programme);* cf. also H.-C. DESROCHES, *Signification du marxisme*, followed by a bibliographical introduction to the works of Marx and Engels, by CH.-F. HUBERT, les Editions Ouvrières, Economie et Humanisme, Paris, 1950.

State is not abolished, it withers away."[21] Whether or not this nineteenth-century vision of socialism is a Utopian one, whether it is possible that direction of the processes of production will one day, as one understands it, become virtually an automatic process, the fact remains that the course of history was different, largely because of the circumstances surrounding the victory of the Russian Revolution.

The fact that the Revolution came to fruition in a backward country, such as Russia, and not in the more advanced countries of the West, the fact of the civil war and "capitalist encirclement", all led to the improvisation of "war communism" and the drive towards the "building of socialism in one single country". To ensure the economic independence of the country, it was necessary to stimulate its economic development. Very early on, the making of a single State plan was seen as the means to this end. Preparation of such a plan was envisaged in 1918, and this was implemented in 1920 with the launching of the first general plan, the plan for the electrification of Russia (known as the Goelro Plan). The 1924 constitution reaffirmed the principle of planning, and specified that the working out of the plan was the responsibility of the government of the USSR, and not of the republican governments.

The essential contribution of ideology to the origins of the planning system is, therefore, this "voluntarist" theme which was mentioned previously, the belief in man's all-powerful capacity for changing his environment. Looked at in historical perspective, Soviet planning does indeed emerge as an essentially empirical structure, owing very little to the application of either past or present theoretical principles. During the early years of Soviet power, the political necessity for controlling the economy by centralization of the administration, and ensuring its survival at all costs in the midst of widespread poverty during the civil war, was a consideration which overrode all others. During the NEP period (New Economic Policy), when there was a partial return to some of the mechanisms of the market economy, planning somewhat resembled what is today known as "indicative" planning, the annual plans which were put into operation at that time being regarded by enterprises as a sort of yardstick, which left

---

[21] *Anti-Dühring*, p. 309.

them free to follow, or not, the indications given, and to work out their own plans accordingly, if they so desired.[22] The launching of the first five-year plan, in 1927–8, and particularly the big turning-point of 1930, which brought compulsory collectivization (which had not been part of the plan) the acceleration of growth rates planned in the very midst of the initial difficulties, and the simultaneous start on a large number of vast projects, together with the systematic practice of "deficit balancing" swept away all that, and gave Soviet planning the general character which it has today. It should be added that Soviet economic science, which had been in a fairly flourishing state in the decade 1920–30, at this time went into an almost total decline, which lasted till about 1955, and that from 1930 almost all the leading economists found themselves excluded from responsible posts.[23] Only in the last few years has one witnessed a revival, and indeed a striking one, in Soviet economic science.

THE "LAWS" OF SOCIALISM

In the form in which it has crystallized since the first five-year plans under the impetus given by Stalin, Soviet planning, therefore, emerges more as a political experiment than as a method of economic administration. As Stalin is supposed to have put it: "Planning is not thought, it is action," which is the sort of voluntarist concept which accords well with the idea of "human practice and the comprehension of this practice", and the desire not simply to "interpret" the world but to "change" it[24] which Marxist philosophy advocates.

In practical terms this means that Soviet plans are not a synthesis of impressive studies by economists looking at the economy of the country as a whole, but plans of action which are more or

---

[22] ZALESKI, op. cit.

[23] In this connection, see particularly the evidence of W. LEONTIEF, The fall and rise of Soviet economics, Foreign Affairs, January 1960; see also the note on V. G. GROMAN, one of the leading economists in Gosplan during the years 1923–8, who was condemned in 1931, in N. JASNY, Soviet Industrialization 1928–1952, The University of Chicago Press, 1961.

[24] K. MARX, 8th and 11th Feuerbach Theses. K. MARX and F. ENGELS, Selected Works, vol. II, Foreign Languages Publishing House, Moscow, 1949, Lawrence & Wishart, London, 1950.

less uniquely valid for that sector of activity in which the State
is immediately interested. This particular trend has not always
been the dominant one, for precisely during the years 1920–8,
interesting attempts were made to lay the foundations of a national accounting system, and to co-ordinate a system of targets and
forecasts. These attempts were subsequently abandoned, but
Soviet economists sometimes like to refer to them nowadays,
especially in arguments with "bourgeois" economists.

In articles and statements by Soviet authors, mention is made of
a certain number of "laws" of socialism and of the development
of societies. Many of these are purely political in content, like
the law put forward by Stalin, and nowadays condemned, about
the intensification of the class struggle with the advance of socialism in a single country, or the "solidarity of the communist
movement, which is a law of the development of Marxist–Leninist parties"[25] Only those "laws" with an economic content need
concern us here. Although they are only very loosely defined, are
not clearly numbered and do not appear to have any very precise
relevance as aims, or principles, of organization, they are worth
examining for a few moments.

The one which is most frequently quoted, and is often described as a fundamental law[26] is the "law of the balanced or planned
development of a socialist economy"[27] This begs the question,
rather like a syllogism, stating that since capitalist economy is by
nature unbalanced, and since the Soviet economy is the reverse
of capitalist, then a socialist economy must be a balanced one.

Such an assertion, of course, only very partially accords with
the facts, for the progress of the Soviet economy seems to have
been characterized rather by a series of ups and downs, as we
will see, and by the almost constant existence of bottlenecks.
However, it cannot be denied that this "law" has some relevance,
if only in taking account of the manner in which the growth
mechanism works.[28] The law can, moreover, be interpreted as an

[25] I. F. ILICHEV, *op. cit.*

[26] L. GATOVSKI, Some problems of the political economy of socialism at
its present stage, *Vopr. Ekon.*, No. 3, 1959.

[27] See also the statement by STRUMILIN, "The task of a planned economy
is the suppression of all disproportions in production." Cf. The law of value
and planning, *Vopr. Ekon.*, No. 7, 1959.

[28] See later, Chapter IX.

attempt at systematization of the so-called "balance" method which is characteristic of Soviet planning. It has also been the occasion of some studies, for example the one in which Academician Nemchinov endeavoured to prove, using Marxist categories and with figures to support his view, that the British economy in 1935 and 1950 was unbalanced, without, however, showing, by reference to the same categories, that the USSR itself was not.[29] Certain of the general objectives of economic policy and especially of regional policy, which we shall mention later (eradicating the fundamental differences between town and country, between manual and intellectual work, achieving a balance in the level of economic development)[30] are presented as aspects of this need for achieving equilibrium.

Another "law" which is very often quoted, although its application is very obscure, is the "law of value". This is a reference to the "labour theory of value" propounded by Marx, after Ricardo, in which he condemned capitalist society and its "surplus value". Paradoxically, it would seem, this law had previously never been invoked in the USSR, since there was, conversely, a long-standing "immutable law"[31] according to which the prices of the various commodities, in a socialist economy, could be fixed without relation to the cost of production. This question has in recent years been the subject of much controversy in the USSR. Most economists now think that the law of value should play some part in socialist planning "in order to regulate working time and the distribution of social labour between different categories of production in proportion to their needs".[32] Going a little further, and in contradiction to one of the fundamental tenets of Marxism, Strumilin even agrees that although work is the basis of the value of all commodities, the value of the products of work "does not take on its full significance" until the moment

---

[29] V. NEMCHINOV, Relationships in expanded production, *Vopr. Ekon.*, No. 10, 1958. See also D. OPARIN, Quantitative relationships in models of expanded production, *Vopr. Ekon.*, No. 11, 1959.

[30] V. NEMCHINOV, Theoretical problems of the rational deployment of productive forces, *Vopr. Ekon.*, No. 6, 1961.

[31] GATOVSKI, *ibid.*, *Vopr. Ekon.*, No. 10, 1958.

[32] S. STRUMILIN, On the determination of value and its application in socialism, *Vopr. Ekon.*, No. 8, 1959.

an exchange is made,[33] thereby coming close to the conclusions of the "bourgeois marginalist" school. The practical import of these discussions will be analysed later.

Nor should one forget to mention the "basic law" of socialism, as defined by Stalin in 1952, which aims at ensuring "maximum satisfaction of the ever-growing material and cultural needs of society" by constantly perfecting socialist production in accordance with the most advanced techniques. This is first and foremost a propaganda statement, of course, but one which should not be discounted insofar as it may serve as an objective or a guide for Soviet economists.

Lastly, there is the "law of priority in the development of heavy industry" or producers' goods, which could also be considered a "law" of socialist economics.

This law was quoted in particular by Shepilov against those "pseudo-economists" — in fact, Malenkov, who was then president of the Council of Ministers — who were accused of disregarding it. The recommendations of the Conference on problems of determining the economic effectiveness of investment (Moscow, June 1958) make a similar reference to the "economic laws of socialism, which call first and foremost for the development of production of the means of production, and require that maximum rates of growth should be achieved in production in general".[34] Some authors, however, seem reluctant to admit that such a law has any widespread validity, and even regard "a marked change in the most important proportions of the economy in the sector of material goods, values, and the regional sector"[35] as a feature of the present time.

Of course, in dealing with all these laws, we are often told that it is a mistake to treat them as "dogma", that "socialist

---

[33] *Id., Vopr. Ekon*, No. 7, 1959. The relevance of this remark is all the greater when one recalls the violence of the controversy, ten or twenty years ago in western Europe, which divided Marxist and non-Marxist economists on this question of value. Cf. particularly H. DENIS, *La Valeur*, Editions Sociales, Paris, 1950; C. BETTELHEIM, *Problèmes théoriques et pratiques de la planification*, Presses Universitaires de France, 1946 (particularly pp. 4–7); J. ROBINSON, *An Essay on Marxian Economics*, Macmillan, London, 1947, particularly the conclusion.

[34] Critères des choix de l'investissement en URSS, *ISEA.*, G, No. 6, p. 105, June 1959.

[35] Ya. KRONROD, Certain aspects of socialist growth at the present time, *Vopr. Ekon.*, No. 9, 1959.

political economy is the study of the economic laws of a social formation, a study which must constantly inspire, and does so inspire, economic policy"; or we are told that "Marxism makes commitment an essential part of any positive essay in social and economic research, and that it regards such commitment as an indispensable condition of all progress in research".[35a]

But however interesting these affirmations may be in the philosophical context, can they be of any real assistance to the economist whose task it is to discover the basic principles on which society can most efficiently be organized?

THE TRANSITION TO COMMUNISM

The approach of the XXIInd Congress of the CPSU, and the Congress itself, in October 1961, focused attention on the transition from the stage of socialism—which is based on the "law of distribution (of income) in accordance with the work done" — to communism, which is based on the principle, also borrowed from nineteenth-century French authors, "from each according to his abilities, to each according to his needs." This transition had already been frequently mentioned by the Soviet leadership.[36] The XXIInd Congress, however, is the one which "will go down in history as the Congress of the builders of communism, the Congress which studied and adopted the great programme for the building of a communist society".[37] The core of the new programme, which was submitted as a draft programme in July 1961, and adopted by the Congress with very few amendments, consists of the broad outline of the new plan, with 1970 and 1980 as its terminal years. This plan is to lay "the material and technical foundations of communism" and to ensure "an abundance of material and cultural goods".

Apart, however, from the reference to abundance, the description of the communist state is left very vague, following in this

[35a] L. GOLDMANN, *Le Dieu Caché*, p. 100, Gallimard, Paris, 1955.

[36] The history of the USSR has reached a vital point, "that of the completion and edification of the socialist society without classes and of the slow change from socialism to communism." Molotov's report to the XVIIIth Congress (17th March 1939) quoted by J. BRUHAT, Que sais-je?, *Histoire de l'URSS*, p. 90, Presses Universitaires de France, 5th ed. 1958.

[37] Report on the programme of the CPSU presented on 18th October 1961 by N. S. Khrushchev.

the example of the Marxist-Leninist masters. Where there is a precise description, the future communist society seems to look very much like Soviet society as it is today, or as it is said to be. The resemblance emerges both in the image of what communist society will be (a classless society in which all citizens will have a say in public affairs, which will raise the cultural level of the masses and ensure the fullest development of the individual, and maintain strong democratic centralism) and of what it will not be (rejection of "soupladle communism", and of the concept of communism as an "association of independent economic organisms", rejection of the withering away of the State, and of universal implementation of the system of free distribution and the elimination of wage disparities "irrespective of the nature and complexity of the work"). Nevertheless, the increases in benefits in kind, which by 1980 are expected to comprise half of the total income of the population (in particular, the greater part of the upkeep of children and also, according to some statements, certain free services such as urban transport and entertainments) are undeniably an important development. And yet, it is not these features of the future communist society which have aroused most general interest in the USSR, as they have in the rest of the world, but almost exclusively the promise of abundance, and a standard of living for the people which will be "higher than that of any capitalist country".

It is interesting to note that, according to the Soviet idea, achievement of abundance is the prerequisite for reaching a state of full communism. This is what leads American economists to advance the theory that communism is reached when the marginal utility of consumption is equal to zero (in other words, consumption no longer increases when goods are free). Judging at least from what Professor Galbraith says, consumption in the United States, which is much higher than it is in the USSR, has already in a great many sectors reached the point where the marginal utility of private consumption is equal to zero, if the forces of advertising do not intervene.[38]

---

[38] cf. A. BERGSON, "The economic aspects of the Party program," Paper read at Harvard on 26th October 1961. *Bulletin of the Association for the study of Soviet type economics (ASTE)*; J. K. GALBRAITH, *The Affluent Society*", The Riverside Press, 1958, especially Ch. X and XI.

CHAPTER IV

THE PROCESS OF PLANNING

THE best known feature of the Soviet economy is its planning system. The term is used here in its generally accepted sense, that is, a body of directives issued to the various economic organs with the object of achieving predetermined aims.

GENERAL CHARACTERISTICS OF SOVIET PLANNING

Control of the economy is an essential prerequisite for a collectivized system. Since nationalization of the means of production does away with the profit motive and the autonomy of decision-making bodies, a substitute must be found for these features of the capitalist or market-type economy. This is represented by *orders* issued to enterprises and other economic organs by, or through, the central authority. A natural solution to the problem of rationalizing this form of administration and making it as "scientific" as possible is found in the formation of overall plans; something, too, must have been contributed by the nature of the Russian character, with its steadfastness in the execution of predetermined tasks, its inclination for the broad, long-term view, its respect for science and culture.

At the present time, however, the State is still far from exercising the same degree of control over all sectors of the economy, and the plans themselves do not cover the entire field of economic activity, so that there are still fairly large unplanned areas on the periphery. For example, the investment figures given in official publications usually do not correspond to total investments, but only to State-planned investments; occasionally, investments by kolkhozy and other sectors which, though part of the planned economy are not part of the State sector, are also included, but even in this case it appears that some part of investment is still omitted.[1]

One of the most striking aspects of Soviet life is that, far from being entirely regulated and balanced, it has in fact a certain number of fields, sectors or types of activity which are either forgotten or disregarded, and which develop on the fringe of official preoccupations. The number of these sectors gradually diminishes, of course, as the area of public ownership increases, and one of the features of Soviet policy in recent years has been the attention paid to aspects of the economy which were previously neglected or sacrificed (consumption, agriculture, construction), though the earlier trend has not been entirely reversed.

One important question concerns the aims of Soviet planning. This will be examined later on, when we deal with the problem of criteria, which is of crucial importance in the implementation of modern methods of administration.[2] In more general terms, however, we must ask ourselves what end the Soviet leadership is pursuing. Economic growth is not the complete answer. The fact is that the Soviet leaders tend to give systematic priority to heavy industry, to carrying through a programme of major projects, enforcing collectivization and bringing the entire economy within the ambit of control organizations, in order to transform the economic basis of society and bring about a redistribution of the national income, thus "paving the way for a technical revolution, which for a Marxist is a fundamental criterion, if not indeed the ultimate one".[3] It has been said that there is a dichotomy in the objectives of the plan and of the planners. In fact in an economy where prices no longer act as scarcity indicators, the plan and its objectives tend to act as a yardstick. But the plan itself is in fact only a means of attaining other ends, which may be, as we have already shown, the suppression of any economic power which is independent of the central power, the building up of a modern economy,[4] or again, along with this desire

---

[1] Some statements include items from which total figures for investment may sometimes be reconstructed; see essays on this subject in the reports of the Economic Commission for Europe, United Nations Organization, Geneva.

[2] See later, Chapter IX.

[3] BOBROWSKI, *op. cit.*, p. 86.

[4] See ZALESKI, *op. cit.*, pp. 289–90.

for industrialization, the desire to change the economic structure by utilizing the most advanced techniques, and to spur on the producers by setting ambitious targets,[5] which sometimes appear to be means to an end and sometimes ends in themselves.

And so it would appear that what the Soviet leadership is seeking is not economic rationality alone; or at least, one can agree that they are doing so only in so far as one adheres to the politico-economic doctrine that the search for economic rationality entails a struggle against the so-called capitalist system, and the "ills" imputed to it: an assumption which would seem to deny the existence of any rationality without some political content.

Soviet planning is, as we know, *mandatory* in character. Soviet plans do not in fact consist solely of a body of general directives, but are broken down into a series of individual directives issued to all economic agencies, and strictly delineating their sphere of activity.

Soviet plans fulfil a certain number of functions. These may be summarized under four main headings:

The function of *forecasting*, which consists of a definition of the objectives which must be achieved, together with appropriate dates and figures;

The function of *administration*, since the plan serves as a basis for the allocation of investment funds, raw materials, components, labour and deliveries of finished products;

The function of *supervision*, in which the results of fulfilment of the plan are used as a basis for the apportioning of rewards, reprimands or penalties;

Lastly, in its final function, which should be mentioned despite the reservation made earlier on, the plan does not constitute an end in itself, but a means to the achievement of steady *growth* in the various sectors of the economy.

Soviet authors do in fact often stress this last point. "Only a complex of measures systematically aimed at ensuring the

---

[5] Objectives $O_2\,O_3\,O_4$ of the basic model by D. GRANICK, An organizational model of Soviet industrial planning, *Journal of Political Economy*, April 1959.

country's growth can be described as planning"[6] writes Academician Nemchinov, for example.

In official documents or statements one often encounters the expression "single State plan". But, as we have already noted, the plan is in fact made up of a mass of individual documents. Firstly, plans are interconnected in point of time: monthly, quarterly, half-yearly and annual plans described as *current* plans; five-year, seven-year, and now ten- and twenty-year plans, described as *long-term* plans. Alongside these plans, there are also other major objectives or plans, for example the objective of 60 million tons of steel by 1960, which was launched by Stalin in 1946 (and which, unlike the objectives of the first five-year plans, was in fact reached a year early) or the fifteen-year plan which was launched in 1957. Like some others, particularly the sixth five-year plan (1956–60) which was launched in 1956 and abandoned in 1957, to be replaced by the seven-year plan 1959–65, the fifteen-year plan now seems to have been shelved; but there is evidence that in the development of the chemical industry, for example, reference was still being made in 1962 to the objectives which it contained.

A new type of plan has emerged, namely the two-year plan, for 1964 and 1965. This plan, preparation of which was called for in the Central Committee's Directives of 13th March 1963, was submitted at the session of the Supreme Soviet on 16th December 1963 by P. Lomako, the chairman of Gosplan. The objectives of this plan replace those laid down in the seven-year plan for the two years in question. At the same time, there has been a return to the formula of the five-year plan for the years 1966–70. The 1964–5 plan is, moreover, divided into six-monthly periods, and not quarters, as was the case hitherto.

It has become the custom to have long-term plans approved not only by the government but also by the Party Congress: thus, the sixth five-year plan was endorsed by the XXth Congress (1956), the seven-year plan for 1959–65 by the XXIst Congress (February 1959), the 1960–80 plan by the XXIInd Congress (October 1961). Between 1960[7] and the beginning of 1963, top-

[6] V. S. NEMCHINOV, The application of mathematical methods in economic research and planning, *Vopr. Ekon.*, No. 6, 1960.

[7] Decision by the Communist Party and the Council of Ministers, 7th August 1960.

level responsibility for long-term plans and current plans was divided between two organizations, and *Gosekonomsoviet* (the State scientific economic council) was responsible for the preparation of long-term plans, while Gosplan (the State Committee on planning) dealt only with current planning. Since 1963, long-term planning has once more become the responsibility of Gosplan, as well as current planning. However, alongside Gosplan there now exists, as we shall see later on, the Sovnarkhoz of the USSR, which relieves Gosplan of its responsibility for the fulfilment of annual plans.

There is a similar interconnection of plans in the territorial sense: plans for enterprises, municipalities, the various regions or territories, the republics, and finally the Union itself. In addition to general or production plans, there are also special plans aimed, for example, at the reorganization of workshops or a whole factory, and varying in their time limits, or plans with a particular objective common to several enterprises or sectors.

In principle all these plans are not contradictory, but interdependent. Indeed the "principle of continuity in planning" is one which has been most frequently stressed of recent years, for instance in N. S. Khrushchev's statement at the meeting of the Supreme Soviet of the USSR in 1957, or the decree by the Communist Party and the Council of Ministers of the USSR dated 26th December 1960.[8] However, the fact that it is so often emphasized may largely be an indication that so far it has not worked very well in practice.

PLANNING PROCEDURES: CURRENT PLANS

How is a plan made? This is a question which arises nowadays in all sorts of different countries which are faced with the task of stimulating their economic development by establishing, or perfecting, a national planning system. Our concern here is not with the range of systems which are possible, or with deciding which of these may properly be described as planning, but with the Soviet system — which after all is a pioneer in the field.

[8] Cf. A. EFIMOV, Problems of perfecting the planning of the national economy, *Kommunist*, No. 4, March 1961.

Foreign economists engaged in a study of Soviet planning often concentrate their attention on problems of choice within the planning system itself, and the degree of rationality thus reflected in the progress of the economy. But achievement of this rationality, although it is the central problem of the economy, does not depend exclusively on the methods which are employed in arriving at decisions; to a very great extent it also depends on the nature of the procedure which is followed, and of the organizational machinery which enables these decisions to be made.

Soviet planning is essentially an enormous administrative machine, the working of which depends on the co-operation of a very large number of individuals and organizations. Its internal mechanism has in fact a singularly limiting effect on the choice of methods which may be employed, and consequently is one of the essential factors governing the degree of efficiency with which it works and the results it produces. This inner structure is also its most original feature, and the introduction in 1957 of a system of territorially based industrial administration, which was altered, but not abolished, in 1962–3 and which so far has not been imitated by any of the countries which follow the Soviet model, only serves to confirm its importance.

Plans are worked out in accordance with a procedure which has now to some extent become standardized. The procedure is roughly similar both for long-term plans and annual or current plans. A brief description will be given, with emphasis particularly on the latter category, which are the real operational plans, the only ones having the four types of function listed previously, and which are necessarily much more detailed than long-term plans; we shall deal particularly with industry. The description is based mainly on my interviews in 1961.

This description of planning procedures will be formal, however, in the sense that its full significance is not apparent until viewed in the context of the problems of the actual working of the economy.[9] The study of problems connected with the location of industry[10] and of the methods of determining and achieving an economic optimum[11] will also ensure a fuller understanding of the

---

[9] See later, Chapters VI and VII.
[10] See Chapter VIII.
[11] See Chapter IX.

implications of the decisions which are made when plans are being elaborated.

Soviet economists, when asked to talk about their planning system, like to remind one that in the USSR, "where everything belongs to the people," the entire economy operates as an administrative whole. This, they say, is a precondition of efficient planning. However, while there is certainly centralization, it is a "democratic centralization". Proof of this is to be found in the fact that there is participation at all levels of the economic administration, from enterprises and workers' councils up to Gosplan, the Council of Ministers of the Union, and the heads of the Party.

Up till recently, responsibility for initiating work on each plan rested entirely with the central authorities. Since about 1959, apparently, it has become the custom to begin work on a plan simultaneously from the base and the summit. This practice is made possible by the greater extent to which economic life is regulated, and is justified by the need for using the previous year's statistics, which only reach the upper echelons after a certain time-lag. The elaboration of a plan for a given year—say 1962—really takes place the year before (1961), and is based on the figures for the previous year (1960); the objectives of the plan for the current year, which have been set at the end of the preceding year, i.e. December 1960 for the year 1961, are also used as a basis of reference, as are the current long-term plan or plans.

This new procedure is itself an indication of the trend towards a greater degree of autonomy at enterprise level, or a relative decentralization of the decision-making machinery, which is generally agreed to have been one of the features of recent years. There has indeed been a whole series of reforms affecting planning during the past few years: in 1955, wider powers were granted to the republics, particularly in the matter of 50 per cent of the excess of production over plan requirements, and all their budget surplus, which they may now use as they wish, and especially for the welfare of the population;[12] there was also a reform in planning methods designed to give greater scope for suggestions at local level; a reform in industrial administration in 1957,[13] and, in 1959, the reform in plan elaboration.

[12] See *Kommunist*, No. 17, November 1955.
[13] See Chapter V.

Every year, the government publishes a decree announcing the preparation of a plan, and the rules to be observed by the lower echelons. Elaboration of the plan begins about April, and is completed by about December. On the basis of its results for the previous year, and the plan for the current year, and taking into account both potential production and existing orders, each enterprise prepares its own draft plan for the following year. This contains its production targets, and a statement of the appropriate requirements. At about the same time, Gosplan starts work on its control figures *(kontrolnye tsiffry)* or basic plan figures, although a first draft is not ready much before the beginning of summer. From top to bottom of this chain there is a simultaneous ebb and flow of information and proposals which will go to make up the content of the plan, and which will in the main be co-ordinated at republic level. In accordance with the terms of the decree of 9th July 1958, which set up "permanent production councils" in enterprises of more than 100 people, enterprise proposals must be examined and approved by the "enterprise collective".[14] When they are ready, they are passed on to the superior authority which, in the case of a large enterprise, will be the sovnarkhoz. In practice, given the constant contact between enterprises and sovnarkhoz, the latter is consulted on proposals at a very early stage, and discussion goes on during the spring months. At the beginning of summer, the sovnarkhoz itself is expected to have completed its draft plan for the total number of enterprises coming under its jurisdiction, and this is then passed up to the next administrative level.

A certain amount of information is shed in the transition from one stage to the next. Thus, the enterprise plan, which as a whole is designated by the name of *tekhpromfinplan* (technical-industrial-financial plan) contains a lot of detailed information about the production programme, the introduction of new techniques, supplies of materials and equipment, employment and wages, costing and accounts, technical and organizational methods.[15]

---

[14] H. CHAMBRE, *Le Pouvoir Soviétique*, p. 138, Librairie générale de Droit et de Jurisprudence, Paris, 1959; — Le Plan Septennal Soviétique, *ISEA*, G, No. 10, p. 24, November 1960.

[15] *ISEA*, G, No. 10, p. 25, and, for an example of the forms used, pp. 336–58.

But only a part of this information is used in the compilation of the sovnarkhoz plan.

Within the sovnarkhoz itself there is, of course, a planning section, one of whose duties is to draw up a certain number of general indicators or norms, which enterprises must use as a guide, which they must implement, and which relate to the various aspects of economic activity already mentioned (increasing of production or productivity, lowering of production costs, or consumption per unit of production, etc.); it would appear that the purpose is one of directing and controlling the planning work of enterprises, rather than acting as a central collecting point for all this information. In addition, from what I was told in my interviews, the sovnarkhoz has no authority to change the total of material requirements for production, which is arrived at by adding up total requirements for all enterprises, except after individual discussion with the enterprises, the object of this being no doubt to prevent distortion of the estimated figure for enterprise requirements by an over-zealous sovnarkhoz bent on implementing the norms for reduction of consumption of raw materials.

Just prior to completion of its plan, that is round about June-July, the sovnarkhoz begins discussions with the Gosplan of the republic to which it belongs. In principle the republican Gosplan does not establish direct contact with enterprises; there is a report that, after the sovnarkhoz had completed its draft plan for 1958, the Ukraine Gosplan, to whom it had been submitted, took steps to summon the directors of the enterprises to Kiev, without consulting the sovnarkhoz, in order to ask them to modify their objectives, but were forced to desist in view of the protests which resulted.[16]

On the basis of the documents which it has received, the republican Gosplan, which by this time has the control figures which have been worked out in Moscow, in its turn prepares its general plan, which is supposed to be completed by about the month of August. The republican plan, although not so detailed, is a more complete document than that of the sovnarkhoz, which is only concerned with industry and construction. It is divided both by branch and by territory.

[16] Report by S. KAMENITSEN, quoted by M. KASER, The reorganization of Soviet industry and its effects on decision making, in *Value and Plan, op. cit.*

Draft plans from the various republics are then sent to Moscow, to the all-Union Gosplan. The draft plan for the whole of the Union must be completed and approved by Gosplan, then by the Council of Ministers of the USSR, by October or the beginning of November.

In the course of this work, Gosplan makes adjustments in the proposals which are submitted to it. The object of these adjustments is to ensure that the individual objectives are in conformity with its own general objectives, and also to ensure the coherence of the plan, that is, to verify that the output totals, and the various requirements of enterprises, sovnarkhozy and republics, tally for each of the products studied. Where there is a discrepancy, the appropriate decisions are taken, which may mean either increasing certain production objectives, or reducing others, if the necessary amounts of raw materials are not available.

These adjustments and checks comprise the main phase of planning. In the earlier period, it might have been said to be almost the only one, since enterprise proposals were only a very secondary consideration so far as Gosplan was concerned. Nowadays, however, it seems certain that the forecasting carried out at enterprise level, and the forecasting and adjustment done at the level of sovnarkhoz and republic are also of considerable practical importance.

However, it is clear that the adjustments made by the all-Union Gosplan are of an entirely different order, since Gosplan alone is in a position to have an overall picture of total requirements and total resources for all the different aspects of production, and to make the decisions which will produce a balanced whole. In practice it appears that the upward or downward adjustments made by Gosplan in the plan proposals which are submitted to it may be very considerable; so far as can be seen, adjustments resulting in a 10 or even 20% reduction or increase in the initial proposals from enterprises are not unusual. There may even be cases, as we shall see later on, of very much greater modifications made either during preparation or execution of the plan, although these are no doubt exceptional, since they are usually the subject of a press report.

The plan, whose objectives are now obligatory, begins its downward journey from the all-Union Gosplan to the enterprises, once more passing through the republican Gosplans and the sovnarkhozy. This phase seems to cover the period from the end of October and the beginning of November to the beginning of the month of December, at which time the general objectives of the plan, possibly after some final revision, are officially approved and published (by the Council of Ministers of the USSR and then, in the form of a decree, by the Supreme Soviet). At each stage of the downward journey, the plans once again become more detailed in content; in fact, what appears to happen is that draft plans are prepared during their upward journey, are then revised and completed to accord with the planning work carried out by the upper echelons, and are finally returned to their authors. The following diagram[17] corresponds fairly accurately to statements made by various Soviet authorities, for example Professor Turetski:

The objectives of the long-term plan will be subdivided, for the period covered by the plan (five to seven years) by sector of activity, by federated republic, by administrative economic region, by enterprise, and by construction site. A systematic approach of this kind helps to stimulate economic initiative on the spot, at the centre of activity. It enables enterprises to build up their reserves, to make advance contracts for delivery of supplies and the acquisition of the requirements necessary for the following year's production, without waiting for the central authorities to communicate details of the annual plans, which are sometimes late in arriving.

In drawing up their plans for the current year, enterprises, construction sites, sovnarkhozy (for the economic administrative regions) and federated republics all use the objectives of the long-term plan as their model. At the same time, they can apply the necessary correctives in the light of practical considerations, taking into account the requirements of the national economy and the need for maintaining equilibrium among the various branches of economic activity . . .

While exercising systematic supervision over plan fulfilment and studying the latest needs of the national economy, the all-Union Gosplan makes adjustments, where necessary, four months before the end of the year, to the objectives laid down for the following year, in accordance with the corresponding forecasts in the long-term plan. These adjustments are ratified by the government of the Union, since they relate to the overall national economic plan. In other cases, adjustments in annual objectives are made in accordance with their importance and their particular sector by the organizations concerned . . . or by the enterprises and construction sites themselves.

[17] Figure 1, p. 75.

Using these revised annual objectives as their guide, enterprises work out their three-monthly and half-yearly plans.[18]

Recent information does not suggest that there has been any noticeable change in the procedures as outlined above. There is a continuing trend as we shall see later, towards reducing the number of categories subject to central planning, and giving correspondingly greater importance to plan elaboration at enterprise level. It was announced, in this connection, that in the RSFSR, some 300 officials of the republican Gosplan, sovnarkhoz and other organizations, and about 100 officials from the Union Gosplan and the State committees, had been sent to give on-the-spot assistance to those concerned locally with the drawing up of the plan.[18a]

Concurrently with these production and investment plans, and in as close a degree of co-ordination with them as is possible, the planning authorities draw up allocation plans, which state in concrete terms the tasks which are to be accomplished in this field, and at the same time indicate who is to be responsible for carrying them out. Elaboration of these plans also takes place at various levels, for although Gosplan is responsible for preparing the overall allocation plan for the national economy, and submitting it for approval by the Council of Ministers, this plan, as we shall see, does not cover all products, but only those on Gosplan's list, these being essential products, while the others are allocated either by the republican Gosplans, or by the sovnarkhozy.[19]

Preparation and organization of the *supply of materials and equipment*, as it is usually called, is a vital aspect of the economic

---

[18] C. TURETSKI, La Planification régionale de l'économie nationale en URSS et le régionalisme, *Revue Internationale des Sciences Sociales*, No. 3, 1959, Cf. also the description given by H. CHAMBRE, Plan d'entreprise et balances régionales dans le plan septennal, *ISEA*, G, No. 10, November 1960, and reports by earlier missions of Western economists: "Les méthodes soviétiques actuelles de planification. Compte rendu et observations d'une mission d'économistes français en URSS", *ISEA*, G, No. 7, August 1959; H. S. LEVINE, "The centralized planning of supply in Soviet industry", report to the US Congress (Joint Economic Committee) October pp. 151–76, 1959, and notes on a visit to the USSR, May–June, 1959.

[18a] Y. CHADAEV, *Plan. Khoz.* No. 11, 1963.

[19] Cf. R. FASSIER, *La répartition planifiée des moyens de production dans l'industrie soviétique*, thesis, Grenoble 1960, pp. 59, 110 (mineogr).

activity of the State, since it is on this that achievement of the planned objectives really depends. This matter of supply organization has always been a sensitive spot in the Soviet economy. One of the most frequent complaints in the Soviet Union has always been the inadequacy of co-ordination between the organization of supplies and planning proper.

Preparation of the supply plan by the Union Gosplan is carried out nowadays in two distinct phases. The aim of the first phase is to draw up material balances and an allocation plan for key products in the national economy (i.e. about 150–200 products only). On the basis of information supplied by enterprise and the sovnarkhozy the republican Gosplans transmit an estsmate of their requirements in these products to Gosplan (theoretically by the 15th May). Gosplan then prepares the material balances and also the allocation plan for these products, and submits them to the Council of Ministers of the USSR who must in principle give their approval before the 15th June of the year prior to the period covered by the plan.

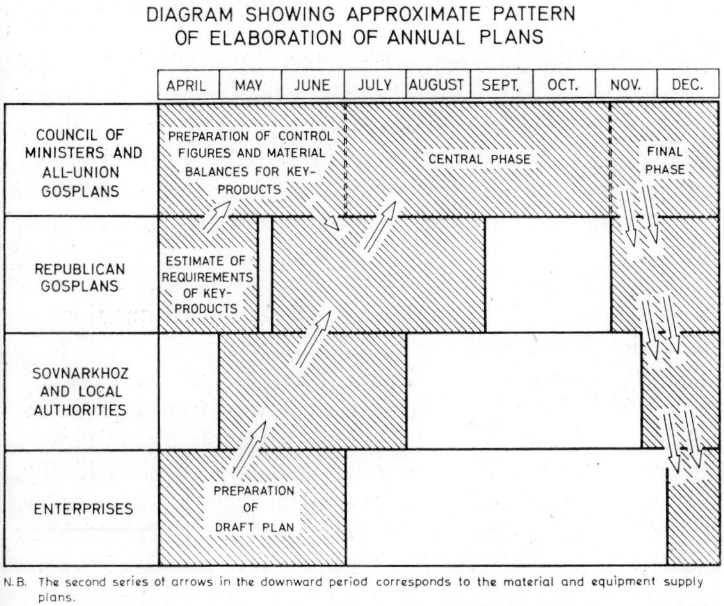

DIAGRAM SHOWING APPROXIMATE PATTERN
OF ELABORATION OF ANNUAL PLANS

N.B. The second series of arrows in the downward period corresponds to the material and equipment supply plans.

FIG. 1. Diagram showing approximate pattern of elaboration of annual plans

The second phase, which is similar to the elaboration of production plans, begins, like the latter, at enterprise level. With those products which are subject to centralized allocation, the work ends with the national supply plan, which is included in the annual plan for the development of the national economy. This plan comprises the approval by the Council of Ministers of the USSR, with a statement of the fundamental objectives and the tasks of republics and ministers; the material balances; the distribution plans by product, noting the republic or ministry concerned; the material consumption norms plus the targets for reduction of these norms. The rest of the document is made up of plans for deliveries between republics, and deliveries for federal purposes, which in principle are approved by the Union Gosplan before the 1st December.[20]

Supply allocations do not cover the total available resources. Reserves are built up at various levels of the organization, one of these, which is subject to central administration, being known as the "Council of Ministers" reserve. These reserves are a provision against emergencies which may arise during fulfilment of the plans.

Draft plans for the supply of products other than those allocated by Gosplan are approved either by the Council of Ministers of the republics upon submission by the central supply directorates of the republican Gosplans (products allocated by the republics) or by the ministries concerned, when they have retained their allocations, or by the sovnarkhozy for products on their list.[21]

As the plan works its way down to enterprise level, it gradually becomes more specific and more detailed on such questions as targets, time factors and consumption norms.[22]

The officials with whom I spoke in 1961 had described the way in which these detailed instructions were transmitted; first of all, they said, the passing down of the supply plans followed that of the production plans after an interval which, ideally, should not be more than about a fortnight (however, as we know, the press report numerous instances of enterprises which by January, February or even later in the year in question have not

[20] FASSIER, *op. cit.*, pp. 110, 122.
[21] *Ibid.*, p. 125.
[22] *Ibid.*, p. 126.

yet received their supply plan, or sometimes even their production plan). Each sovnarkhoz, as producer or consumer, is given notice, at the same time as the specialist supply agencies, of the quantities of the various products which it must receive, or deliver, every quarter. At each stage on the plan's downward journey, increasingly detailed indications are given with regard to quality, and origin or destination, of the products in question. For example, if the Union Gosplan has estimated that for a given construction project in the Ukraine, requiring 1000 tons of metal, 900 tons should come from the Ukraine itself and 100 tons from the Urals, the specialist supply department of the Ukraine Gosplan will add some supplementary details; thus, of the supplies to be provided by the Ukraine, 600 tons, for example, should come from the steelworks at Zhdanov, and 300 from Stalino (now Donetsk). The sovnarkhoz may add some further details (quality, delivery dates, etc.). At the final stage, producer and consumer enterprises make contact, and exchange a commercial contract[23] containing all the required specifications. Once this contract has been signed, the producing factory is under an obligation to deliver, and the consumers, for their part, are bound to provide exact specifications of their requirements. Penalties are incurred in cases of nonfulfilment of a contract.

I was informed at the Moscow Town sovnarkhoz that an enterprise which has completed its draft plan may thereafter — that is, from June onwards — make contracts relating to its orders for the following year. These orders will be incorporated in the supply plan, which itself is not finalized until the autumn. This information tends to confirm, if indeed confirmation is needed, that plan preparation at enterprise level is by no means a mere formality, affecting as it does the orders issued by superior authority.

LONG-TERM PLANS

In the preparation of long-term plans, such as the seven-year plan for 1959–65, the part played by enterprises and regional organizations, as compared with the role of the central organi-

---

[23] In this connection, see later, p. 158.

zations, is much more restricted than in the case of annual plans.[24]
Elaboration of the seven-year plan, which we may take as a model of the long-term plan, apparently consisted of the following
phases:

(a) *Adoption of general directives by the Party and the government.* These directives, unaccompanied by figures, or with only
a very few figures, presumably stated the general aims of economic policy and the broad trends of the plan.

(b) *Elaboration of "control figures" or plan indicators by Gosplan.*
These forecast production, in physical quantities, and growth
rates for the various sectors of production, and, in addition, total
investments, the allocation of these by sector and by republic,
the level of consumption and external trade. The republics and
their Gosplans were consulted on this question at the beginning
of 1958.

(c) *Adjustments and detailed definition of plan objectives; downward and upward movement of plans.* Each enterprise and, at higher
level, the sovnarkhozy and other intermediate organizations,
and the republics, are requested to prepare their production
and investment objectives for the period covered by the plan, in
accordance with the broad trends mentioned previously. Passing
through the sovnarkhozy, these proposals go up to the republican Gosplans who, in the light of the overall objectives which
have been fixed for the Union and their own republic, adjust and
finalize them as binding objectives and then return them to their
authors. At the same time, the republican Gosplans use the information received to suggest amendments in the "control figures"
to the Union Gosplan, wherever this is judged necessary.

(d) *Approval by the Council of Ministers of the USSR and by
the Party.* In the case of the seven-year plan, approval was given
by the Central Committee (November 1958) to the "basic figures
for the development of the national economy of the USSR for
the period 1959–1965", first presented in the form of "theses"
by N. S. Khrushchev. At this point, yet another phase may ensue,
namely discussion at national level.

(e) *Discussion at national level.* In the case of the 1959–65 plan,
this discussion, which had been called for by the Central Com-

---

[24] Report by French economists, *op. cit.;* R. BORDAZ, *La nouvelle économie soviétique,* Grasset, 1960; H. S. LEVINE, *op. cit.*

mittee, took place in the period between the Central Committee meeting in November 1958 and the XXIst Party Congress in February 1959. It took place, according to what is no doubt a time-honoured procedure, in enterprises, construction sites, kolkhozy, sovkhozy, research centres and institutes, units of the armed forces, local soviets and administrations throughout the country, and involved "over 986,000 meetings in which more than 70 million persons took part, and 4,672,000 Party members made speeches, contributing suggestions, observations and amendments".[25] In the event, however, it seems unlikely that this discussion had much effect in modifying the original proposals.

Elaboration of the ten- and twenty-year plan (1960–80) which was carried out by Gosekonomsoviet and approved by the XXIInd Congress in October 1961, also seems to have been the occasion of some form of consultation with authorities or personalities at republic level; nevertheless, in this instance, the role of the central authorities appears to have been by far the more important.

CONTENT OF PLANS AND PRODUCT CLASSIFICATIONS

We have only indirect knowledge of what Soviet plans contain. Only the broad outlines of these plans are in fact published. Thus, we know the 1959–65 plan in the form of a "Resolution by the XXIst Party Congress of the Communist Party of the Soviet Union based on the report of comrade N. S. Khrushchev: Basic figures for the development of the national economy of the USSR for 1959–65 (unanimously adopted 5th February 1959)".[26] In addition to this document, we have the speech by N. S. Khrushchev, and the various supplementary methodological or statistical data, elucidating some particular point or announcing corrections and dealing with related problems which are to be found in review articles, books or pamphlets, and also in the statistical yearbook.

On annual plans, too, the amount of information available is incomplete. For example, on the 1961 plan, we have a 45-page booklet containing the report by V. I. Novikov "on the State

[25] Decisions of the XXIst Congress.
[26] Foreign language editions, Moscow, 1959, 174 pp.

plan for the development of the national economy of the USSR for the year 1961" presented to the Supreme Soviet on the 20th December 1960, the closing address (22nd December) and the text of the law of the same day approving the plan.

The information to be found in articles in periodicals is often fuller than in official documents. For example, an article appearing in the December 1961 issue of *Planovoe Khozyaistvo* gave a whole series of figures relating to the 1962 plan. The article ended with a table showing the main objectives of the 1962 plan by republic, broken down into seven columns: global industrial production (index 100 in 1961), State investments, numbers of wage-earners and salaried staff, labour productivity in industry and construction, reduction of expenditure per rouble of industrial market production, reduction of costs in construction and assembly work, retail trade turnover.[27]

On the other hand, there is no information on the specific content of the plans for enterprises, territorial administrations or the Union as a whole. In the entire post-war period, no Western economist, so far as is known, has ever succeeded in finding out the complete plan for an enterprise, a sovnarkhoz, a republic or the Union itself. However, a certain number of forms used in the preparation of plans have either been passed on, or published. For instance, the forms and tables used in the preparation of the seven-year plan for 1959–65 were handed over, without the figures, to the French economists' mission which visited the USSR in May 1958 to study planning methods; they were translated into French, and produced a document of considerable length.[28] A fair number of these tables are filled in by republic, by ministry and service of the USSR, and sometimes by large economic regions, to say nothing of those comprising part of the plan for each enterprise, sovnarkhoz and oblast. Finally, numerous descriptions of methodology are furnished by Soviet authors.

How many industrial products are covered by the central plan? How many figure in the production and consumption "balances" which are a feature of the Soviet planning system? There is no simple answer to this question: a study of the planning forms reveals that there are in fact numerous types of tables

[27] 1961: the decisive year for the seven-year plan, *Plan. Khoz.*, No. 12, pp. 3–14, 1961.

[28] *ISEA*, G, No. 10, November 1960.

and balances, and consequently numerous different classifications, which may explain why there are sometimes considerable discrepancies in the information gleaned from conversations with Soviet economists.

All sources seem to be agreed, however, that at the present stage the number of plan indices, and more specifically the number of products covered, is greater in annual plans than it is in long-term plans, and that the number of products covered at Gosplan level has fallen in recent years, as greater responsibility is assumed by the lower echelons, and is markedly smaller than the number of products covered at these lower levels. Thus, it has been observed that the number of headings for the State plan for 1958 was 40% less than in the 1957 plan.[29] The directive for the drawing-up of the annual plan for 1959 also shows that the annual classification had been reduced to 1047 headings, instead of 5000 in 1952.[30] According to what I was told in 1961, there were only a few hundred products (300–400) for which complete balances were made at Union level; in the republics and sovnarkhozy, the usual estimate of products figuring in material balances is several thousands; in the RSFSR, according to Urinson, the classification of the principal products runs into about 1100 items, of which 50% are covered by the Union plan, and the rest by the republic plan. Of this total, 850 items relate to branches of heavy industry, and 250 to branches of light industry.[31] Again, according to Academician Nemchinov, there are: (a) approximately 150 supply balances covering important products such as coal, sheet metal, timber, which are expressed in physical quantities, or totalled in the "conventional units" so often used in Soviet statistics (conventional tons of fuel, tractors expressed in units of 15 h. p., etc.) and which are approved by the Soviet government; (b) about 1600 balances relating to categories of products which have already been subject to more detailed breakdown and preparation by the Union Gosplan and the republican Gosplans; (c) about 10,500 balances drawn up by those organizations concerned with distribution, and which

[29] According to R. Fassier, La répartition planifiée des moyens de production dans l'industrie soviétique, op. cit., p. 111.

[30] Quoted by B. Kerblay, ISEA, G, No. 10, p. 18.

[31] M. S. Urinson, op. cit., Chap. II.

represent the major part of the value of production.[32] In his original article the same author stated that, in 1959, 285 balances had been calculated, for general planning purposes, and 10,500 balances relating to supplies of materials and equipment.[33] And lastly, there is mention by another source of 400–450 main objectives contained in the national plan, and elaborated by the central Gosplan, and approximately 15,000 headings included in the plan but originating with local agencies or enterprises.[34]

The striking feature is that the number of products covered in this way is relatively small, when one considers that the number of products making up an industrial classification can easily go into some tens of thousands, when a detailed breakdown is made of all the categories of products appearing for example in catalogues, price-lists or trade schedules, etc. It certainly seems much smaller than one would have imagined, knowing the volume of work involved in Soviet planning;[35] in practice these supply balances do not by any means cover the total value of industrial production.

But it is in matters relating to the allocation of products that the content of plans, and the classifications used, are of greatest importance; in fact, as we have already seen, the organizations responsible for planning the allocation of supplies, and implementing and controlling it, vary according to the importance of the products to be allocated.[36]

It may be useful to say a few words about the categories into which products were divided prior to 1958. At that time, there existed for legislative and economic purposes, three categories of products: (a) the so-called *base products*, that is, the most im-

[32] V. NEMCHINOV, Application of statistical mathematical methods in Soviet planning, Report to the International Conference on input-output techniques. Geneva, September 1961.

[33] V. NEMCHINOV, The application of mathematical methods in economic research and planning, *Vopr. Ekon.*, No. 6, 1960. (Résumé by H. WRONSKI, L'URSS et les pays de l'Est, *Revue des Revues*, Strasbourg, No. 2, 1961.) On the use of mathematical methods, cf. Chapter IX.

[34] *Planirovanie mestnovo khozyaistva i kulturnovo stroitelstva raiona*, Izdatelstvo VPCh i AON pri TSK KPSS, 312 pp., Moscow, 1961, p. 12.

[35] On this question, reference can be made to observations and theories by the French economists' mission *(ISEA, G, No. 7.)*

[36] See particularly FASSIER, *op. cit.*, pp. 48–54 and bibliography on this question.

portant products; the number of these continued to increase until 1952, at which date it was 2000, and they still numbered 760 in 1958; for each of these products a production and consumption supply balance was drawn up, and they were allocated in accordance with plans made by the central authorities; (b) *products planned according to a centralized procedure*, which were of lesser importance and were the responsibility of the central supply directorates of the appropriate ministries; and (c) *products not subject to centralized planning*, which were mainly the production of local industry over which districts, regions or republics had a certain amount of jurisdiction.

After April 1958, these categories were revised, and the distinction now is between: (a) *products subject to central allocation by Gosplan;* shortly after the change, these comprised 1200–1500 categories of materials and equipment, of which 150–200 items, previously referred to, are the subject of supply balances approved by the Council of Ministers, while the rest are directly allocated by Gosplan; (b) *industrial products allocated by republic*, which went into some thousands (rather more than 3000 at the end of 1958); and lastly, (c) *products subject to decentralized allocation* and (d) *agricultural products*, which are the subject of special arrangements.

REGIONAL PLANNING

Plans prepared by the central authorities include a regional section. Traditionally, this was worked out for each republic; in the case of the RSFSR, however, there was an additional category covering the Urals and Siberia at least. As we have seen, a greater degree of importance is now attached to the "large economic regions" (13 up till 1960, thereafter 16, and now 17)[37] and it is assumed that this category will tend to be used more extensively. We are also told that, whereas the 1959 plan covered 57 branches of industry, and all the sovnarkhozy of the Russian republic, the 1960 plan was intended to go further by estimating the new productive capacity to be introduced into each economic ad-

[37] See above, Ch. II.

ministrative region in the course of the year;[38] presumably, therefore, this had not previously been done.

In a sense, however, it is true to say that up till now there has been no real regional planning in the USSR. This is not to say that Soviet planning is a purely top-level exercise; on the contrary, all levels of the economic system, and all territorial levels, take part in the elaboration of the State plan, each in their appropriate sphere. But if, by regional planning, one is to understand an overall analysis of the various factors or problems affecting the economic life of a given territorial unit, which is aimed at influencing development, or giving rise to decisions which will be acted upon, then it must be said that up to the present time nothing like this has existed. The sovnarkhozy, in particular, were not set up with any such purpose in mind. Opinions may vary as to whether the experiments carried out elsewhere under the heading of regional planning can truly be described as such, or what the virtues of the system really are;[39] what one cannot say is that the USSR has been a pioneer in the field.

There is considerable awareness of this shortcoming in the USSR, and of the need for introducing what they describe as "complex" planning. During my visit, this question was under consideration both at Gosekonomsoviet and in the Committee for the study of productivity (SOPS for short),[40] a committee which had been attached to Gosekonomsoviet since 1960; on the other hand, officials whom I met in the provinces seemed to have little information, or to be rather reticent on the subject. During my stay, there was a conference in Moscow (March 1961) on the improvement of planning methods, and regional problems figured largely in it. A report on its work has since been published.[41]

[38] L. CHADAEV, Problems of improvement in production planning and in the construction of the councils of the national economy, *Plan. Khoz.* No. 4, 1960.

[39] For a rapid review of the problems arising in the case of France, see for example our article, La planification régionale en France, *Revue de l'Action Populaire*, Paris, February 1961.

[40] „Soviet po izucheniu proizvoditelnikh sil". Founded in 1915, SOPS had up to 1960 been attached to the Academy of Sciences of the USSR.

[41] See particularly the article "Principal problems of complex development planning in the economic regions", by a team of experts from SOPS, *Plan. Khoz.*, No. 5, 1961; TOKAREV and ALAMPIEV, *ibid.*, No. 7, 1961. A. VEDICHEV, Improvement of complex planning of development in the economic regions, *Ekonomicheskaya Gazeta*, 2nd April 1961.

Official endorsement of these studies and of the reforms proposed was given in decisions dated March 1962.[42] The criticism levelled at the existing system was that, generally speaking, planning by sector still continued to take priority over planning on a territorial basis. In the first instance there was denunciation of the inadequacy of regional planning at the level of the large economic regions. "Plans for the large economic regions, which are worked out in the territorial divisions of Gosplan of the USSR, and Gosplan of the RSFSR, are in fact no more than a formal arrangement of the regional plans for the various sectors drawn up under a limited number of headings, and their inner coherence is not checked by the use of balances".[43] Lower down the scale, each economic sector was apparently planned separately by the various organizations concerned: sovnarkhoz, oblast and other local authorities, and ministries of the Union, without there being any real co-ordination.

At this conference, it was decided that co-ordination should be strengthened simultaneously at both these levels. Firstly, in the seventeen large economic regions, the aim was to create councils for economic co-ordination, whose duty it would be to make recommendations on the development of those regions. The nature and functions of the councils were to vary considerably, according to the status of the large regions in question; if they were divisions of the RSFSR and the Ukraine, they could be administered by the supersovnarkhozy which were set up in 1960 in these republics;[44] if they comprised several small republics, the attempt at co-ordination would be made through periodical meetings of the republican planning organizations, under the direction and with the co-operation of the central authorities of the Union. According to Lomako, the first meetings of these councils for the ten large regions of the RSFSR took place from November 1961 to January 1962.

The work of the co-ordinating councils would be directed towards producing soundly based plans for the development of each of these large regions, plans which were described to me as

---

[42] See P. LOMAKO, deputy-chairman of the bureau of the Party Central Committee of the RSFSR, "The committees for coordination and planning have started their work", *Pravda*, 23rd February 1962.

[43] *Plan. Khoz.*, No. 5, 1961, *op. cit.*

[44] See Ch. VI.

makety (models) by Nekrassov, the chairman of SOPS, corresponding member of the Academy of Sciences. These models would be used as a basis for the long-term overall development of the large regions. Such long-term plans take on a special significance when viewed in the context of large-scale construction projects, such as the Nurek Dam on the Vakh river in Central Asia, which involve vast geographical areas and have far-reaching implications.

So far there has been no indication whether these regional plans were to be integrated into one of the existing long-term plans. It seems that this question had still not been settled at the time of the XXIInd Congress, since P. N. Demichev, the first secretary of the Moscow Party Committee, proposed that major economic surveys should henceforth be included in the plans, and it would appear that these surveys must have been of a regional nature.[45]

Between meetings of these councils, which apparently were to consist of some 50–100 members (secretaries of the Party committees of the oblast, krai and ASSR in question, chairmen of the executive commissions or of the councils of ministers of the territories concerned, chairmen of the sovnarkhozy and a certain number of other elected members, directors of large factories or specialists) work was to be carried on by permanent commissions, and possibly scientific centres, whose duty it would be to coordinate the work of new institutes and research centres in the large regions.

At the level of economic administrative regions and oblasts, the need for a similar effort at co-ordination was also felt. The conference held in Moscow in March 1961 had considered it essential that a plan should be drawn up in each oblast or krai covering all types of production and economic activity, independently of the existing administrative arrangements for particular enterprises or industrial establishments. To this end, a commission was to be set up at this level, which would be responsible for working out a single overall plan for the area in question. This was to be aimed particularly at maximizing utilization of all the resources of the region, and was to cover expansion of industry, agriculture, transport, construction and services,

[45] *Pravda*, 20th October 1961.

while leaving the actual administrative responsibility for enterprises and industrial establishments unchanged.

The most favourable conditions appeared to be those in which one republic contained only one sovnarkhoz and one oblast or krai; in such cases the republican Gosplan was to be the competent authority. When the boundaries of oblasts and economic administrative regions coincided (as they did in the majority of cases), conditions were not too difficult; but in the fairly frequent instances where one economic administrative region in fact comprised several oblasts, elaboration of this single overall plan would certainly present some difficulty.

The need which has become apparent in recent years for effecting co-ordination simultaneously at two or even three different territorial levels (economic administrative regions, large economic regions, and republics) was no doubt one of the motives for the reform of territorial divisions. In any event it will be seen that after the creation of the new enlarged sovnarkhozy in November 1962, the co-ordinating councils of the ten large regions of the RSFSR and of the three large regions of the Ukraine were abolished, while in Kazakhstan the duties of the co-ordinating and planning Council devolved upon the Council of ministers of the republic. Those Councils which have been retained (Baltic countries, Transcaucasia) are attached to the all-Union Gosplan. In this way, the new sovnarkhozy would seem to be the successors both of the large economic regions and of the old sovnarkhozy.[46]

However, the degree of co-ordination which can be achieved by the sovnarkhozy is still limited, since their jurisdiction does not extend over all economic activities, and moreover no co-ordinating council of the type previously mentioned seems to have been attached to them.

On the other hand, it would seem that the co-ordinating powers of the republics must have become wider. In fact, since November 1962, the plans elaborated by republican Gosplans have related to the overall economy of the Republic, and not simply to those

---

[46] On the 23rd December 1964, after the fall of Khrushchev, it was reported that the economic region of Central Asia had been abolished. It was reported at the same time that there had been a minister in Tashkent in charge of problems concerning the four regions is question.

enterprises and organizations administered by republican and local authorities, as was formerly the case. Their task in this connection is to confirm the objectives planned by the various State authorities, to solve practical problems arising during the execution of the plans, to supervise fulfilment of the National Plan, and in fact to be directly responsible for the work of the supply and purchasing services.[47]

[47] J. PAWLIK, *Gospodarka Planowa*, No. 10, 1963; *Planirovanie narodnovo khozyaistva SSSR* (Planning of the national economy of the USSR), (ed. M. V. BREEV), Moscow, quoted by E. ZALESKI, *op. cit.*, 1964.

CHAPTER V

CO-ORDINATION OF PLANS AND DETERMINATION OF OBJECTIVES

THE foregoing description of planning procedure and plan content has shown us planning, as it were, from the outside. It is now time to consider in practical terms the way in which these plans are dovetailed one into another, and to take a preliminary look at the methodology of their elaboration.

CO-ORDINATION OF PLANS

The problems of plan co-ordination are undoubtedly among the most complex facing the Soviet planner. There are several aspects to these problems: co-ordination of the various plans in point of time, for one thing; or again, co-ordination of the various elements comprising the plans; and lastly, co-ordination of the various plans in the territorial sense, of which we have just been speaking. We shall deal rapidly with the problems arising under the first two of these headings, although we cannot, of course, hope to say all there is to be said on the subject.

In principle, annual plans are based on the five-year (or seven-year) plans, in the sense that they are conceived as being transitory phases in the implementation of the latter. But there is always the possibility of a hiatus occurring at the moment of changeover from one long-term plan to the next, a danger which Soviet authors have not been slow to recognize,[1] all the more so because it has frequently happened that long-term plans were not approved until after the beginning of the period which they were supposed to cover. Those responsible for annual plans might thus be left without any guiding line in their work.

[1] See, for example URINSON, *op. cit.*

A new feature — or so at least it was described — of the seven-year plan for 1959–65, as compared with the five-year plan which preceded it, was that it not only indicated what the final objectives were to be, but also gave stage-by-stage indications of the objectives for each of the intermediate years. The same idea was put into operation not only for plans at republican and Union level, but also for enterprise plans and those for inter-mediate territorial units. In this way, an enterprise or organization engaged in preparing its plan for a given year had to bear in mind both the objectives laid down within the framework of the seven-year plan for that year and also for the terminal year.

However, the problem of co-ordination between annual plans and long-term plans was still not solved, for during the second year of its execution, that is in 1960, it became clear that the objectives of the seven-year plan had lost a great deal of their validity because of widespread over-fulfilment of industrial objec-tives during the first two years, and also because of other changes in the original estimates. After the 1961 plan had been approved, in December 1960, new measures were announced, which received the widest publicity. It was announced that in future, in addition to the regular annual plans, revised objectives would be prepared each year for the fifth year ahead. Thus, in preparing the plan for 1962, the planners must also apply themselves to the task of determining objectives for the year 1966, which in turn will entail the revision of estimates for the intermediate years. In this way, it is thought, the planners will have at their disposal, at any given moment, and at any given level of the economic system, an up-to-date appraisal of the objectives covering the next five years. This procedure has been given the name of *un-interrupted five-year planning*, or more simply, *uninterrupted* or *continuous planning*. It should be noted that this process of revision will continue to be supervised by the Union Gosplan, which is responsible for annual plans, and not by Gosekonomsoviet.

Have these reforms been successful in giving planning the desired continuity? Studying reports on this subject in the Soviet press, one cannot fail to be struck by the number and extent of the revisions to be made in plans while they are in course of execution, and the amount of disorganization which must result. This was true in the past also. Eugène Zaleski, who has made a detailed survey of the execution of the first five-year plan,

1927–28–32, notes in striking fashion the successive and far-reaching revisions which it underwent, and which often took no account of the extent to which the plan then current had actually been implemented; these revisions were such that during the final years of the plan it was next to impossible to say which of the series of objectives that had been announced were effectively in operation.[2] Over the economy as a whole, the amount of disorganization has no doubt been less of recent years. But lower down, at local and enterprise level, one is still struck by the extensive revisions which are called for, and the amount of inconvenience they must cause.

There are numerous complaints about this. For example, So-ich, chairman of the Kharkov sovnarkhoz, notes that "in 1960, the Kharkov sovnarkhoz were called upon to make 400 changes in production: in 1961, 500. These adjustments give rise to endless correspondence, and are the source of frightful anomalies, for the changes we are ordered to make are never synchronized". One of the consequences is that enterprises which are the victims of these changes "find themselves unjustly classed with those enterprises which fail to fulfil their plan, and suffer the appropriate consequences".[3] Davydov, chairman of the sovnarkhoz of the Buryat republic, complains that the 1961 plan assigned objectives for foundry production for the whole of his sovnarkhoz which were "three times higher than existing factory capacity; despite my protestations, no correction was made, and the objectives assigned for the 1962 plan are still 50% above factory capacity".[4] Similarly, at the time of the XXIInd Congress, Krotov, director of the "Uralmash" factory at Sverdlovsk, one of the most important machinery factories in the USSR, complained that Gosplan had not yet been able to determine a production plan covering four or five years, which he considered indispensable for the main types of equipment, and also that many additional orders were in fact issued to enterprises during the year. He also pointed out that preparation of the annual plan required an enormous amount of work (six to eight months) and the collaboration of numerous individuals and organizations, and that, despite the efforts which were made, plans were usually late in reaching the enterprises. He

---

[2] *Op. cit.*
[3] SOICH, Directorate or Combine, *Ukrainian Pravda*, 24th January 1962.
[4] *Ekonomicheskaya Gazeta*, 5th February 1962.

also suggested that, if the principle of continuous planning of production, investment and supplies were to be effectively implemented the period for current planning should be extended to at least two years, which would enable plans to be approved at least one year before completion of the previous plan.[5] If such a course proved practicable, would it in fact serve to eliminate revisions to plans during their execution, or would there not be a danger, on the contrary, of its giving rise to still further revision?

But the real problems of plan co-ordination are those arising from the multiplicity of organizations responsible for approving and implementing plans, and also from the existence, side by side, of what most recent reports agree are three distinct types of plans: production plans, capital construction plans (what we call investment plans) and supply plans.

V. Gavrilov, secretary of the Krasnoyarsk obkom, criticized the proliferation of planning organizations, disclosing, for example, that "the investment plan for our sovnarkhoz passed through 19 departments and administrations of the supersovnarkhoz and Gosplan of the Russian republic, and the production plan involved 17 organizations." It often happens that the year has begun before these plans, or the supply plan, have been endorsed; or it can happen that a factory scheduled under its quarterly plan to start a new line in production is unable to do so because it will not receive the necessary equipment until the following quarter, and is nevertheless penalized for its failure. The writer called for a reform in planning procedure for annual plans, and a reduction in the number of organizations involved.[6] Another author, the assistant director of a department of Gosplan, noted that in 1960 only 80 out of the 218 new plants proposed for the chemical industry of the RSFSR had in fact been started, and blamed delays in construction[7] arising from the fact that too many projects had been started in relation to the resources available:

Planning which is not co-ordinated with the supply of materials and equipment often results in the creation of an artificial shortage of certain products and types of equipment. To achieve proper distribution of those products of

[5] *Pravda*, 27th October 1961.

[6] V. Gavrilov, Plan, production and life: costly anomalies, *Izvestia*, 6th February 1962.

[7] There are innumerable complaints on this subject.

which there is both a central and a regional shortage, it is necessary to maintain a vast apparatus of supplying and purchasing organizations.

This state of affairs is the result of erroneous ideas. It is a common belief that an intensive, i.e. non-realistic, plan, which serves to mobilize all the efforts of workers in a collective enterprise, is always justified. The argument is as follows: these plans are not fulfilled within the time limit, but a sector which has received generous allocations will show a high rate of growth, even though the plan is not fulfilled.

In this article, which appeared at the time of the XXIInd Congress, and which is certainly based on expert knowledge, the author concludes that it is natural that those responsible for administering the various sectors of industry should try to speed up the rate of growth, but adds that if their recommendations are accepted by the planning authorities without due provision of the requisite means of production, or at the expense of other sectors, then the consequences will be disastrous. He also recommends:

  (a) that some attention be paid to the evils of "unrealistic" planning;
  (b) that there should be an increase in the estimated financial and material reserves in annual plans;
  (c) that there should be more efficient co-ordination of developments in the various sectors;
  (d) that a greater part should be played by the supervisory organizations, both at the centre and in the sovnarkhozy, especially in the matter of co-ordination of decisions;
  (e) lastly, the introduction of a simple and efficient system of providing information on the state of available resources by the use of electronic computers.[8]

Putting the matter more forcefully, Spiridonov, who was then first secretary of the Party organization in the Leningrad oblast, and is now president of the Supreme Soviet — not, perhaps, a promotion — said in his speech at the XXIInd Congress:

Those in control of industry, and we, the local Party cadres, have the impression that the Union Gosplan and the RSFSR Gosplan are nothing but an assemblage of various services, described as sector administrations and

[8] V. MARKIEVICH, Improving the methods of planned economic administration, *Kommunist*, No. 15, October 1961.

departments, in which the right hand often does not know what the left hand is doing, while the heads of these services spend their time dealing with innumerable shortages, and correcting the errors of their own administrations, which are no less numerous.[9]

In this context, one final point is the announcement, also at the XXIInd Congress, by A. N. Kosygin, then first deputy-chairman of the Council of Ministers of the USSR, and said to be in charge of the overall co-ordination of Soviet planning, that a new procedure for investment planning was being introduced into the 1962 plan, and that there would henceforth be close co-ordination between investment planning and the supply of construction materials and equipment.[10]

What importance should be attached so far to the procedure of *continuous planning* which the decree of December 1960 sought to establish? It has been pointed out that, in practice, the federal republics had to prepare the annual plan for 1962 without having received from Gosekonomsoviet the control figures for 1966; similarly, the plan for 1963 had to be elaborated by the republics in the absence of any version of the objectives for 1967 which was consistent with the revisions in the seven-year plan then being implemented at Union level.[10a] On the other hand, the preparation of a preliminary plan for the years 1964 and 1965, and of a new five-year plan for 1966–70, both called for by the decree of 13th March 1963, seems to indicate that implementation of the recommendations outlined by N. S. Khrushchev in this matter may have become a secondary consideration.

The basic idea of the new procedure was that adjustments or revisions in the plans should not be made in isolation by a few central planning organizations, but should form part of a new coherent revised version which, on each occasion, would indicate objectives for several years ahead. But this would assume that it is possible to allow a certain time to elapse before putting into effect the changes which appear necessary, whereas on the contrary the growing complexity of production tends to make them increasingly numerous and urgent.

[9] *Pravda*, 20th October 1961.
[10] *Pravda*, 23rd October 1961.
[10a] Cf. E. ZALESKI, Les réformes de la Planification en URSS, *Cahiers de l'institut de Science économique appliquée* (ISEA), August 1964.

At all events, the *continuous planning* attempt is an interesting experiment, which has not failed to attract attention in other countries which have adopted a planning system — whether or not of the mandatory type — and have found that a convenient procedure for the revision of objectives is one of the most necessary improvements to be made, if planning as an institution is to continue to make sense.

CHOICE OF MAIN OBJECTIVES

We shall now try to describe in broad outline the methods used in determining plan objectives. However, as has already been indicated, the picture will not be complete until we have examined the problem of economic criteria, which we reserve for a later chapter. What we shall attempt to ascertain here are the stages of the process by which the planners decide on the objectives to include in their plans. For the moment, we shall dwell mainly on the action of the central planning authorities. We shall examine firstly the choice of main objectives in the plan, and, in the following section, the system of supply balances which is one of the principal methods used in Soviet planning.

There is in fact very little information available in Soviet writings concerning the way in which decisions about the broad general trend of a plan, and its main objectives, are made. To provide some basis for comparison, it may be helpful if we follow a practice already adopted elsewhere[11] and begin by taking a look at how nowadays, in the West, and for instance in France, the elaboration of a plan or economic programme is conducted. In Western planning, as we know, the first step is to ascertain, by means of an estimate of the growth of the national income, which itself is based on estimates of the growth of population and productivity, what the future level of consumption is likely to be, given the variable elasticity of demand for different goods and services. With the aid of an input–output table, corrected if necessary to take account of probable technical changes, an estimate is made of the level of intermediate production and, consequently, of investment which will be necessary to meet the estimated level of consumption.

[11] Report by French economists, *op. cit.*, pp. 46 and 59.

Soviet planners approach the problem in a rather different way. Their starting-point is not evaluation of final demand, as is the case with programming of the Western type, but evaluation of industrial production and its growth potential. "Experience has convinced the Soviet authorities that there was less risk of error in directly determining the volume of key products, than in arriving at it indirectly by evaluation of final demand."[12] Or again, as R. Fassier says:

> Under the Soviet system of full planning, the choice of objectives, and the determination of general lines for the utilization of production goods are governed, not by consumer demand, as in the case of a market economy, but by an economic policy and the priorities accordingly laid down by Party and State. [. . .] These priorities are determined mainly on the basis of the fundamental proportion, decided at the outset of the planning process, between the output of producer goods and consumer goods, which itself is based on the Marxist notion of an expanding social production. Similarly, in the domain of industry, the prime importance attaching to heavy industry, and to engineering in particular, seem to be determining factors in the choice of priorities.[13]

This primary aim of creating a production apparatus which is apparently a part of the ideological framework, and the system of priorities to which it consequently gives rise, are facts which emerge clearly from all the available information on the subject. But indications about the technical decisions which must logically be involved are singularly vague in character. Also, in practice, the major decisions governing the rhythm of growth and the broad trends in economic development, in other words the respective levels of production of a number of key products, which serve as indicators, seem to be arrived at on an essentially empirical basis. Some degree of economic calculation may be involved, but there are also a certain number of *a priori* assumptions based on the example of the capitalist countries or on strategic considerations, on the preoccupation with speeding up the transformation of the country, preferably by use of the most advanced techniques available, or quite simply on the personal preferences of the leaders themselves; Stalin, for example, seems to have had a predilection

---

[12] B. Kerblay, "Remarques sur les formulaires de la planification soviétique," in *Le Plan septennal soviétique, ISEA*, G, No. 10, November 1960.

[13] Fassier, *op. cit.*, p. 46.

for steel and coal, and a distrust of oil, which had a distorting effect on the economic development of the USSR over a long period. The abandonment of the sixth five-year plan and preparation of the seven-year plan (1959–65) coincided with the making of several major decisions, such as the priority subsequently given to oil and natural gas, as opposed to coal, and the powerful stimulus given to the chemical industry, activities in which the USSR had been far outdistanced by developments in the capitalist countries, particularly the United States.[14]

Another example of this "voluntarist" aspect of planning is the still fairly widespread reluctance to determine objectives by means of forecasts based on the examination of previous trends, such forecasts being criticized as "bourgeois mechanistic methods".[15]

But since it is difficult, in practice, to evaluate the exact incidence of all the measures which, taken together, make up government policy, this means that Soviet planning is still denying itself a source of information which could prove very useful to it.[16]

The foregoing remarks should not be taken as meaning that plans are not drawn up in a coherent fashion. The whole complicated mechanism of planning and the making of balances are designed precisely to ensure coherence. Nor is there any suggestion that very numerous calculations of costs are not made; innumerable examples could in fact be quoted in the field of power alone. But it would seem that these exercises are only of secondary importance, and that they are carried out once the main objectives and the principal priorities have been decided upon.

---

[14] In raising this question, it must be added that the change of policy with regard to oil and gas would not have been possible without the great effort in prospecting which had previously been made during the fifth five-year plan (1951–5) as a result of which 364 deposits of oil and gas had been discovered, mainly in the Volga and Ural regions, Cf. ZOLOTAREV and STEINGAUS, Energetika i Elektrifikatsia v SSSR, *Gosenergoizdat*, Moscow, 1960.

[15] EFIMOV, *op. cit.*, March 1961.

[16] R. Pressat, of the National Institute of Demographic Studies in Paris, who spent some time at the Institute of Economics of the Academy of Sciences of the USSR shortly before my visit, particularly made this point, cf. Vues sur la planification de la main-d'oeuvre en Union soviétique, *Population*, pp. 235–48, April–June 1961.

Soviet planners themselves complain of the rudimentary nature of the methods employed. An authority such as A. Efimov, director of the Institute of Economic Research, attached to Gosplan (or, between 1960 and 1962, to Gosekonomsoviet) and already well known to French planners, described in the following terms the problems facing institutes which are concerned with the study of planning: the main one is the problem of growth rates in the national economy, and the broad proportions to be maintained in its principal sectors; for example, between industry, agriculture and transport, or between coal and oil extraction, rail and road transport, etc. He commented that although the research organizations were already engaged in practical surveys of this kind, they were "still a long way from providing a solution to the problem of the economic basis of the plan. To be precise, only the first steps in a scientific approach to this important problem have been taken".[17]

No doubt, an insight into the lines along which Soviet economists are working may be afforded by some preliminary studies, such as the one carried out in fact by the Institute of Economic Research, in which an attempt was made to analyse the complex relationships existing between the growth of labour productivity on the one hand, and the consumption of power, the value of fixed capital in industry, and wages and income of labour on the other hand; these studies, which were begun in 1957, no doubt helped in determining the growth rates for productivity which are laid down in the plans.[18] But whatever interest such studies may have, they do little to illuminate the problem of intersector choice.

This deficiency is all the more serious since the problem facing Soviet planners is in fact much more acute than it is in the Western type of programming, where the question is fundamentally one of providing incentives. In a Western-type economy the alternatives proposed by the planner or economic counsellor, regardless of the extent to which they have been elaborated, or the importance of the calculations on which they have been based, are in fact subject to constant review, verification and correction through the interaction of commercial operations, which themselves are

---

[17] A. EFIMOV, Economic research and planning, *Ekonomicheskaya Gazeta* 4th September 1961.

[18] B. BRAGINSKI and D. KARPUKHIN, *Plan. Khoz.*, No. 8, 1961.

necessarily a reflection of the state of the market, unexpected changes in technical conditions, etc. It may sometimes be thought that the operation of this built-in corrective goes too far. To take only one example, anyone who has observed the pattern of the development of fuel supplies in western Europe over the last seven or eight years will certainly have something to say on this subject. But the almost total absence of any such safety device in the Soviet Union has many other disadvantages: initial errors or misconceptions arising at the time when major decisions are made cannot be detected or corrected in time; the resultant losses have a cumulative effect, and the correctives when finally applied may be just as drastic as they are elsewhere, if not more so. For example, despite the fact that coal output in all the major industrial countries has tended to remain static or to fall during the past few years, because of continual changes in the fuel balance, the Soviet Union's seven-year plan envisaged an increase of 22 % in coal output between 1958 and 1965; though the increase in the first three years, from 1958 to 1961, was only 3 %, the twenty-year plan still calls for an increase in production from 513 million tons in 1960 to 1190 million tons in 1980, i.e. an increase of 2·3 times. What will happen if, as it is certainly not absurd to suppose, these targets turn out to be grossly in excess of requirements?[18a]

We must now return to the question of the role of demand in plan-making. Although, as we have said, choice of the main production objectives is not governed by estimated demand, it would still not be entirely correct to say that the only part played by demographic factors is in determining the available reserves of manpower. According to the information I was given at Gosekonomsoviet, estimates of demographic trends and of final demand did play a considerable part in the elaboration of the long-term ten- and twenty-year plans. But unlike current Western practice, in which estimates of global demand are based on estimates of the rise in income of the population, and of the elasticity of demand by categories of products, the manner in which demand seems to be estimated by Soviet planners is basically *normative*. For example, on the question of food, dietetics insti-

---

[18a] Production in 1963 was 532 million tons (an increase of 7% in five years) and the production objective for 1965 was reduced to 553 million tons (instead of an original objective of 600–620 million tons).

tutes take the distribution of the population by age and sex, and make allowance for local habits, and then indicate what the requirements are for a balanced diet, and what will be the chances of achieving this in the given time. Other institutes are similarly engaged in determining scientific consumption norms for textiles, housing and the principal services (transport, education, social services, entertainment). Looking at the question from the point of view of the Western economist, one may ask if the total of all the different types of expenditures by the population can be calculated by this method, and whether the conclusions arrived at have any validity. How, for instance, does one establish a norm for consumption of motor-cars or other consumer goods, and how can one be sure that the resulting estimate will be adequate to meet all demands and will not give rise to any particular difficulties or problems? As we know, this is not a purely academic question, in view of the ambition of many Soviet citizens to own a motor-car, and the little hope that they have of doing so under present planning provisions. Soviet economists do not seem to feel quite the same degree of diffidence on this subject as Western economists, and appear confident of their ability to judge, in almost all contexts, what it is proper for their fellow-men to produce and to consume. It should, of course, be said that in the Soviet view, the problem of the satisfaction of consumer needs must be considered in dynamic terms, apart from certain deliberate exceptions, such as the "individual motorcar"; the solution to the problem lies in the achievement of high levels of consumption which will help to bring about the "transition to communism".

Are market surveys carried out in the Soviet Union? The experts at Gosekonomsoviet to whom I put this question told me that, far from being neglected, this field of research is in fact constantly being developed. Judging from their explanations, however, it seems that none of these are long-term surveys, and that the period covered is barely more than two years at most. If the aim is indeed to study the level of future demand for various categories of products in relation to the amount of money available, then it would seem that the practical purpose of these studies is mainly to estimate potential sales of commodities which have either been produced already, or have been ordered. With the state of relative plenty which has now developed, the question of sales is in fact beginning to raise certain problems.

The whole of this approach is doubtless based on the implicit assumption that consumer demand, as defined in Western economies, is a meaningless concept, since it is to such a large extent influenced by advertising, and that it is much more important to fulfil the vital needs of the population as a whole — needs which are perfectly well known — than to stimulate excessive demand among certain sectors which one must then set about satisfying.

The foregoing observations were made mainly from the standpoint of the economist. Looking at things now from the angle of the engineer, and turning once more to the field of investment goods as opposed to consumer goods, one may ask how choice does operate among different production objectives within a given sector. On this point, we have very little direct information. However, reports by foreign technicians indicate that decisions which involve a choice between different products, and which are based mainly on technical considerations, seem to be very carefully weighed. This seems to be the case particularly in the chemical industry, an industry which is developing rapidly, but where investments require several years before their effect is felt in production, and in which experience elsewhere has shown that indications based on the movement of prices and market pressures are not necessarily the surest guides.[19]

THE INSTRUMENTS OF PLANNING: NORMS, BALANCES AND NATIONAL ACCOUNTING

Once the main (or priority) objectives have been determined, the task of fixing secondary objectives and verifying the inner coherence of the plan is carried out by means of the so-called *balance* method. This enables the planners to make a comparison between the available resources of industrial products and the supplies of these products which will be needed for production operations, and to ensure coherence among the various branches of the economy.[20]

[19] One must recall that a considerable expansion of this industry was decided upon in Russia five or six years ago.
[20] See particularly R. FASSIER, *op. cit.;* E. ZALESKI, *op. cit.*, also various unpublished notes by E. ZALESKI, whom I should like to thank here for having let me see them.

A material balance consists of a balance sheet of resources and requirements, which is drawn up for a particular product for a given period, and which gives precise details of the existing or anticipated level of supplies, and the main pattern of their distribution. The balance method is universally employed, not only in the central planning organizations, but at all levels of planning: enterprises and central directorates under the former system, enterprises, sovnarkhozy and Gosplans of the federal republics under the present system. At Union level, balances are made both retrospectively, in the form of tables drawn up by the Central Statistical Office, and prospectively, as tables prepared by Gosplan, there being separate balances for the elaboration of economic plans and for their implementation.

Balances are made not only for materials, but also for manpower. In principle, the balances are expressed in physical units of measure; but there are also general balances which are expressed in monetary terms (particularly national product and income, financial operations, fixed capital and national assets, balance of the national economy) of which more will be said later on.

Material inputs, which comprise the "requirements" (or "use") side of the material balance, are determined by means of technical indices known as *norms*. These *supply norms* have been defined as "processed information determining the maximum quantity of raw materials, equipment or fuel which will be used in the manufacture of a commodity or the execution of a piece of work at a given level of technique and organization".[21]

These norms are an essential instrument in planning, not only for ensuring rational utilization of resources, but also for encouraging growth in productivity and economy in administration. They are in fact administrative in character: preparation and approval of norms, and the fixing of targets for their "planned reduction", are amongst the most important aspects of Soviet economic administration. Norms are also used in matters relating to production costs; expenditure on raw materials, fuel, equipment and electric power has a direct bearing on the costs of production, and the fixing of norms and of targets for the

---

[21] *Ekonomika sotsialisticheskoi promyshlennosti*, Gospolitizdat, Moscow 1957, quoted by R. FASSIER, *op. cit.*

reduction of these norms, is designed to bring about a reduction in costs.

We cannot make a detailed examination of the distinctions which are drawn in the USSR between the different types of norms, for example, norms for the utilization of basic products or related items, individual norms (for example, for finished products) or aggregated norms, valid for a particular branch of industry, or of the methods employed in determining these norms. Suffice it to say that the problem of establishing correct norms, which will be valid for the economy as a whole, is virtually insoluble in view of the multiplicity of activities, hence the temptation to go on increasing the number of norms. In 1952 the number of technico-productive indices approved in the plans for the supply of materials and equipment rose to 2230 for consumption of ferrous metal sheet alone. Mostly, these norms were determined by "statistical-accounting" type methods, and one of the most widely used for a long time was the method of "average progressive norms", in which the activities of the best firms were used as a basis; the average norms were then fixed below the general average. Use is sometimes made of theoretical exercises, or laboratory experiments, in determining norms.

Stocks of industrial products in the hands of the users are also subject to limitation through fixed norms, but it can be said straight away that this is one of the instances in which the provisions of the plan are most likely to be ignored in practice. Although the aim is generally to maintain stocks at the minimum level compatible with continuity in production, in order to ensure economy in the use of raw materials, it has been observed that stocks in the hands of the users are nearly always much larger than the level planned; in respect of hot rolled iron, reserves in the industry as a whole were 154% more in 1950, and 54% more in 1955, than the amount estimated in the plan (40 days' reserve instead of 29); although it had been estimated that there would be a considerable reduction in these stocks each year, it was in fact found that the level rose, or remained constant.[22] The excess of idle stocks and unnecessary reserves raises a grave efficiency problem for Soviet industry, since it represents an accumulation of unused material resources, and the American

[22] Examples quoted by R. FASSIER, *op. cit.*, pp. 67 and 87.

economist R. Campbell has shown that the level of stockpiling was in fact noticeably higher in the Soviet economy than in the American economy.[23]

In the present context, we shall omit specific problems relating to the making of balances, on which there are numerous publications available to the Western reader, and confine ourselves to the major problem of plan elaboration facing the central planning authorities, in other words the problem of coherence between the different balances, and the appropriate choice of production objectives. It need only be said that the number of material balances has gradually increased with the passage of time, having grown from a score or so during the first five-year plan to several hundreds during the second five-year plan, and to an even greater number after the Second World War. As previously noted, there has been no further increase in the number of balances made by the Union Gosplan, and a greater amount of detailed work now takes place at republican and sovnarkhoz level.

The problem confronting the Soviet planner is that of solving an equation with several unknown quantities. In the initial stages, the planner does not know where supplies are to be directed (since plans for the user sectors do not yet exist) nor does he know what is to be produced by these same sectors. So far, there seems to be no mathematical method used in solving this simultaneous equation; it would in any case call for the use of a criterion or maximizing factor, and it is not clear how this could be defined in a planned economy where there is no proper price system in operation.

The method which is used to solve this problem consists of elaborating separate provisional plans for the various sectors, in the form of a working hypothesis. This first version is drawn up assuming the most favourable conditions for growth in each sector, and taking into account the existing priorities. The next stage consists of adjusting the draft plan for the different sectors so as to ensure coherence in the balances.

By this method the principal bottlenecks can be identified fairly rapidly. Elimination of bottlenecks is carried out with due atten-

[23] R. W. CAMPBELL, A comparison of Soviet and American inventory output ratios, *The American Economic Review*, September 1958.

tion to the principle of supplying in full the needs of priority branches and projects. The method employed is that of so-called "leading links", which enables the planners to single out, in their final demand, one or several products which are deemed to be of key importance, and to calculate the various amounts of direct or indirect consumption which will be required to produce a given volume of these products. The same method is then applied to products of the second and third degree of priority, and so on, until the resources available for allocation have been exhausted.

This method of successive approximation, or "iteration", is difficult to implement in cases involving revisions in the plan. In fact every change made in a resource item or in the use of any product must theoretically have repercussions on all resource items and the use of all products, because of the interplay of interdependences. All the indications would seem to suggest that in practice, Soviet planners do not go so far in correcting the balances when there are changes in the plan. Generally, it is only those balances which reflect interdependences of primary importance which are recalculated. For example, when there are changes in the production plan for motor-cars, they will correct the balances for ferrous and non-ferrous metals, for tyres and paint and other products used directly in the manufacture of motor-cars, but not the balances for those materials whose production will be affected by the change in demand for these same ferrous and non-ferrous metals, etc.[24] Since changes in the plans, either before or after they are put into operation, are assuredly inevitable, this means that in practice Soviet plans are never perfectly coherent, even on paper.

On the subject of *value balances*, one of the most important of these is the balance of income and expenditure of the population; its object is to study the equilibrium of the market under three heads: overall equilibrium between income and expenditure; equilibrium within a given region or town or locality; and equilibrium between consumer preferences and the goods and services offered. In principle, study of the overall equilibrium appears to be a simple matter in the USSR, because of the "planned wages funds", the "retail sales plans", the "State Bank cash plans" and the results of kolkhoz accounting and procurement plans for

[24] See A. EFIMOV, *Perestroika upravlenia promyshlennostiou i stroitelstvom v SSSR*, p. 107, Moscow, 1957.

agricultural products. As for the balance of the national economy, this "system of variables which reflects the overall process of social-economic growth and the reciprocal interrelationships and proportionality of economic factors and of the different branches of the national economy",[25] Soviet economists are enthusiastic in their praise of it. Academician Nemchinov, for example, regards it as a "much more effective" instrument than any of the same nature to be found in the West. This balance, which was undertaken in the early days of the Soviet experiment, was subsequently discontinued, and was not resumed until the 1950's. Various improvements have been made in it since that date (including the introduction of intersector and interregion balances). So far, however, it would not appear that this balance, or any of the other general balances, has played any very specific part in the work of planning; its role is rather the provision of general economic information which is of assistance in the elaboration of production and investment plans.

We should add a word here about the balance of the economic administrative region, which has been drawn up by the sovnarkhozy for each product since the reform of 1957. The task of the sovnarkhoz administration here is to determine which requirements will be covered by resources controlled by the sovnarkhoz in question, and which resources must come from outside, particular attention being paid to the utilization of local resources, so as to limit contributions from other regions. Thus, although regional balances do not lead to the making of a true "complex plan", as we have said before, they do seem to serve a wider purpose than the simple pinpointing of local requirements; in particular they provide a basis for the planning of transport, by enabling a preliminary estimate to be made of the tonnages which will have to be transported to the economic region in question.[26]

What tentative assessment can one make of the Soviet planning system at this stage? One's overriding impression is of a system which is admirable, and yet rudimentary. Admirable it un-

[25] R. V. RYABUSHKIN, Problems of methods in the national economy, *Voprosy Ekonomicheskoi Statistiki (Problems of economic statistics)*, p. 19, Gosstatizdat, Moscow, 1958.
[26] R. FASSIER, *op. cit.*

doubtedly is, when one considers this vast structure, with its proposals and directives infiltrating every sector of an immense country, its norms, indices and balances designed to cover all contingencies, its complex of plans linked one to another, its incessant reforms aimed at adapting the system to ever-increasing pressures or mitigating the worst of its defects, and the very vision of social and economic growth and transformation of which it is the expression, and by which a whole people is inspired. And yet it is rudimentary too, because of the still inadequate procedures governing choice in the various objectives, and above all because of the still persistent lapses in co-ordination among its diverse elements.

CHAPTER VI

ECONOMIC ORGANIZATION AND ECONOMIC HIERARCHY

IN AN economy which is based on a system of administrative orders, the everyday conduct of affairs depends to a great extent on the nature of the hierarchical organization within which enterprises and other economic agencies function; before proceeding to the problems of plan fulfilment, we should therefore first examine this organization.

Its influence is all the greater in that the fulfilment of Soviet plans, as we have seen, never goes according to schedule, but is subject, at all levels of the economic structure, to unforeseen contingencies and bottlenecks which call for adjustments of various kinds. This is in large measure due to the system of priorities in planning, and the role of those in charge of the administrative or political machine is therefore essentially one of resolving problems or difficulties as they arise.

Some information about the economic hierarchy has already been given in the preceding chapters. We now take up the question again, beginning with a study of the history of the sovnarkhozy, which had been the principal echelon of industrial administration since 1957, and which continued to be so even after the reform of 1962–3 had reduced their number by more than half. The description which follows applies to the situation as it was at the time of this reform.

THE SOVNARKHOZ EXPERIMENT: THE REFORM OF 1957

Prior to 1957, Soviet industry was administered mainly on a vertical basis, that is, by branches of industry. Hundreds of thousands of industrial enterprises and construction sites all over the country were under the control of a score or more of ministries, and several hundred specialist directorates, the great majority of these being based in Moscow, the capital of the Soviet Union.

This situation arose as the result of a historical process. During the period of the first five-year plans, which was marked by industrialization and the collectivization of agriculture, administrative organizations (people's commissariats, or *narkomaty* for short) had been created, with special responsibility for the various branches of industry; these narkomaty administered most of the industrial enterprises and construction organizations. The State agricultural sector (sovkhozy and machine tractor stations) was directly controlled by the appropriate agricultural narkomaty at all-Union level, and in the same way transport and the majority of commercial organizations were also subject to centralized control. The republican organs were responsible for local industry only, in other words those industries producing non-durable consumer goods, local building materials and fuel, and for certain communal economic undertakings, such as local education, health and culture, and for part of agriculture.

With the growth of the Soviet economy, the disadvantages of this system soon became apparent. The growing number of large factories in widely different areas all over the Soviet Union, and the resulting number of production units, all coming under the jurisdiction of the same organization, did not make for efficient administration. There had been a gradual tendency to increase the number of ministries (as the people's commissariats had been renamed in 1946) and the number of directorates, in an attempt to achieve a greater degree of specialization, and there seemed to be a continual necessity for creating new ones. The ministry of machinery, for example, had been split into three ministries, dealing respectively with heavy machinery, medium machinery and machine tools. In addition to the ministry for precision machinery and automation equipment, and a ministry for the electrotechnical industry, there were also ministries of a more traditional kind, such as the ministries for mines, timber or oil. By 1955 the number of economic ministries had risen to 53, compared with 18 in 1932, and the total number of ministries and directorates was 438.[1]

[1] A. VEDICHEV, Three years of the new régime. An economic study, *Plan. Khoz.*, No. 7, 1960.

The process was not, of course, a continuous one, and from time to time efforts were made to cut down the number of ministries: 10 were abolished in 1948-9, and several more in 1953, but there was always a tendency for the number to creep up again.

Alongside this specialization in administrative organizations there was a growing tendency for enterprises in different industrial sectors within the same geographical region to be sealed off into watertight compartments. Each ministry or directorate tended to become a self-contained empire, with its own suppliers and customers, often manufacturing some of the equipment and raw materials which it needed itself, with little or no regard to geographical location. The result was a fantastic general post of materials of the most diverse sorts over the length and breadth of the Soviet Union. One factory would send the machines it produced thousands of miles away, while an enterprise in the vicinity which used these same machines would be supplied, through its appropriate purchasing agency, with machines which had also travelled thousands of miles. This lack of liaison among factories operating in close proximity to each other was also an obstacle to specialization: for example, in Kharkov the engineering factories came under twenty different Union ministries, and almost every one had its own foundry-shop, although it would have been possible to set up communal specialized workshops. In the Rostov sovnarkhoz, "the Krasny Aksai factory, which produced agricultural equipment, received steel castings from Stalingrad, the Novocherkassk electrical equipment factory received theirs from even farther away, while the foundry of the stamping-press mill at Azov was producing more on the spot than it could use. All this because these factories were controlled by three different ministries."[2]

During the years prior to the 1957 reform, this state of affairs had been the subject of frequent criticism, notably at the meeting of the plenum of the Central Committee in July 1955, and a change had already begun to take place, as a result of several measures; the first of these, following on the plenum of September 1953, gave wider powers to the republics in various fields, such

[2] P. I. ABROSKIN, Study of the history of the Rostov sovnarkhoz, *Voprosy Istorii*, No. 10, 1959, summarized by R. PHILIPPORT, L'URSS et les pays de l'Est, *Revue des Revues*, No. 4, Strasburg, 1960.

as the transfer of certain industries from the jurisdiction of the Union to the republics, and a reduction in the number of products subject to centralized planning and allocation.

The reform in the administration of industry and construction enterprises, which was embodied in the law of 10th May 1957, and came into force on 1st July of that year, was first put forward in the form of "theses" presented by N. S. Khrushchev. These were the subject of "national discussion" for three months. The Institute of Economics of the Academy of Sciences of the USSR figured largely in the discussions. Its scientific council held one, or several, meetings in this connection, notably featuring studies on cross-haulage. However, it does not seem that the opinions of the economists attached to the Institute, or possibly even the opinions of Gosplan officials, carried much weight in the final decisions. Two of the officials whom I interviewed in 1961 in fact said that they had not thought the Party's reform would be so radical; one of them, a veteran of the first five-year plans, who described himself as a centralist "by habit and by ideology" told me quite frankly that in his opinion the reform had gone too far and that the powers of the sovnarkhozy were now excessive.

It is certain that the reform did not go through without some opposition; moreover, it became law and was put into operation, as we know, during one of the most serious political crises of recent years (meetings of the praesidium and then of the Central Committee of the Party in June 1957, followed by the dismissal of all N. S. Khrushchev's opponents from the Central Committee). In a curious publication entitled *Reports on the December and January plenums of the Central Committee of the CPSU*, which appeared in Moscow in February 1957, a certain Karasev, a candidate for the Central Committee, stated that the intended reorganization would be a gradual one only. "However," he adds, "some comrades are of the opinion that this reorganization should be rushed through at top speed. These comrades are most certainly mistaken . . . There must be no abrupt severance of existing inter-enterprise links."

Thus, there were two schools of thought. Nevertheless, at the meeting of the Supreme Soviet and the plenum in February 1957, called only two months after the previous one in December 1956, the floor had been held mainly by local Party cadres who condemned the evils of centralization, and a definite decision had in fact been taken in favour of a realignment of the economy on a horizontal basis, which entailed the suppression of most of the industrial ministries; N. S. Khrushchev was empowered to prepare theses implementing this principle to a very considerable degree. However, none of his colleagues came forward to lend public support to the proposed reform, either at that time or in May when the theses were published and the session of the Supreme Soviet took place. According to commentators at that time, all the indications seemed to point to the fact that implementation of the industrial reform had been made difficult by the opposition to Khrushchev, strengthened by resistance from those officials who were having to leave Moscow as a result of the creation of the sovnarkhozy.

At the time of the reform, there already existed, in the major industrial centres, specialist directorates for the various branches of industry *(upravlenie)*, which were attached to central administrations in Moscow, and which acted as intermediate links in the administration of the enterprises of the particular agglomeration or region. The purpose of the reform was "to bring the administration into closer contact with enterprises, and to increase participation by the people in the administration of industry" (article 1). To this end, it was laid down that "administration of industry and construction would be founded on the territorial principle on the basis of economic regions" (article 2). The reform consisted of freeing these local administrations from control by the central directorates and ministries in Moscow, the majority of which were then abolished, and placing them under the control of new councils for the national economy *(Soviet Narodnovo Khozyaistva* or *Sovnarkhoz* for short). As will be seen, the branch directorates still, however, preserved their separate existence and even a certain degree of autonomy.

The nature of the reform will be readily understood by anyone with a knowledge of French administration; one need only imagine a not impossible situation in which those branches of the administration functioning in the *départements* or regions (public services, rural works, etc.) which up to the present were responsible directly to the appropriate directorate or ministry in Paris, have been placed under the authority of the *préfets* of the various *départements*, or under new authorities specially created in the *départements* or regions. In a certain number of cases, the authority of the sovnarkhozy also superseded that of the ministries of the various republics. Thus, in addition to the abolition of some ten or so central ministries (mainly in the heavy engineering sectors) and the amalgamation of several others, about fifteen or so categories of ministries in the republics (paper, light industries, oil, etc.) were also superseded at the same time, and the enterprises and organizations under their control were placed under the authority of the sovnarkhozy.

THE SOVNARKHOZY: ORGANIZATION AND FUNCTIONS

As its name indicates, the sovnarkhoz is a council. It consists of a chairman, several vice-chairmen and members (for example, in Kharkov there are 4 vice-chairmen and 17 members, in Kiev there are 5 vice-chairmen).[3] The sovnarkhoz is directly responsible to the Council of Ministers of the republic, and the Council of Ministers of the USSR has no authority over it except through the republican Councils of Ministers (article 5). It is not a representative local organ, but the representative of republican power. In terms of French administrative law, therefore, the creation of the sovnarkhozy was not *decentralization* but *deconcentration* — a distinction which may help to clear up certain arguments which have occasionally arisen among Western economists.[4] Only in relation to republics, oblasts or towns can one properly speak of a measure of decentralization.

The authority of the sovnarkhoz does not extend over the entire field of economic activity, but is confined to industrial enterprises. Nor is the sovnarkhoz responsible for the whole of industry, but solely for large-scale industries, since small-scale industry is the responsibility of local soviets, towns and oblasts. The distinction between large-scale and small-scale industry is not entirely clear-cut. It depends both on the size of the enterprise and the nature of the activity. In the main, those enterprises

---

[3] See Quelques aspects de la situation du directeur de l'entreprise soviétique, *Rapport d'une mission française en U R S S* (MM. Abbou, Delamotte, Lachaux, P. Stoetzel, M. Watine, head of delegation), April 1961, 31 pp. (roneo).

[4] Cf. O. HOEFFDING, The Soviet industrial reorganization of 1957, *American Economic Review* (Proceedings), May 1959.

coming under the jurisdiction of the sovnarkhozy employ a minimum of 200 or 250 workers, but there are cases where enterprises of this size, or even larger, come under the local soviets. On the other hand, the food industries and those industries serving the needs of the local population are generally the responsibility of local organizations; a major food industry, such as a brewery, however, will usually be controlled by the sovnarkhoz. Similarly, a large brick-works or cement-works comes under the sovnarkhoz, but small factories producing building materials are administered by the oblast.

These are not hard and fast distinctions, and in the years after the reform, the area of competence of the sovnarkhozy seems to have continued to extend, both *vis-à-vis* the local soviets and the Union. Thus, it is said that a part of light industry came under the control of the sovnarkhozy in 1960. It was reported that in certain regions or territories of the RSFSR the sovnarkhozy were made responsible not only for industrial enterprises which had formerly been administered by the local authorities, but also for building trusts. From the point of view of the enterprises in question, the advantage of the transfer was said to be that Gosplan, or at least Gosplan of the RSFSR, would generally fulfil the needs of the enterprises and organizations administered by the sovnarkhozy much more thoroughly than they would the needs of those controlled by the local authorities. However, there has also been mention of areas where the reverse was happening, and enterprises were being returned to the care of the local authorities.[5]

According to official data, the pattern of development of the various categories of industrial enterprises, classified according to value of production *(valovaya produktsia)* and administrative responsibility, has been as follows, since 1950 (in percentage):

It will be seen that from 1952 there was a reduction in the proportion of industry coming under the direct control of Union administrations, and that by the end of 1956 this was no longer predominant. From the reform of 1957 up until 1962, there would not appear to have been any major change. This infor-

[5] I. MAYEVSKI and A. FOMIN, New improvements in economic planning methods, *Vopr. Ekon.*, No. 10, 1960.

TABLE III.

Enterprises in the Soviet Union from 1950 to 1960

	1950	1952	1956	1957	1959	1960
Enterprises controlled by — the Union	67	70	45	6	6	6
— Republics, oblasts, raions	33	30	55	94	94	94
of which, controlled by the sovnarkhozy				71	72	72

SOURCE: *Nar. Khoz.*, p. 213, 1960, and *Nar. Khoz.* p., 41, 1955.

mation, however, does not entirely tally with what one gathers from other sources.

The majority of the industrial sectors, and particularly such important sectors as steel or oil production, were therefore entirely under the jurisdiction of the sovnarkhozy. On the other hand, the armaments industries, and allied industries (nuclear energy), and certain industries in which techniques are very advanced and growth rapid, were still presumably the responsibility of the Union. There is no means of telling to what extent all these industries actually figure in the above table.

Although the administration of enterprises was very largely taken over by the sovnarkhozy in this way, the construction of factories seems for the most part to have remained a central responsibility. For example, in 1959 the ministry of electric power-stations was abolished, and the administration of power-stations and the responsibility for meeting local power needs passed to the republics; but at the same time a ministry for the construction of electrical power-stations was created, and this continues to come under the Union administration. In 1960, whereas the proportion of the value of total production represented by industries administered by the republics reached 94%, the corresponding figure for building organizations controlled by the republics was no more than 80%, and the figure for total investments was 76% (as compared with 5% in 1953).[6]

It is also known that, of 8000 building enterprises administered by the councils of ministers of the federal republics, only 3500

[6] URINSON, *op. cit.*

were the responsibility of the sovnarkhozy, while 3400 were attached to the republican ministries of construction, and over 1000 to the local soviets.[6a]

The sovnarkhozy employ a fairly large number of administrative staff: there are about 800 at Kharkov, and some 1500 at the Moscow Town sovnarkhoz; in the latter case there are some 400 people employed in central organizations of the sovnarkhoz, and 1100 in the various industrial directorates. These figures, so far as one can gather, do not include the supply and purchasing agencies now attached to the sovnarkhozy, of which we shall be speaking later on.

There were, in 1961, 15 technical directorates *(upravlenie)* in Moscow (as against 23 previously) and 20 in Leningrad: the executive departments *(otdyel)* at Kharkov consisted of a planning department, a technical division, and departments for production, investments, finance, transport, external relations and economic accounting; finally, the executive division concerned with supply of materials and equipment and with sales ranked as a directorate.

The functions of the sovnarkhozy are, essentially, to supervise the industrial enterprises for which they are responsible. Leaving aside those functions which have to do with planning proper, and which we have already touched upon, they may be summarized under the following headings:

(1) Appointment of directors;
(2) Supervision of the fulfilment of plans, with particular reference to the award of bonuses to staff and directors, and supervision of accounts, alongside that exercised by the banks;
(3) Payment to enterprises of the investment capital laid down in the plan and financed by the budget, these payments being made through the directorates *(upravlenie)*, and supervision of the working capital of enterprises so as to ensure growth in productivity and rationalization of production;
(4) Responsibility for the construction or starting-up of the new factories provided for in the plan, and which come within the scope of the sovnarkhozy;

[6a] M. I. BARYCHEV, *Sovietskoe Gosudarstvo i Pravo*, No. 8, 1963.

(5) Study of problems allied to industrial production, particularly house building, in collaboration with local authorities and other relevant bodies;

(6) Finally, participation in the distribution and price-fixing system.

The directorates have a consultative voice in the allocation of investment funds to enterprises, mainly for the purpose of ensuring that expenditures correspond closely to the objectives of the plan. In practice this affords the sovnarkhozy, and more especially the directorates in question, a considerable amount of power, and some authors have expressed the fear that real power may still lie with the "vertical" or technical administrative organizations, as it did prior to 1957, at the expense both of territorial co-ordination and enterprise autonomy.

The decision of 26th September 1957 by the Council of Ministers of the USSR, which defined the powers of the sovnarkhozy, gave them the right, for purposes relating to the improvement of local working and living conditions, to utilize any locally produced raw materials which were surplus to the requirements of the plan or not covered by it, and to place the appropriate orders with enterprises, on condition that there was no encroachment on the objectives laid down in the plan. To this end, the sovnarkhozy were also empowered to enter into reciprocal aid agreements with the other economic regions, and with ministries and administrations for local industry. As we shall see, however, there was serious opposition to the granting of these powers, which represented a real step towards decentralization.

Another function of the sovnarkhozy is participation in discussions with the unions for the making of collective agreements. However, if it is true that collective agreements in the USSR are more a "technique for encouragement and organization than a vital institution", since their provisions are for the most part copied from the public statutes, this particular function need not be taken very seriously.[7]

Alongside the sovnarkhozy, there exists a consultative body, the technico-economic council *(tekhniko-ekonomicheski soviet)*

[7] L. GREYFIE DE BELLECOMBE, *Les conventions collectives de travail en Union soviétique*, pp. 112 and 59, Mouton & Co., The Hague, Paris, 1958.

which is of some importance. This is described as a "social organization", by contrast with a State administrative unit, in that it is purely consultative in character, and its members are unpaid. The council consists of leading specialists, workers, engineers, directors, scholars, instructors, Party and union members, with, it seems, a special place for local inventors. Numerous sovnarkhoz officials take part in its discussions. It is divided into sections corresponding to the various industrial sectors or techniques. In 1961 the Kharkov Council altogether comprised some 1000 members.

Nomination of members to the technico-economic council is a matter for the sovnarkhoz; however, prior to nomination, candidates are seemingly put forward by representatives of local enterprises, and town and regional organizations.[8]

As a new juridical form of collective participation in State administration of industry and construction, the technico-economic council has a say in all matters which come within the province of the sovnarkhoz.[9] In practice it would seem that its main purpose is to assist in furthering technical progress in industry, within the context of the major objectives of the plan, and in collaboration with national and local scientific institutes. According to the Watine mission,[10] its task is also to help the sovnarkhoz authorities in providing technical assistance for enterprises. Compared with the efforts of the local productivity councils which have been set up in various Western countries, notably France, there may be greater emphasis on experimentation with new techniques than on the dissemination of already accepted ones.

CONSEQUENCES OF THE CREATION OF THE SOVNARKHOZY

One of the factors most frequently quoted in favour of the setting up of the sovnarkhozy was the reduction in cross-hauls. In drawing up their production and distribution plans and making

---

[8] G. A. YAMPOLSKA, The technico-economic council attached to the sovnarkhoz, a new form of collective participation in state administration, *Sov. Gos. i Pravo*, No. 11, 1959. Commentary by M. MOUSKHELY, L'URSS et les pays de l'Est, *Revue des Revues*, No. 4, Strasbourg, 1960.

[9] *Ibid.*

[10] *Op. cit.*

the regional balances for those products which came within their jurisdiction, the sovnarkhozy did in fact try to ensure that suppliers and customers should be fairly near each other, a point which had not received so much attention when industry had been "vertically" administered.

At the Institute of Economics of the Soviet Academy of Sciences, I was told that the effect of the reform had been, for the USSR as a whole, an annual saving of 2 billion old roubles (200 million new roubles, or 1100 million francs at the official rate) in transport alone. No information was given as to how these figures had been calculated, but they seemed to be based on a comparison between the amount of transport actually used and the amount which would have been required for implementation of the supply plans for previous years, taking account of the level of production which had been reached. In the Kharkov sovnarkhoz I had likewise been informed that the result of the reform had been a saving of not less than 20% on the total transport requirements for the years 1958, 1959 and 1960, the saving being more marked at the end of the period in question than at the beginning. Again, for the USSR as a whole, the average length of freight journeys by rail, which had risen by 39 km, or 5%, in the three years prior to 1957, had remained unchanged during the three following years, which might indicate a greater degree of regional integration. In the Russian republic, while the total volume of consignments had risen by 8% from 1957 to 1958, intra-regional consignments were said to have increased by 10% over the same period; similarly, intra-regional consignments of cast or forged steel, in the years 1957 to 1959, had risen from 29% to 47% of the total consignments.[11]

At the XXIInd Congress, Beshchev, the Minister of Transport for the USSR, gave further details from which it is possible to check the foregoing information: after the reform in the administration of industry and construction, the average length of freight journeys by rail fell by 25 km, and the resultant saving was 300 million roubles (the total cost of transport was 20 billion

[11] The expression "intra-regional consignments" is not, however, made clear: does it really mean consignments within an economic administrative region, as opposed to total consignments? The latter examples have been taken from VEDICHEV's article, *op. cit.*

roubles).[12] In the article announcing the setting up of the co-
ordinating councils for the large regions, P. Lomako also indicated that, from the time of the 1957 reform until 1960, the sovnarkhozy in the Urals had been able to cut down imports of steel
castings and ingots from other sovnarkhozy by 58% and 77%
respectively, and that, in the case of the sovnarkhozy in western
Siberia, the proportions had been even slightly higher.[13]

One is tempted to make a brief check on these figures, by comparing the variations in industrial production and in the total
volume of transport for Russia as a whole over the last few years,
but the results are not very conclusive; the increase in the volume
of transport was less than the increase in industrial production, as
measured by the official index, but the difference was no greater
than it was prior to 1957; however, there are numerous other
factors which may affect the figure for the total volume of transport in one way or another (particularly the development of new
sources of power, and the opening up of new lands in regions far
from the centres of population).

Another advantage which had been attributed to the creation
of the sovnarkhozy was the increase in enterprise specialization.
It was this point which P. Lomako had in mind, for example,
when explaining the reduction in "imports" of raw materials into
the Urals and western Siberia which was mentioned above.

It was also said that the problem of allocating scarce raw materials or manpower had been eased by the setting up of the sovnarkhozy, in that they could arbitrate locally in cases where there
was a shortage in one sector and a surplus in another, whereas it
had formerly been necessary to refer the matter to Moscow.
However, as will be seen later on, it is not certain that any very
marked progress has been made in this direction.

What was undoubtedly true was that the creation of the sovnarkhozy narrowed the gap between enterprise and administration. The industrial enterprises attached to any one sovnarkhoz
were in fact relatively small in number, a few hundred at the most:
about 700 in Leningrad, 400 in Moscow Town (for 800,000 workers employed), and much fewer in the smaller sovnarkhozy. This
relatively small number made for a greater degree of direct per-

[12] *Pravda*, 28th October 1961.
[13] *Op. cit.*

sonal contact between the directors of enterprises and sovnarkhoz officials. All the officials whom I met emphasized the advantages of such a system. According to a French engineer, who was the representative of a firm building four complete factories in different parts of the USSR, and who by 1962 had already spent more than twelve months in the Soviet Union over the three previous years[14], the most tangible benefit brought about by the reform was the fact that a sovnarkhoz chairman could appeal directly to Moscow to speed up delivery of equipment required by an enterprise when there was a bottleneck in the administrative machinery. Whether he was successful, of course, would obviously depend to a great extent on his own personal qualities.

Praise for the sovnarkhozy was not unmixed with criticism. One of the most frequent and most serious allegations about them was that they tended to foster a spirit of "narrow localism".

The introduction of a regionally-based system of administration for industry and construction made it possible to rationalize economic links within the territory of the sovnarkhoz. It was, however, impossible to avoid pressure from local interests, which proved an obstacle to co-operation between neighbouring sovnarkhozy. The result was unprofitable production and uneconomic transport of metals, oil and cement.[15]

There were numerous reports of lack of co-operation among officials, or among enterprises attached to two different sovnarkhozy. A cartoon in *Krokodil* depicted a father preventing his child from lending a toy to a friend, and saying: "She doesn't belong to our sovnarkhoz."[16] It was likewise reported that two trawlers at sea could not transfer fish or water to each other without referring the matter to Moscow — and even with the radio it would take at least two weeks to get a decision.[17]

One particularly harmful features seemed to be the tendency on the part of sovnarkhozy, in cases of non-fulfilment or over-

---

[14] I should like to express my thanks to him here for the information which he so kindly provided.

[15] P. ALAMPIEV, V. KISTANOV, P. SUKHOPARA, The main problems in the improvement of regional organization of production, *Plan. Khoz.*, No. 7, pp. 23–29, 1960. Résumé by E. ZALESKI, L'URSS et les pays de l'Est, *Revue des Revues*, No. 3, Strasbourg, 1961.

[16] *Krokodil*, 10th March 1958, quoted by M. KASER, *op. cit.*

[17] Under the flag of their own economic council, *Pravda*, 22nd March 1962.

fulfilment of plans, to give first priority to deliveries within their own sovnarkhoz.

It was reported of the Perm sovnarkhoz, for example, that their plan for industrial deliveries in 1960 was only 99% fulfilled outside the sovnarkhoz, but that within the area of the sovnarkhoz it had been fulfilled to 124%; the corresponding figures for the Stalino sovnarkhoz were 94% and 113%.[18] In some instances the degree of non-fulfilment of the delivery plan outside the boundaries of the sovnarkhoz was apparently very much greater. In 1958, for example, the Karaganda sovnarkhoz fulfilled only 80% of its planned deliveries to other sovnarkhozy, and the figure for South Kazakhstan was only 87%.[19]

In other cases the sovnarkhozy were accused of misusing money and supplies granted to them for the development of important industries by diverting them to meet local requirements.[20]

From the point of view of Soviet planning, these were grave distortions, since they amounted to priority in deliveries for particular regions, instead of particular sectors, and this was not at all the purpose behind the reform of 1957. The republican Gosplans endeavoured to keep a very close watch on the sovnarkhozy, and even to revoke the powers which had been granted to them, by the decision of 26th September 1957, for the satisfaction of local needs. According to the terms of a resolution dated 17th April 1958, which determined the hierarchical responsibility for fulfilment of deliveries to the various organizations engaged in preparation and execution of the supply plan, federal republics, sovnarkhozy and enterprises were bound to ensure priority for planned deliveries to other federal republics and economic regions, and for general State requirements, regardless of the level of plan fulfilment. A decision of 22nd January 1959 deprived the sovnarkhozy of their right to divert supplies of material, and this function passed to the republican Gosplans and councils of ministers.

The fear of "localism" did not date merely from the creation of the sovnarkhozy, and it was no doubt this fear which, until the

---

[18] *Kommunist*, No. 7, pp. 52–53, 1961.

[19] V. KOLTSOV, *Vopr. Ekon.*, No. 2, 1959.

[20] See in FASSIER, *op. cit*, the example of the Gorki sovnarkhoz in 1958, and the comments of Zverev, Finance Minister of the USSR, in his report on the 1959 budget.

reform of November 1962, lay behind the refusal of wider powers to them, which would have brought not only large-scale industry but also other economic activities under their jurisdiction. This fear was again manifested at the time when the new interdistrict organizations for agricultural administration were set up in March, 1962. Chairmen of sovnarkhozy, it was said at the time, would not belong to these new committees, for the links between agriculture and industry must be at State level, and not at local level; localist tendencies in the supply system for machinery to kolkhozy and sovkhozy were particularly to be avoided.[21]

Among other criticisms levelled at the sovnarkhozy, it was sometimes said that they had done nothing to lighten the weight of bureaucracy. "When the sovnarkhozy were set up, we said to ourselves: 'Now there will be fewer headquarters meetings.' We thought that because they were near at hand the administrators would come to the factory;" in fact, nothing of the sort happened, and there was a simultaneous increase in the number of operational meetings *(operativka)* on the spot, time-consuming activity which was deplored by the workers and engineers of the Red Sormovo factory at Gorki.[22] More frequently, one found the sovnarkhozy being accused, in fact, of wielding insufficient power, and consequently being unable to play a sufficiently strong co-ordinating role. For instance, one author expressed regret that they were unable to use the investment funds which came under their jurisdiction as they thought best.[23] It was also said that, despite appearances, industrial administration continued to function on a vertical basis, as it had done in the past, mainly because the "branch administrations" of the sovnarkhoz still retained their autonomy.

There was particularly severe criticism on this score. Davydov, the chairman of the Buryat republican sovnarkhoz (eastern Siberia) who had complaints on the subject, proposed that the planning sections in the industrial administrations should be abolished, and that all planning work should be concentrated in the

---

[21] Speech by Voronov, first deputy-chairman of the bureau of the Party Central Committee of the RSFSR, at the plenary session of the Central Committee on agriculture, *Pravda*, 7th March 1962.

[22] *Izvestia*, 7th February 1962.

[23] ABROSKIN, Report on the history of the Rostov sovnarkhoz, *op. cit.*

central sovnarkhoz apparatus.[24] A similar opinion was expressed by Soyich, the chairman of the Kharkov sovnarkhoz, who stated that a "directorate" was only a small organization at the head of some twenty-five enterprises engaged in similar or allied forms of production, and went on to suggest that "most of the directorates should be abolished, and that combines *(combinaty)* should be set up, with a leading enterprise at their head, which would be directly subordinate to the sovnarkhoz".[25] The main argument in favour of the sovnarkhozy was that they were a homogeneous and relatively small organization capable of dealing with all problems affecting the enterprises within their territorial jurisdiction. But experience had shown that, in a number of instances, reference to the sovnarkhoz was more or less openly dispensed with, and there were sometimes cases of enterprises receiving orders direct from the branch directorates of the republican Gosplans, or even from the Union Gosplan, or cases where direct contact was established between those directorates and their opposite numbers in the sovnarkhoz, while the central organization of the sovnarkhoz might not necessarily be informed.[26]

The introduction of a territorially-based industrial administration had in fact been accompanied by an increase in the powers of the Union Gosplan, which had acquired wide responsibilities in matters of current administration; it had absorbed the chief supply departments *(glavsbyts)* of the former ministries, and had become responsible for the elaboration of interrepublican delivery plans, and the fixing of prices for the principal goods and services. In practice, therefore, the Union Gosplan had become the main supervisory and co-ordinating authority for the sovnarkhozy, through the republican councils of ministers and Gosplans; in the years that followed, this position had been further strengthened, because of the criticisms to which the territorial system of administration was subject (excessive attention to local interests, use of investment funds and resources in a manner prejudicial to the national interest, failure to fulfil interrepublican delivery plans).

[24] *Ekonomicheskaya Gazeta*, 5th February 1962.
[25] *Ukrainian Pravda*, 24th January 1962.
[26] See examples quoted on this subject in A. Nove, The industrial planning system: Reforms in prospect, *Soviet Studies*, July 1962.

In an effort to achieve a closer degree of co-ordination between the sovnarkhozy of the large republics, a first step towards
reform was taken with the creation of republican sovnarkhozy, or
"supersovnarkhozy" *(vysshie soviety narodnovo khozyaistva*, or
V.S.N.Kh.) in the second half of 1960 in the large republics, i.e.
in the RSFSR, the Ukraine, Kazakhstan and Byelorussia. The
V.S.N.Kh., under the authority of the appropriate republican
Gosplan, is responsible for co-ordination of the activities of the
sovnarkhozy in the republic.

The result of this reform seems to have been to increase the
supervisory and co-ordinating powers of the republican authorities over the activities of the sovnarkhozy, and to have separated
them from the strictly planning functions of the republican Gosplan. However, there is very little information available about the
activities of these new organizations between 1960 and 1962. It
was being said in Moscow that Radio Armenia, that well-known
source of a number of good stories circulating in the USSR, had
held an enquiry into the nature and functions of the supersovnarkhozy, but had been forced to conclude that "nobody knows".
Nevertheless, it is known that they were given the right to re-
allocate investment funds and materials, which had been taken
away from the sovnarkhozy, and assumed by the republican
Gosplans. Anyway, it does not appear that this new body is
giving much satisfaction. The chairmen of the Kharkov and Buryat republican sovnarkhozy, whose comments were quoted previously, are reported as complaining about intervention by the
supersovnarkhozy of the RSFSR or the Ukraine, on the grounds
that they were simply an additional echelon functioning alongside
the republican Gosplan, and further complicating administration.

ADMINISTRATION OF OTHER SECTORS OF PRODUCTION

Before proceeding to an examination of the economic hierarchy as it now is, following on the 1962–3 reforms and the organization of the new sovnarkhozy, we shall consider the administration of the other sectors of production.

Up till November 1962, the sovnarkhozy, as we have seen, were
responsible only for large-scale industry and, in a great many
matters, it was the oblast which remained the competent authority. The principal administrative organ of the oblast is the exec-

utive committee *(oblispolkom)* which is the representative of
Soviet power in the area, and is assisted by a council which meets,
in principle, every two months.

In the large cities the authority of the oblast is replaced by that
of the municipality. Thus, small enterprises in the city of Lenin-

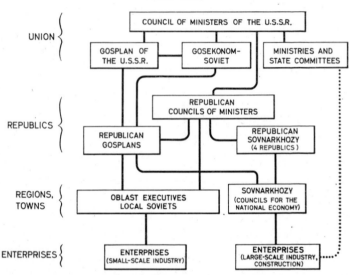

FIG. 2. Simplified diagram of the organizational structure of
   industry and construction (1960–62)

grad are responsible, not to the executive committee of the oblast,
but to the municipality *(gorsoviet)*. This rule seems to have been
tightened up recently, and small enterprises situated in the city
now come exclusively under the jurisdiction of the municipality.

Small-scale industry, in principle, is the responsibility of the
oblast. In the case of Leningrad the sovnarkhoz has control over
a cellulose combine, an aluminium factory, a cement factory,
factories turning out machinery, a large shoe factory, a chocolate
factory, while the oblast is responsible for the clothing industry,
small shoe factories, a lemonade factory. The functions of the
oblast organizations are very varied, since they may cover all

questions arising within the area. They include, in particular, responsibility for house building, sometimes in collaboration with the sovnarkhozy when it is a question of providing housing for workers in proximity to factories administered by the sovnarkhozy; the organization of public services, such as road maintenance, municipal transport, canals (transport problems as a whole, however, are the responsibility of the ministries of the republics in respect of roads, and of the Union in respect of railways), the administration of primary, secondary and technical education (the sole exceptions being higher education and certain institutes); hospitals and health services, which are responsible both to the local authorities and to the Ministry of Health. The number of officials attached to the oblast or town authorities (Gorsoviet and its planning section Gorplan) is, consequently, generally much higher than those attached to the sovnarkhoz.

Town and oblast organizations have the same powers over the enterprises which are attached to them as the sovnarkhozy have in their particular field. These enterprises are sometimes grouped in the form of "trusts" (like the Moscow Restaurant Trust), a term which was also formerly used to describe a union of large-scale factories. Similarly, small workshops which were formerly separate enterprises have been attached to larger enterprises, so that the number of industrial enterprises now controlled by the Leningrad oblast is only 185, each employing an average of 200 people, and the largest of them 600; in one raion of this oblast, for example, a small wood-stripping yard, a grindstone workshop about 500 yards away, and a sawmill some 10 miles distant now comprise one single enterprise. Producers' co-operatives (artel), which were dissolved in 1960, were also amalgamated in the form of small state industrial enterprises.

The industries administered by local authorities are responsible for satisfying local consumer needs. The existence of a clearcut distinction between small-scale industry, whose activities are directed towards local consumption, and large-scale industry, which is concerned mainly with the manufacture of producers' goods and certain items which are properly described as articles of mass consumption, is one of the characteristics of Soviet industrial administration. It seems to be recognized that current consumer needs cannot be satisfied except by a sort of haphazard production which can scarcely be described as industry, and in any case rates no priority. One might quote, on this subject, the case of the small enterprise turning out meat mincers, an article much sought after by the public; the local sovnarkhoz had applied to the planning department of the oblispolkom for the transfer of the enterprise in question, so that it might be turned over to the manufacture of a certain machine part, in order to facilitate reorganization of the large factory which up till then had been producing these parts. "But what would have become of their output of mincers?" said the man who was telling me this story, and who, for his part, must have tried to oppose the transfer. The oblast authorities work "for man's needs", he also added, which in this case could only be interpreted as an indirect, although probably unwitting, reflection on the way in which large-scale industry functions.

Still, it was rather rare to hear it said that this division of industrial administration between sovnarkhozy and local soviets was abnormal. At the XXIInd Congress, Polyanski did give this as his personal opinion, but then went on to say that, if the independence of the local authorities continued to increase, it was not in order that they should organize their territorial economy so as to become self-sufficient; on the contrary, he said, what was necessary was to increase the interdependence of the various territories.[27] It seems that the fear of "localism" is still being expressed.

This state of affairs is often more openly criticized, however, in the small republics. For example, the president of the Council of Ministers of Estonia complained about the division of industry between the sovnarkhoz and the other administrative organs.[28] The chairman of the Azerbaidzhan sovnarkhoz for his part deplored the overlapping of work between the republican Gosplan and the sovnarkhoz.[29] The chairman of the Latvian sovnarkhoz referred to what looks like an original solution of the problem. In 1958 or 1959, the administration of local industry in this republic was handed over to the sovnarkhoz, which in return was instructed to submit an overall plan for industry to the government. In this way, considerable progress was made, a notable

[27] *Pravda*, 24th October 1961.
[28] *Izvestia*, 13th May 1962.
[29] *Izvestia*, 17th May 1962.

example being the wool hosiery industry, a traditional industry in Riga, where the supply position was greatly improved. Nevertheless, the sovnarkhoz has no say in financial control over local industry; this remains the prerogative of the local authorities, although they are not well equipped to undertake it. The reason for this rough and ready compromise seems to be that in Latvia, as in the rest of the USSR, a large part of the local authorities' budget for cultural needs and construction comes from the profits of the enterprises under their control, which they cannot for this reason afford to relinquish. The author of the article in question suggests that the State should increase the funds which it allocates to local authorities for these municipal undertakings, so that the whole of the administration of industry, including financial administration, could then be properly centralized under the control of the sovnarkhoz.[30]

All the same, one wonders whether what seems feasible in a small republic, where the interests of the consumers are possibly less neglected than they are elsewhere, would necessarily be an improvement in the rest of the USSR. Judging from the examples quoted above, the sin of "localism" cannot be avoided except at the expense of the consumers' interests.

The building of houses and various urban installations is another of the responsibilities of the local soviets, but the various republican ministries have also a say in this matter, which again raises problems of co-ordination. N. Kondratiev, member of the Kharkov city council, and chairman of the local planning commission, disclosed that in this city, which has only one builder (the Kharkov building trust) and one customer (the building section of the executive committee) the principle of balanced town planning is often in fact disregarded. The funds necessary for these development schemes come, in part, from various republican ministries, such as the Ministry of Education, the Ministry of Public Health, the Ministry of Commerce and the Ministry of Communal Economy. Some of these ministries draw up their own plans in great detail and do not necessarily approve, insofar as they are concerned, the plans submitted by the towns. As a result, despite existing standards, new districts are often completed before street lighting, and schools, shops, cinemas and other

[30] *Izvestia*, 24th January 1962.

services have been provided; the resultant inconvenience affects not only the inhabitants, but also the builders, who are obliged to return time and again to the same building sites.[31]

In matters relating to town planning, it is particularly difficult to ensure effective co-ordination of all the various services concerned; this is a problem which is no doubt common to all countries. But it will be observed that the apparent simplicity of the Soviet solution — one builder, one customer — is in fact no guarantee that co-ordination in planning is any better than it is elsewhere.

The administration of agriculture is another domain in which, up till recent times, the local authorities had a say. A major reform in this connection took place at the beginning of 1962. Under the previous system, briefly, the oblasts had, through the medium of the districts (raiony) a certain amount of jurisdiction over the kolkhozy; in practice, the district Party secretaries seem to have had close control of the kolkhozy in their area. The sovkhozy, on the other hand, were responsible to their own organization. G. I. Voronov, first deputy-chairman of the central Party bureau for the RSFSR, put the matter very forcibly at the plenary session of the Party Central Committee on agricultural problems in March 1962, when he said that "the system was rotten to the core" and amounted to nothing but a "rubber-stamp administration."[32] As is so often the case in the USSR, it seems impossible to mention personalities, or institutions, which have been discredited, without going in for violent denunciation.

The new system was based on the creation, at republican level, of new ministries for the production and supply of agricultural products, to which there were to be attached interdistrict administrative councils which would control the kolkhozy and sovkhozy in their area. In Byelorussia, 29 of these councils were announced, an average of 1 for every 5 districts and 93 kolkhozy. In the Russian republic G. I. Voronov spoke of 382, and later 418, of these bodies.[33] The number of collectives administered by each one of these councils might vary from 15 to over 100.

[31] *Izvestia*, 3rd April 1962.

[32] *Pravda*, 7th March 1962.

[33] Speech to the Party Central Committee bureau, *Pravda*, 28th March 1962; see also speech by N. S. Khrushchev at the same meeting.

The duty of these councils was to organize production in agricultural undertakings, to see to the distribution of supplies to them, and to exercise the necessary control over them. The executive council of these organizations consists primarily of the first secretaries of the district Party committees *(raikom)*, plus agricultural specialists and the head of the inspectorate. The main feature of these new administrative councils is that they seem to combine the functions of procurement and supply with those of supervision and direction of production.

At republican level, the Ministry of Agriculture was to become the Ministry of Agricultural Sciences, while a section of the party was to be specially organized to deal with agriculture. The same organization was set up at Union level. According to Olshansky, who was then Minister of Agriculture of the USSR, the Ministry of Agriculture had in fact been transferred to a sovkhoz outside of Moscow, and it was intended to move 32 agricultural institutes to other sovkhozy (although this had not so far been done).[34]

THE 1962–3 REFORMS AND THE PRESENT ORGANIZATION
OF THE ECONOMY

In the light of proposals put forward in a speech by N. S. Khrushchev on the 19th November 1962, and later adopted as decisions by the plenum of the Party Central Committee in November 1962,[35] a reform in economic organization and the economic hierarchy took place in January and March 1963.

One of the first of these decisions was to reduce the number of sovnarkhozy, which, as we have already seen in Chapter II, now number only 47. The new expanded sovnarkhozy were made responsible both for the administration of heavy industry and of local industries. On the other hand, building enterprises were removed entirely from their jurisdiction and became the responsibility of a new organization, the State building committee *(Gosstroi)*.

The reform in agricultural administration which had taken place at the beginning of 1962 was confirmed, and in consequence

[34] *Pravda*, 7th March 1962.
[35] *Izvestia*, 24th November 1962.

the former districts (raiony) ceased to function as organs of economic administration. Instead, there were set up industrial districts and rural districts, the latter corresponding to the areas of the new so-called kolkhoz-sovkhoz (or sovkhoz-kolkhoz) administrations for agricultural production.

Just as the entire Party organization was split into two halves which were responsible, respectively, for agriculture, and industry and construction, so the former oblast or krai soviets were superseded, in the majority of cases, by district councils dealing either with industry and allied activities, or agriculture.[36]

There is now a clear-cut territorial distinction between the boundaries of the sovnarkhozy and the oblasts, which means that the sovnarkhoz authorities are less subject to political control by the oblast Party cadres.

At the top administrative level, *Gosekonomsoviet* was abolished. Gosplan once more took over responsibility for long-term planning, as well as current planning. Alongside Gosplan, a new organization was set up, namely the sovnarkhoz of the USSR, which relieved Gosplan of its responsibility for annual plan fulfilment. At republican level, its opposite numbers, in those republics where they existed, were the four republican sovnarkhozy, which were retained, and the new regional sovnarkhozy. In addition Gosstroi was set up, as we have mentioned, and the State committees were redefined: these ceased to be committees attached to the Council of Ministers, and were instead attached to a number of different organizations.

By the decree of 13th March 1963, there was set up a *Supreme council for the national economy of the USSR* (supersovnarkhoz) which is the main administrative organ for industry and construction; it is directly responsible to the government, and its resolutions and orders are immediately binding on all State organs. Gosplan, the sovnarkhoz of the USSR, Gosstroi and a certain number of State committees are responsible to it.

Those in charge of the above organizations were, until recently, Ustinov (who was previously responsible for armaments) for the Supreme Council, P. Lomako (who, as we saw earlier on,

---

[36] As mentioned earlier, this organization was abolished and the former situation re-established in the autumn of 1964, after the fall of N. S. Khrushchev.

played a part in the creation of the large economic regions) for Gosplan, V. Dymshits (formerly chairman of Gosplan) for the sovnarkhoz of the USSR, and I. Novikov for Gosstroi.

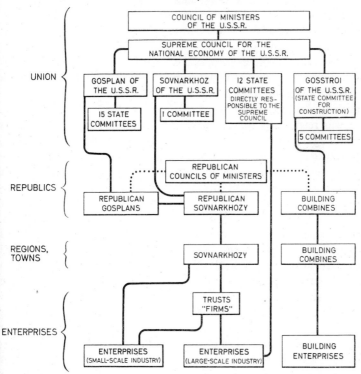

SIMPLIFIED DIAGRAM OF THE ORGANIZATIONAL STRUCTURE OF INDUSTRY AND CONSTRUCTION AFTER THE DECREE OF 13TH MARCH, 1963.

FIG. 3. Organizational structure of industry and construction after 1963.

After the separation between current planning and long-term planning, when the latter function was taken over by Gosekonom-soviet in 1960, Gosplan had in practice assumed wider powers, and had in fact become a sort of all-Union supersovnarkhoz. But it lacked the formal right of supervision over sovnarkhoz activities as a whole, since this was strictly speaking the function of the republican councils of ministers or sovnarkhozy. The purpose of the decree of November 1962 was to regularize this situation. The text of the decree reads: "To transfer the functions of Gosplan of the USSR, which is at present engaged in the year by year work of long-term plan fulfilment, to the new organization (the sovnarkhoz of the USSR) and also to provide the latter with the necessary administrative powers. To transform Gosekonomsoviet into Gosplan of the USSR by giving it responsibility for long-term planning".

According to the decrees of January and March 1963, the new Gosplan was thus responsible not only for the elaboration of current and long-term plans, but also for the fixing of wholesale and retail prices and material consumption and utilization norms. It was responsible for supervising plan fulfilment, particularly with regard to the development of new industrial capacity, and for ensuring co-ordination between Soviet plans and those of the "socialist world". It should be noted that the sovnarkhoz of the USSR and Gosplan of the USSR henceforth became federal-republican organizations. This means that their opposite numbers in the regions and republics are now directly attached to them, and are no longer responsible to the republican councils of ministers, as was previously the case. This was a move toward centralization which lessened the autonomy which the Union republics had for some years enjoyed in matters of economic administration. Gosstroi and a certain number of State committees also became federal-republican organs.

The diagram on page 133 illustrates, in summary form, the hierarchical organization of industry and construction as it now is, following on the reforms. It has been based particularly on a diagram showing the structure of the Soviet government which was published by *Ekonomicheskaya Gazeta* on 4th January 1964,[37] and on various other data.[38] The activities of the State committees attached to the USSR Gosplan cover most of the main branches of industry, such as non-ferrous metals, or the chemical

[37] Reproduced and commented on by Z. FRANK-OSSIPOF, *Bulletin du Centre d'Etude des Pays de l'Est*, No. 1, Bruxelles, 1964.

[38] See M. LESAGE, The structure of Soviet government, *Le Courrier des Pays de l'Est*, Paris, 23rd April 1964.

industry, for example. Those committees which are attached to the Supreme Council are concerned with particular problems (military equipment, the aircraft industry, shipbuilding, electronic equipment and radio-electronics, utilization of atomic energy, geology, inventions and discoveries, weights and measures, electricity generation and electrification, the gas industry, medium machine building, the last three being described as "state production committees of the USSR"). In addition, the "State committee for co-ordination of the work of scientific research" (directed by M. Rudnev) and the Federal Investment Bank are apparently attached to the Supreme Council for the national economy; on the other hand, certain other important economic organs, such as the Central Statistical Office, Gosbank, and organizations concerned with agriculture, are directly responsible to the Council of Ministers.

It should also be noted that, although the chairmen of Gosplan and the USSR sovnarkhoz have the title of deputy-chairmen of the Council of Ministers of the USSR, they do not rank as first deputy-chairmen, this title being reserved for the chairmen of the Supreme Council of the national economy. "Where a conflict arises, Gosplan does not arbitrate, but acts rather as an expert, and decisions are made either by the first deputy-chairmen of the Council, or at a higher level."[39]

At the time when these reforms were introduced, it was argued that one of the reasons for them was the need for stricter control over material allocations, particularly in order to facilitate the extra arms effort which the USSR found itself compelled to make at that time. It was held that such an effort would involve complex decision-making and would therefore necessitate a greater degree of centralization. However, it will be observed that even after the reforms, the economy still retained the territorial structures which it had acquired in 1957, and that the top administrators continued to be dispersed throughout the country. It also appears that the net result of the reforms was in fact to reduce the amount of work devolving on the central planning autho-

---

[39] E. ZALESKI, op. cit. 1964. See also articles by A. NOVE, The Liberman proposals, Survey, April 1963, and B. KERBLAY, Les propositions de Liberman pour un projet de réforme de l'entreprise en URSS, Cahiers du monde russe et soviétique, No. 3, 1963.

rities. In conclusion it can be said that although these reforms may not in themselves be regarded as having brought about a greater degree of rationalization in enterprise administration, they have paved the way for future solutions in this direction.[40, 41]

[40] On these final points, see particularly J. R. AZRAEL, Politics and management, *Survey*, October 1963.

[41] For events since the fall of N. S. Khrushchev, the suppression of sovnarkhozy at the end of 1965, and the reestablishment of industrial ministries, see Postscript.

CHAPTER VII

PROBLEMS OF ECONOMIC ADMINISTRATION

THE operation of the Soviet planning system raises a great number of day-to-day problems. In the present chapter we shall confine ourselves to those concerned with distribution, with a particular aspect of plan fulfilment, with co-ordination of the activities of enterprises and with the bonuses awarded to enterprises.

PROBLEMS OF DISTRIBUTION

A great many of the problems which have been mentioned in earlier chapters are in fact connected with supply and distribution. Indeed, the supply system, which was discussed in the last chapter in connection with the elaboration of plans for the "supply of materials and equipment", seems to be one of the major weaknesses of the Soviet economy. We shall deal briefly with the most serious of the problems arising on this score.

The Soviet distribution system cannot be compared with systems of a similar order which occasionally operate, for example in wartime, in Western economies. In the latter case, the distributing agency usually confines itself to the issue of priority certificates or vouchers to designated users, who are then free to choose their own suppliers. Soviet distribution plans, on the other hand, specify which supplier shall supply the user. Hence the "compulsory nature of the contracts drawn up between previously designated enterprises, on the basis of approved prices, leaving only a very small margin of independence to the contracting parties."[1]

As we have already seen, the allocation of orders and the direction of customers to particular suppliers are the responsibil-

[1] R. FASSIER, *op. cit.* p. 6.

ity either of the central interrepublican supplies directorate attached to Gosplan, in the case of key products, or of the supply and disposals directorates of the federal republican Gosplans, in the case of other products subject to central allocation. Orders for products not subject to central distribution are placed by the sovnarkhozy.[2] As in other countries, supply may be effected either directly from one enterprise to another, or through stores, the proportions of the different types of supply being determined by the government according to circumstances.

In the main centres, both before and after the reform of 1957, there existed a very large number of supply organs. For example, at the end of 1956, before the reform in industrial administration, there were, in the Russian republic alone, about 1500 supply organizations and almost as many disposals organizations for the 29 industrial ministries and the 7 ministries of construction. These organizations were for the most part situated in the big cities. By decree of the 17th April 1958, it was decided to place all warehouses, stores, depots and other supply outlets under the direct control of the sovnarkhozy or of the main supply and disposals directorates attached to the federal Gosplans.[3] The number of these supply outlets nevertheless remained very high, and the fact that they were nominally attached to the sovnarkhozy does not seem to have solved the problems which arose when they came under the dual control of the sovnarkhozy and the central directorates.

All the available evidence confirms the persistent difficulties created by the supply system, the clumsiness of administrative procedures, the resultant delays and frequent bottlenecks in supplies which affect producers and consumers alike. The example of the razor-blades, although not perhaps entirely typical, is likely to remain a classic by reason of its comic character. At the beginning of December 1961, the *Izvestia* correspondent noted that all the men in Novorossiisk were wearing beards, not as a result of a sudden vogue, but because no razor-blades were due until the end of the year. The newspaper reported that the same phenomenon was to be observed in many other regions: from Moldavia, Krivoi Rog, Lvov, Kursk, Tiflis came letters from men complain-

---

[2] *Ibid.*, p. 137.
[3] *Ibid.*, pp. 161–162.

ing that they were unable to shave, for not all towns can boast an organized black market selling blades at three times the normal price. "There is a monstrous regiment of beards." This state of affairs had already arisen at various times in the past, and *Krokodil*, in its issue No. 4 of 1960, had published a cartoon entitled "The beard Plan". A large proportion of the blades sold in the country come from a factory in Leningrad. The newspaper correspondents reporting on the latest crisis were told by the directors of the factory that it was different from the 1959–60 one. At that time, production had far exceeded demand, and they had run out of storage space for the blades, "the factory being in a difficult position because for a long time Gosplan had been unable to achieve proper co-ordination between production and demand." In 1961 the position was reversed: the factory could have satisfied the total demand, but had been obliged to cut down production, because the suppliers of the steel necessary for making the blades had not fulfilled their undertakings.[4]

Complaints about the lack of co-ordination between the planning of production and the supply of materials and equipment are legion.[5] This failure in co-ordination frequently leads to artificial shortages of many products and materials. In order to distribute products which are centrally, as well as regionally, in short supply, an enormous supply and sales apparatus has to be maintained.[6] It often happens that deliveries of raw materials do not arrive until after the date fixed for delivery of the finished product.[7]

The situation is well summed up by the experiences of those engaged in transport. According to the collective editorship of the magazine *Gudok*, the stations are congested because of the multiplicity and the scattered nature of loading and unloading points.

> Transport routing is difficult and tortuous. On its journey between supplier and consumer, merchandise is generally loaded or unloaded anything up to five or seven times. All this is a legacy of the system of administration by sector and the materials supply system.

---

[4] *Izvestia*, 5th December 1961.
[5] See, for example, MAZUROV, first secretary of the Party in Byelorussia, Congress, *Pravda*, 20th October 1961.
[6] *Kommunist*, No. 15, October 1961.
[7] KROTOV, *Pravda*, 27th October 1961.

The editors note that materials handling absorbs a great deal of manpower (about 4 million persons, not including handling in the factories), that the USSR is very backward in mechanization, that with the exception of a few stores there are no fork-lifts as there are in foreign countries, and that losses of goods in transit, especially cement and inorganic fertilizers, are "enormous". They make the following suggestions:

> It is abundantly clear that the present system for the supply of materials and equipment, whereby each consumer receives his fuel and raw material supplies direct from their place of production, must be reorganized. There should be a system for deliveries and sales based on large specialized depots situated in the user areas, and which would have available all the supplies required by enterprises which are not connected by rail, and which receive their freight in large amounts.[8]

But it is undoubtedly easier to make suggestions than to put them into practice, and the above observations were not made yesterday.

The most frequent criticism made of the supply organizations relates to centralization and lack of responsibility. "Because of the extremely centralized nature of distribution, the central supply administrations are scarcely able to ensure supply of the requisite quantity of goods," writes R. Levin from Tallin; he adds that they are even more out of touch when it comes to establishing the most rational links between producers and consumers.[9] Another correspondent points out that one of the drawbacks of the situation is that the officials of the supply administrations are in no way responsible for the results obtained by enterprises, and that they often cut down supplies to enterprises and sovnarkhozy, change their suppliers, alter dates, etc., without any warning.[10] It must, in fact, be borne in mind that the supply organizations have no personal commitment; enterprises which are bound to each other by commercial contracts have to bear the responsibility, particularly the financial responsibility, for non-fulfilment of their undertakings, but the supply organs, for their part, are purely administrative bodies, whose involvement does not extend beyond the

[8] *Pravda*, 28th February 1962.
[9] R. LEVIN, Are experiments necessary only in physics? *Izvestia*, 7th April 1962.
[10] V. GAVRILOV, *Izvestia*, 6th February 1962.

reprimand which may eventually be issued to those in charge of them.

It was hoped that this weakness would to some extent be cured by closer co-ordination in the planning of production and supply. As far as the building of new factories is concerned, this was said to have been done already. According to a statement by Kosygin, principal supply administrations for materials and equipment had been set up within the Union and republican Gosplans, and also within certain ministries. "The task of these administrations is to ensure that enterprises in the course of construction receive all their equipment in good time." Nevertheless, according to the same source, these administrations were as yet not producing satisfactory results.[11]

It is in matters of supply that the distinction between priority and non-priority projects or products most clearly emerges. Thus the building of the new steelworks at Novo-Lipetsk, in Central Russia, which will be using iron ore from the ore-deposits at Kursk, was given top priority. However, by the beginning of 1962, work was badly behind schedule, and it looked as if the first blast-furnace would not be started up at the stated time. The machinery had not been delivered in time, which was not surprising, since building had begun even before the designs were completed; in particular the ore-treatment plant would not be ready for a long time, so that production could not, under any circumstances, exceed half of the factory's potential capacity. Nevertheless, an emergency plan was put into operation — without success, as it turned out — to get the blast-furnace started on time. To this end, the necessary supplies were diverted from enterprises belonging to no fewer than thirty-two different sovnarkhozy; the number of building workers was double that estimated; the wages fund was spent ten times over.[12] In such conditions, it is not surprising that projects which do not head the priority list have some difficulty in obtaining their fair share of supplies.

Elsewhere there was mention of a factory for the production of agricultural insecticides, which was to be built at Ufa, in the south Urals.

[11] Speech at the XXIInd Congress, *Pravda*, 23rd and 24th October 1961.
[12] The cost of last-minute emergency measures, *Pravda*, 20th January 1962.

> The principal supply administration for chemical equipment in the Russian republic handled deliveries to this factory as if it were dealing with some quite ordinary building project. And of course it did the job badly. Responsibility for supplies was therefore transferred to a higher level, namely the principal supply administration for chemical equipment for the Union.

It does not appear, however, that the latter organization achieved any better results. The same passage goes on to criticize both the Gosplan directorate and the State Committee for the chemicals industry.[13]

Manufactures or industries which do not belong to any clearly defined sector seem to be in a particularly unfavourable position. This emerged in the course of an inquiry which *Izvestia* made into the pharmaceuticals industry, following a complaint from a certain number of chemists in Perm, who gave a long list of medicines which were unobtainable. The administrative body responsible for this industry is the pharmaceuticals directorate of the Ministry of Public Health of the RSFSR. When the plan is being drawn up, this body is responsible for calculating the country's overall requirements and for reporting on them to Gosplan which, in due course, issues production instructions to the industry. In practice these orders are executed with great inefficiency; the supersovnarkhoz either refuses to produce a certain number of medicines, or does not produce them in sufficient quantity; their chemicals directorate is theoretically responsible for the pharmaceuticals industry, but in fact takes no interest in it. The RSFSR Gosplan complains about the division of its responsibilities with the ministry. As for the factories making pharmaceutical products, they are described as being nobody's baby. The sovnarkhozy to which they are attached take very little interest in them, and hand them over, for administrative purposes, to organizations which, except in the case of Moscow Town, are all incompetent; supplies to the industry are, naturally, very badly organized.[14] One author revealed that 30% of work stoppages in enterprises were the result of failures in the supply system.[15]

---

[13] In defence of those who defend the harvest, *Izvestia*, 21st April 1962.
[14] Pharmaceutical questions, *Izvestia*, 20th April 1962.
[15] E. RUSANOV, *Vopr. Ekon.*, No. 11, 1962.

What more can be said about the supply system, apart from agreeing wholeheartedly with all the criticism it arouses in the USSR itself? Is its clumsiness due to organizational errors which it should be possible to correct without too much difficulty? Are the administrative abilities of those in charge not always as good as they might be? Or do these difficulties arise because Soviet planners are, from the best of motives, doggedly trying to solve a problem which is really insoluble under present conditions? At first sight it would seem that these are all to some extent contributory factors. If the administrators were all excellent and the system were working badly because of its very nature, then one would think that pressure to reform it would be greater than it in fact is; in this connection, one may recall observations by visitors from the West who have had dealings over a long period with Soviet industrial administrators, and have been very much struck, from one visit to the next, by the improvement in the quality of the personnel with whom they have been in contact. But conversely, a system which assumes qualities in men which they do not possess cannot altogether be a good system.

However, one should not press this point too far for, after all, even if its results are bad, the system does work, and in a more or less orderly fashion; none of the reports reaching us over the past few years suggest that the Soviet industrial machine has so far ever come to a complete halt, or been seriously impaired by a widespread and radical breakdown in supplies, such as the fuel crisis which overtook Great Britain in February 1947 and which disorganized industrial production for some considerable time.

IMPLEMENTATION OF INVESTMENT PLANS

We shall leave aside for the moment the financial aspects of the implementation of the plans and the problems of controls in so far as they affect enterprises.[15a] In the remainder of this chapter, we shall be dealing with two very important problems which relate to plan fulfilment and which are of considerable immediate interest. The first is the search for a greater degree of specialization and rationalization in industrial establishments; the second is the problem of "success indicators", in other words

[15a] These will be discussed in Chapter IX.

material inducements offered to enterprises and their personnel to ensure efficient execution of the plan. First of all, however, we should say a few words about the procedures for implementation of planned investments.

Although implementation of the provisions of plans is binding on all concerned, the Soviet plan is not itself a budgetary document, automatically entailing an allocation of funds, any more than are the indicative plans of the non-socialist countries. When it is a question of carrying out an investment proposal, for example the building of a new industrial establishment, a procedure is required for putting the decision into effect.

First of all, a precise technical project must be submitted. The bodies responsible for doing this are the "project-making organizations," which carry out specialist surveys relating to the various sectors of industry, and which for the most part function in Moscow.

These organizations are then given the task of submitting a complete and detailed project covering all the technical and economic aspects of the investment proposal (site of the proposed establishment, building plans, plant to be ordered and raw materials to be used, etc.). When the work is completed, it must be approved by an organization which specializes in building problems *(Gosstroi)*, and which is situated in Moscow, or by similar organizations in the republics. In addition to the initial decision inviting the collaboration of the appropriate Institute, the decision to implement the proposal is made by the sovnarkhoz, and subsequently approved by the republican sovnarkhoz, if the total sum of the investment is under 2·5 million new roubles, and by the Council of Ministers of the USSR, at the request of Gosplan, if the figure is higher.

When the project has been approved in this way, the minister of finance then endorses it, provided the necessary funds are available. The appropriate sovnarkhoz is then instructed to participate in supervising the building of the establishment in question, to appoint a director, to organize production, to see that the factory goes into production, and to watch over its operations once they have begun.

It will be noted that financial clearance is necessary before work on the implementation of any investment decision can begin. If in fact provision has been made in the current annual plan for an equivalent sum in relation to the investment in question, then, theoretically, financial clearance is given automatically. However, there is often a delay, particularly in the case of important projects, between approval of a project in principle, and completion of the detailed project. It may be that circumstances have necessitated a change in the size of the project, or some other aspect of it. Or again, projects for which no provision has been made in the annual plan (for example, supplementary estimates for road-building) may be submitted to Gosplan for approval. In all such cases the approval of the Finance Ministry must be sought, and it seems that many have been turned down.

The appropriate funds which are set aside for this purpose in the budget, and handed over to Gosbank, are subsequently transferred to the enterprise or building organization in question, either through the branch directorates of the sovnarkhoz, or with their knowledge.

It should be noted that consideration of the financial situation of an enterprise plays no part at all in the decision to allocate investment or any other funds. The only factor which counts in the end is the productive capacity of the enterprise.

Does the success of large-scale, multiple-purpose projects depend on the use of special economic-administrative structure, which are better adapted to solving the various problems which arise than are conventional structures? As we know, this is sometimes the case in non-socialist countries, where certain hydro-electric schemes, for example, have called for this kind of administrative solution, notably in the United States (Tennessee Valley), in France ("mixed economy companies") and in many of the developing countries. There are no comparable examples that we know of in the USSR. However, in connection with the building of the Dnieper dams, the first of which was constructed under the first five-year plan, a special commission was set up which engaged in economic studies prior to the war; in addition the co-ordinating councils which are designed to operate at the level of the large economic regions, and which were discussed earlier on, have a certain co-ordinating role to play, particularly in matters affecting several small republics and where major hydraulic projects are involved. But in this case it seems to be a question simply of research and co-ordination, and not the creation of *ad hoc* control bodies.

THE NEED FOR SPECIALIZATION AND FOR "CO-OPERATION" BY ENTERPRISES

One of the objectives announced in the text giving the "control figures" for the seven-year plan (1959–65) was enterprise "specialization" and "co-operation". Enterprise co-operation is more or less what is known in the West as "sub-contracting", that is, the division of a manufacturing process among several enterprises each specializing in a particular aspect of manufacture, with one of them retaining responsibility for the finished product. "Co-operation" also entails certain rights and obligations. In fact enterprises which are linked co-operatively with another enterprise receive the supplies which they require through that enterprise, and not directly through the supply channels.

The need for specialization and co-operation, which is one of the most complex problems facing Soviet industry in its bid for rationalization, once more raises the problem of the organizational structure of industry. The reform in the administration of industry and construction which took place in 1957 was in part an effort to find a more effective solution to this problem, and it had been expressly stated, in all the regions from which evidence is available, that one of the main tasks of the new sovnarkhozy would be to encourage specialization in production among the enterprises for which they were responsible. This question is all the more interesting since it might have been supposed that industrial administration would be more conducive to specialization when it was based on sectors of activity, as was the case prior to 1957, and not on the territorial principle which is now in operation.

In order to grasp the importance of this problem in Soviet industry, one must bear in mind the characteristics of Soviet enterprises as they were several years ago, and as they still are to some extent today. As we have seen, most Soviet factories are large establishments, or at any rate larger than their counterparts not only in western Europe, but even in the United States. However, it does not necessarily follow that production of comparable commodities is any higher than it is elsewhere. Productivity, which is generally lower, is not the only reason; indeed, the great size of these factories may mean either that each stage in the manufacture of a given product is being carried out within the same establishment (integration), or that a large number of different articles are being produced.

Both types of production are common. For example, the big ZIL factory (the Likhachev works) which employs some 40,000 workers in south-east Moscow, was still producing in 1961, when I visited it, lorries, buses, motor-cars, bicycles and refrigerators; moreover, production was highly integrated; with the exception of tyres, accumulators and headlamps, almost all vehicle components were manufactured in the factory itself, as well as a fair proportion of the machinery and equipment, for which there were several workshops. Similarly, the Skorokhod shoe factory in Leningrad, which at that time employed 11,000 workers, was linked with a tannery, and produced over a hundred types of footwear.

On the other hand, many factories in fact make the same products; A. Smirnov, head of the all-Union trade administration of Gosplan, revealed that, throughout the country, there were 70 factories turning out refrigerators (few of the models were really up to date), 45 factories making washing machines (of which only 7 were making semi-automatic models) and 60 enterprises producing electric irons (of which only one model was up to date).[16] The number of models of radio and television sets on show in various shops also appears to be fairly large. All the evidence suggests that the degree of standardization is much smaller than one would have expected in a country with a wholly planned economy.

The official statements which preceded or accompanied the 1957 reform contained many criticisms of the administration of ministries and technical directorates in this connection. In his report to the Supreme Soviet on the occasion of the submission of the law on the reorganization of industry and construction, N. S. Khrushchev had renewed his criticism about the absence of real links between enterprises, and had shown that it was the division of ministries into watertight compartments that prevented the setting-up of specialist factories. For example, there were still no factories specializing in the manufacture of motor-car engines, because the ministry for the automobile industry sought to keep production of all motor-car parts in factories under its control.[17]

[16] A. SMIRNOV, Removing the obstacles, *Izvestia*, 24th December 1961.
[17] *Report to the Supreme Soviet*, 7th May 1957.

One writer stated specifically that, because of the existence of industrial ministries, factories could generally go in for specialization only in respect of the finished product, and not for the more advanced form of specialization represented by manufacture of components, or in other words specialization in technical processes.[18]

At the same time, there are other reasons for this lack of enterprise specialization. One reason, for instance, is that when it comes to maintenance, enterprises are almost entirely left to their own devices:

> 60% of basic maintenance and practically all running repairs are carried out in repair shops attached to the enterprises. Centralization of repairs is very rare... Maintenance of machines is much more costly than if it were done by specialist enterprises. In addition, production of spare parts is badly organized... There is a particular shortage of screws, nuts and bolts, and the cost of producing these parts in the workshop is sometimes three times the normal price.[19]

In the motor-car industry, the proportion of semi-finished products bought outside the enterprise is only of the order of 28–50% in the USSR, as against an American figure of 50–70%; the corresponding figure for machine-tools, tractors and agricultural machinery is 15–20%.[20]

This state of affairs seems to be bound up not only with the organizational structure of enterprises, but with the whole nature of Soviet planning. The trouble seems to lie in "success indicators" (or "plan indices") and especially in the peculiarities of Soviet statistics. As we shall see later, the success of an enterprise in attaining its objectives was, and still is, largely measured by the volume of its production, expressed either in physical quantities, or in value terms, according to the sum of its gross output *(valovaya produktsia)* which corresponds roughly to our

[18] V. I. PAVLOV, The development of the economic region (based on the experience of the Yaroslav sovnarkhoz), *Moscow–Gosplanizdat*, 1961.

[19] P. BUNICH, Ways of reducing the cost of maintenance and of modernization of fixed capital, *Finansy SSSR, 1960*, No. 10, summarized by M. LAVIGNE, *L'URSS et les Pays de l'Est*, No. 4, Strasbourg, 1961. Maintenance work absorbs 10–12% of the labour force in industry and uses up not less than 40% of the total number of machine tools in the country.

[20] GUZALIEV, Levels of specialization in industrial production, *Plan. Khoz.*, No. 2, 1963.

turnover figure. As a result, the enterprise has an interest in concentrating on those products which have the highest value. Consequently, enterprises prefer to deliver only finished products (which include the value of a number of components, certain of which may be manufactured outside the enterprise) and do not pay enough attention to spare parts (which count only in respect of their own value). The shortage in supplies of spare parts to Soviet industry and commerce, to which we referred earlier, is notorious. But these enterprises are not only suppliers, they are also each other's customers. The lack of spare parts and of inter-enterprise services strengthens the tendency to self-sufficiency among enterprises, and prevents them from specializing.

Another factor which also tended to encourage self-sufficiency was the "tightness" of plans, which was much more noticeable a few years ago than it is now, and the chronic shortages which were a peculiar feature of the Soviet economy. Since there was a tendency for products never to be available in sufficient quantities, directors were haunted by the fear of a breakdown in supplies which might prevent them from attaining the production targets assigned to them. It was in an effort to overcome these difficulties that they resorted to methods which have frequently been described, such as maintaining representatives in supply offices, using personal influence,[21] rendering each other unexpected and quite "unplanned" services, sometimes even with the connivance of the authorities,[22] or simply diverting goods belonging to the State; Soviet literature and the Soviet press abound in such examples. In these conditions it is clear that a director who agreed to the transfer of a product hitherto manufactured in his factory to some other factory would very likely be laying up additional trouble for himself.

In this respect there has certainly been some change. As we know, since about 1957, annual plans have been providing for

[21] See particularly on this subject the standard work by J. S. BERLINER, *Factory and Manager in the USSR*, Harvard University Press, 1957. See also later.

[22] For instance, the State Control Committee of the RSFSR uncovered a vast illegal barter network between Karelia and various other regions, some of them in very distant parts of the USSR. Wood from Karelia was being bartered for metal and manufactured products. Several ministers and senior officials of the autonomous republic of Karelia were compromised or accused in connection with this scandal. *Sovietskaya Rossiya*, 26th May 1962.

an annual increase in industrial production of only 7–9%, instead of 11–14% in the period immediately prior to that date; it is striking to note that, until 1961 at least, the results announced were by no means correspondingly lower (annual increases in industrial production of 10–11% according to the official indices) which would lead one to suppose that this change was perhaps more a reflection of the desire to effect an improvement in administrative methods than of the acceptance of less ambitious aims. For all that, the supply problems of Soviet industry are still a long way from being solved.

There is another factor, of a more general nature, which may help to explain the lack of specialization. Because they are, so to speak, more interested in glory than in profits, enterprises or industrial establishments seem to have a tendency to concentrate on tasks, or products, which appear to them to be of particular interest, and no doubt their superior authorities are not always able to limit these activities so as to take account of what is being done elsewhere.

So enterprises have been urged, since 1957 at least, by the sovnarkhozy to which they are responsible, to specialize their production. According to V. I. Pavlov, this specialization may take the form of

(a) stopping production of identical finished products by a number of enterprises, and concentrating it in one single enterprise;

(b) stopping the operation of identical stages in the manufacturing process by a number of enterprise workshops, and setting up specialized factories or workshops instead; or

(c) setting up factories or workshops which will specialize in particular technical processes (and will thus be able to work for several categories of users, if need be).

Summarizing experiments carried out by the Yaroslav sovnarkhoz, Pavlov pointed out that these three types of specialization had been tried out successively in the years 1958, 1959 and 1960. However, examples quoted for the different industries in this economic administrative region show that these efforts affected enterprises in the same sectors of industry in other distant economic administrative regions, as well as enterprises in the Yaroslav sovnarkhoz[23] and could not therefore be attributed to one single sovnarkhoz. Many reports on the sovnarkhozy, especially those situated in large towns, have quoted examples of concentration of one type of production in one factory, or a small number of factories, which then worked for various branches of production; P. Lomako, for example, quotes the case of the Chelyabinsk sovnarkhoz, where the number of factories producing what appears to be rivets was reduced from 70 to 3, and also an example from the Leningrad sovnarkhoz, in which production of welding electrodes was confined to factories specializing in this work.[24]

In the course of a visit to a very large enterprise, I learned something of the problems of implementing this policy of specialization. A plan for the reorganization of the ZIL factory, which we mentioned previously, had been adopted during the months prior to my visit in 1961. This plan, which had been approved at high level and was to be implemented over the next few years, being scheduled for completion in 1962 or 1963, was not supposed, in principle, to affect fulfilment of the objectives already assigned to the factory in the context of the seven-year plan. According to the reorganization plan, production of bicycles was to be transferred to another factory which was then in the course of construction in the Bryansk region, while production of buses was to be moved to a factory at Lyukinovo, in the same region, which had formerly been making china and earthenware products. Similarly, manufacture of certain parts (springs, brakes) was to be transferred to a factory which was being built at Serdobsk, in the middle Volga region, while certain other parts (gearboxes) were likewise scheduled for transfer. The Moscow factory would then be able to concentrate its efforts on the production of main parts and the assembly of lorries, thereby increasing both production and rate of return (however, despite its requests, the factory had at that time still not obtained permission to stop production of refrigerators).

It will be noted that the towns we have mentioned, although relatively near Moscow (a few hundred miles away at most) were all situated in economic administrative regions other than Mos-

[23] V. I. PAVLOV, op. cit.
[24] P. LOMAKO, Pravda, 23rd February 1962.

cow Town. One of the questions which inevitably arise after this kind of reorganization is the nature of the future relationship between the new factories and the parent factory. In the case of independent items of production, such as buses or bicycles (the first of the instances above-mentioned), the question is probably only of secondary importance; it is much more pertinent in the case of manufacture of individual parts of a whole, such as the lorry parts mentioned in the second instance.

When a situation of this kind arises in a large-scale Western enterprise, whether private or nationalized, the new establishment will, as we know, generally continue to function under the same administration unless there is some special arrangement; in this way the transfer is effected with the minimum of difficulties. In the USSR a similar solution would no doubt have been found under the old administrative arrangements with the economic ministries, prior to 1957. Nowadays this is no longer the case. As part of another sovnarkhoz, the new factories will still be able to receive technical assistance from the ZIL factory in Moscow which was responsible for setting them up, but on all questions relating to production objectives, raw materials supplies, finance and the inevitable current adjustments to plans, and involving several of these factories simultaneously, it will be necessary to refer to both sovnarkhozy, the one in Moscow and the one in the area in which the new factory is situated, and also to their common superior authority (the sovnarkhoz of the Russian republic) and all the appropriate supply organs. This point, though I was already well aware of it, was clearly brought home to me during my visit in 1961. The net result of this reorganization will probably be to clog the administrative machinery of what had previously been a single unit.

It may well be that in the case of establishments as important as the ZIL factory, a little high-level intervention could speedily remove any administrative bottlenecks which threatened to impede the normal flow of production; but this would not necessarily be so in the case of smaller or less well-known enterprises. Fear of such complications may very well be an obstacle to decentralization and enterprise specialization.

This point has not escaped the Soviet authorities. They have arrived at a solution which seems expressly designed to avoid a situation whereby the creation of a new decentralized establishment results in the disruption of the original enterprise; this is known as the "satellite-enterprise" scheme, which I heard about particularly during my visits to Kharkov. It involves not the creation of a new enterprise but the linking of an already existing small enterprise with a large enterprise, for which the former will produce components, or carry out a specific stage in the manufacturing process. In the Kharkov sovnarkhoz, several small enterprises are now linked in this way with the big "Ordzhonikidzhe" tractor factory, which employs about 30,000 workers. One of these small enterprises is now turning out oil-filters for the tractors. One of the advantages of this solution is that it eliminates one echelon in the command system. Creation of a "satellite-enterprise" is one of the ways in which the transfer of an enterprise from the jurisdiction of the local authorities (town or oblast) to that of the sovnarkhoz can be effected.[25]

The "satellite-enterprise" solution, however, would only be feasible for enterprises belonging to the same sovnarkhoz, or at least that is what I understood from the statements of the various officials whom I met in Kharkov (sovnarkhoz and tractor factory). Under the existing administrative arrangements, it would not be possible, at least in theory, for preferential links to exist between two enterprises belonging to different sovnarkhozy. This attitude is no doubt dictated by fear of a recurrence in disguised form of the trusts and industrial "empires" which existed prior to the 1957 reform; it is none the less a serious obstacle in the drive for enterprise rationalization.

Given the present structures, it is clearly not an easy matter, even within a single sovnarkhoz, to establish links between individual enterprises which will facilitate streamlining of administration and a higher degree of specialization. In an article which we have already quoted, the chairman of the Kharkov sovnarkhoz expressed the opinion that the best way of solving the problem would be to "eliminate most of the sovnarkhoz directorates and set up 'combines' with a pilot-enterprise at their head, which would be directly responsible to the sovnarkhoz". In the case of the machine-building directorate of the Kharkov sovnarkhoz, it would be easy to create such an organization by taking the tractor factory as a pilot-enterprise and grouping around it the

[25] I had been given similar examples in Leningrad (see earlier, p. 128).

other enterprises concerned (of which at least three seemed to be fairly large). Reorganization along these lines would help to simplify and improve economic administration, which was strongly criticized on account of its extreme cumbersomeness. In particular it would "clear the way for further technical progress through technological and workshop specialization, and for the mechanization and automation of production. It would also facilitate the setting up of specialized repair-shops and tool-shops".[26]

This text makes it clear that the situation with regard to specialization and co-ordination among enterprises was not considered satisfactory. With the creation of the sovnarkhozy, enterprises were brought into closer contact with their supervisory authority, but links between neighbouring and allied enterprises, which could be particularly helpful when adjustments have to be made to current plans, are still apparently inadequate.

A similar type of solution was reported from Lvov, where five separate enterprises manufacturing footwear formed themselves into a "production association", also known as a "firm", under the leadership of one of their number, while four tanneries formed a similar association around the largest of their group. The first secretary of the provincial Party, who was reporting this, took care to point out that no new administrative machinery had been set up, no doubt to allay what is certainly one of the greatest fears in the minds of the authorities; the departments and services of the pilot-enterprise were to be responsible for all the work required, particularly for drawing up the balance sheet and financial plans. This development, which in Western terms would be described as a concentration operation (merger), was apparently approved only after some difficulty, since the matter had to be taken up to the Council of Ministers before payment of salaries in one of the new "firms" could be authorized.[27]

The two above-mentioned examples were subsequently quoted with approval by the chairman of the Ukraine supersovnarkhoz, who said that it would be a good thing if the proposed amalgamation of enterprises centred on the tractor factory at Kharkov were to take place. There was also approval of the idea of amalgamating several light industrial enterprises, as had been done at

---

[26] Soyich, chairman of the Kharkov sovnarkhoz, "Directorate or combine", *Ukrainian Pravda*, 24th January 1962.

[27] *Izvestia*, 18th February 1962.

Lvov, provided that the enterprises belonged to the same economic administrative region; the proposal to abolish the industrial
directorates was not condemned out of hand. There was also a
reference to the absorption of several small peripheral enterprises
by the steel-works at Nizhni-Tagil (Urals), with the suggestion
that similar steps be taken by the steel-works in the Ukraine.[28]
Other reports also approved the experiment at Lvov, where the
number of these new "firms" had risen to about forty, representing some two hundred enterprises.

The November 1962 decisions endorsed the experiment with
"firms", without however extending its scope as far as might
perhaps have been expected. After this date we hear of "firms"
comprising several enterprises (and which would now be more
properly described as industrial establishments) situated in different oblasts but not in different sovnarkhozy. The desire to carry
the experiment further was possibly one of the motives behind
the amalgamation of the sovnarkhozy. We also note that the new
firms occasionally took over the functions of the old sovnarkhoz
sector administrations, which in their turn had been reorganized
accordingly, thus implementing certain of the proposals described above.

Arrangements of this kind can occasionally give rise to a number of difficulties. The following example again relates to the
Kharkov sovnarkhoz. At Glukhov, on a branch-line near the
Moscow–Kiev line, in the Sumi oblast which is part of the economic administrative region of Kharkov, but some 200 miles away
from the latter (the Kharkov sovnarkhoz covers a long area along
the frontier between the Ukraine and Russia), the Council of
Ministers of the Ukrainian republic decided in 1960 to organize
production of electrical equipment by transferring part of the
production of the electro-technical factory at Kharkov to what
had, up till then, been a dilapidated workshop making carts and
sledges. The Kharkov factory was to continue as "parent-factory" to the new factory, under the authority of the Kharkov
sovnarkhoz. There were several arguments in favour of this decision: ease of communication, the existence of an electro-technical institute, reserves of manpower which at least during the first

[28] KUZMIN, chairman of the sovnarkhoz of the Ukraine, "A promising
development", Izvestia, 18th May 1962.

stage would obviate the need for new housing, and the fact that the local population welcomed the development.

However, despite all these favourable circumstances, everything seems to have gone wrong during the factory's first two years of existence. Despite the fact that the parent-factory in Kharkov had only delivered a quarter of the estimated amount of machinery in 1961, and that no building had been done, the new factory, which employs some 300 people, found that it had been assigned an ambitious production plan, and a list of customers to supply in various parts of the USSR. The customers were soon complaining about non-fulfilment of deliveries. From the reports made by the correspondent of Izvestia, to the effect that "the parent-factory in Kharkov and the sovnarkhoz consistently left those in charge of the Glukhov factory to their own devices", it is clear that the links between the parent-factory and its subsidiary remained very tenuous, no doubt because of the intervention of too many superior authorities, and that the two factories could in no way be regarded as belonging to a single coherent administration.[29]

The foregoing examples all relate to links between enterprises belonging to the same sovnarkhoz. The difficulties of establishing such links when the enterprises are attached to different sovnarkhozy seem to be even greater. However, this applies only to enterprises which come under the jurisdiction of sovnarkhozy or republics, and which, it should be recalled, accounted for 94% of industrial production as at 1st January 1961. The situation is not the same for those enterprises which continue to be administered by all-Union State committees; they are subject to centralized supply and purchasing arrangements which must favour long production runs and specialization; at the same time, it would seem that if they also wish to enjoy the advantages of co-operation (sub-contracting) by handing over some of the more routine processes to smaller but more narrowly specialized enterprises, they are liable to encounter all the aforementioned obstacles.

These remarks are not, of course, in any way intended to convey that Soviet industry is lacking in examples of successful specialization, or that progress is not gradually being made in this direction. On the contrary, there have been numerous reports, either

---

[29] *Izvestia*, 4th January 1962.

from visitors to the USSR or from other sources, referring to the
size and the degree of specialization of some of the new factories
or workshops, and to the efforts which have been made to set
up highly mechanized production units and long production
runs. Nevertheless, it seems to be a fact that there are still many
obstacles in the way of specialization and rational distribution of
activities among enterprises; the most serious of these obstacles
seem to be inherent in the nature of the Soviet economy. Some
of them are closely connected with the structure of the economic
organizations through which enterprises are administered, while
others stem from the nature of the obligations imposed on those
enterprises by the planning system.

As we have seen, co-operation between enterprises which do
not belong to the same sovnarkhoz is difficult to organize; in
fact there may well be little chance of its operating at all, since
the sovnarkhoz is naturally disinclined to concern itself with
successful specialization except within its own area of responsibility. "In many cases, sovnarkhozy have introduced specialization and strengthened inter-enterprise links only when it was
in the interests of their own economic administrative region."[30]
Moreover, even within the area of one particular sovnarkhoz,
there are still instances of neighbouring production units being
engaged in the same activities, because of the number of different
authorities involved.

> In certain regions, it is still the practice for the sovnarkhoz, the exec-
> utive committee and various administrations to set up their own little
> "personal" enterprises. For example, in the Vyborg district of the
> Leningrad oblast, there appear to be 9 quarries working the same
> deposits alongside each other, and administered respectively by the
> sovnarkhoz, the oblast, the ministry of transport, the ministry of
> construction, etc.[31]

There is still frequent criticism of the lack of specialization in
factories. Thus Krotov, the director of the Uralmash factory at
Sverdlovsk, whom we have already quoted, admits that there is
not nearly enough specialization in factories making various
types of equipment. Dymshits, who was at the time first deputy-
chairman of Gosplan (he later became chairman), made a similar
statement at the XXIInd Congress about building materials, in

[30] P. LOMAKO, *op. cit.*
[31] P. LOMAKO, *op. cit.*

which he urged that specialized regional or interregional factories should be set up under the direction of the sovnarkhozy, with a view to greater rationalization of the building industry.[32] But at the same congress, Spiridonov stated that "due to the departmentalization of the administrative structure, the planning organs were displaying the same inability as their predecessors in implementing the principle of specialization and rational co-operation." Moreover, in place of this principle there had developed the principle of pseudo-"already established" co-operation, which simply regularized the links which had existed between enterprises under the earlier ministerial régime.[33]

It was partly in an effort to remedy this situation, and to eliminate the difficulties encountered in establishing co-operation where different economic administrative regions were involved, that the "supersovnarkhozy" were set up, at the end of 1960, in the four main republics. But these bodies, which only took over the functions previously fulfilled by the republican Gosplans, did not prove very satisfactory, as we have seen. The setting up of the co-ordinating and planning councils for the large economic regions was also aimed at effecting some improvement on this point. Questions of specialization and co-operation in production were foremost among the specific problems with which they had to deal.

However, it was clear that these new organizations would not be able to do much to overcome the difficulties which arose, for even two enterprises which were linked by a "co-operative" arrangement and came under the same co-ordinating council would still be subject to the same administrative structures as before, with all the concomitant risks of alterations to their objectives under the current plan.

In any event the commercial agreements (delivery contracts) which are exchanged between enterprises, and whose object is to ratify the co-operative link between them, continue to be imperfect instruments, since they are subject to the State plan for the supply of materials and equipment, and to the issue of allocation certificates *(naryady)*. "In fact, the administrative authorities have the power at any time to withhold allocation certificates, or to

[32] *Pravda*, 28th October 1961.
[33] *Pravda*, 20th October 1961.

alter quantities or types of merchandise, or delivery dates: in this case, the agreements become void."[34] As we know, this is by no means a purely academic point, for the changes which are made in current plans, and which are usually not synchronized, may add up to several hundreds for one sovnarkhoz alone. And so, as long as implementation of a plan for which every enterprise is individually responsible continues to be subject to such contingencies, it is reasonable to suppose that there will be a serious obstacle in the way of increased specialization and co-operation among enterprises.

At all events, we note that even after the 1962-3 reforms in economic administration, the same complaints were still being made. The author of one recent article deplored the fact that there were 14 different types of oil-filter in use for 14 models of tractors from 16 to 130 h. p., whereas given a reasonable degree of specialization 5 would have been enough; he went on to complain that "effective nation-wide specialization is often hindered by sovnarkhoz officials, whose attitude to this problem is one of narrow localism".[35]

"SUCCESS INDICATORS"

It is the duty of the directors and staff of enterprises to fulfil and to exceed the objectives laid down in the plan. As an inducement to do so, bonuses may be awarded to them; these are in widespread use and represent an important part of total earnings. These bonuses are generally supposed to average about 20–40% of salaries, but in certain cases or certain sectors, notably in the building industry, for example, it seems that they may even be much higher. In theory, therefore, there should be no conflict between the two considerations by which directors of enterprises and their staffs are presumably motivated, in other words fulfilment of the plan, according to instructions, and personal profit. However, this is only according to theory. In practice there may be a very serious divergence between the conduct of the directors, who are busy fulfilling the letter of the plan for their enterprise

[34] N. GALPERIN, Civil law and the supply of materials and equipment, *Vopr. Ekon.*, No. 10, 1960. (Summary by M. de SOLÈRE, *Revue des Revues*, No. 4, p. 55, Strasbourg, 1961.)

[35] *Pravda*, 7th February 1964.

in such a way as to obtain for themselves, and those under them, the biggest bonus possible, and respect for the actual spirit of the plan, as embodied in its overall objectives.

It seems to be a particular function of Party control to prevent such conflicts from arising, but in this it is still not entirely successful. In fact this is one of the most serious weaknesses of the Soviet planning system. It will, therefore, be readily appreciated that the definition of the plan indicators on which the performance of the enterprise will be assessed (the problem of "plan indicators" or "success indicators") is one of the most controversial questions in Soviet economic life.

The problem no longer arises in quite the same way as it did formerly. Until recent years, the indicators used to gauge the success of an enterprise were almost exclusively indices of the volume of production. This was expressed either in physical quantities (units, tons, metres) or more usually—in order to take account of all output and unfinished production—in gross value of output expressed in the prices of a base year *(valovaya produktsia)*. All Western writings on the Soviet economy have drawn attention to the results of this system, beginning with the work of J. S. Berliner, which was based on the evidence of many former directors of Soviet enterprises who fled to western Germany, and which is concerned with the pre-war or the immediate post-war period.[36] Thus, to take a now classic example, a factory with a plan for nails expressed in tons will be tempted to concentrate on production of the largest nails possible; if the plan is expressed in units, on the other hand, the temptation will be to produce the smallest nails, in order to turn out more of them; in either case, the proper product mix will tend to be disregarded.

In order to appreciate the full significance of this problem, one must bear in mind that the director of a Soviet enterprise, particularly in days gone by, but still to some extent today, is faced with a task which it is well-nigh impossible to fulfil in its entirety. If he carries out to the letter the various instructions which he receives, he is unable to fulfil all the plan objectives and thus ensure the appropriate bonuses and rewards for himself and his staff; either the production targets assigned to the enterprise are

[36] *Op. cit.*

too high; or it might be possible to achieve them, except that raw materials have not been allocated in sufficient quantities; or again, it may be impossible to observe the norms laid down for productivity, quality and economy in the use of materials. If the system is to work—and work it does—directors are forced to make a number of decisions, and to take certain steps, which are in contravention to the existing regulations, sometimes openly so, and this involves grave risks.

The clever director has always been the one who refused to let these difficulties get him down, and knew how to "wangle" his way out of them. In the old days he sometimes "adjusted" his figures upwards or downwards, or had recourse to one of a number of practices known as *blat*, which is the term used to describe the use of personal influence in order to induce the responsible authorities to fix easier production targets, or the bank officials to turn a blind eye to some use of enterprise funds not provided for in the plan; or again, he might call on the services of the *tolkach*, who specialized in obtaining goods in short supply by means of bribery and string-pulling.[37]

As long as output was virtually the only standard on which the performance of enterprises was judged, there was a tendency for enterprises to sacrifice all other objectives to this end. The index of gross output *(valovaya produktsia)* was sometimes a very convenient one for this purpose. Since the value of gross output includes the price of all raw materials used in manufacture, production targets could sometimes be reached, as we have seen, simply by increasing the quantity or the quality of the materials used; this may well be the real reason for the weight of so many Soviet products, which are often noticeably heavier than comparable foreign articles.

Nowadays, far more attention is paid to the fulfilment of objectives in productivity, economy of raw materials, costs and even profit, which formerly, as a rule, were hardly ever achieved. In particular, enterprise "profits" have become important since the enterprise is entitled to keep a sizeable proportion of such profits for itself.

Some examples are given here, to show that the problem of "plan indicators" is still as relevant as ever. There are regular

[37] J. S. BERLINER *op. cit.*

discussions on this subject in the press. In answer to Antonov, the aircraft engineer, an *Izvestia* correspondent agreed that "although there is always accord between moral motives and the interests of society, the same cannot be said of material motives."[38] According to another correspondent, "we often criticize capitalist competition, and quite rightly . . . When a capitalist tries to oust a competitor, he is not motivated by love of his fellow-men . . . But we often put love of the plan indicator before love of the consumer."[39] Another writer, complaining of the drop in the production of high-quality fish, and fresh or frozen fish, in favour of tinned fish, also remarked: "All this clearly shows that things are geared not to consumer demand but to fulfilment of the gross output plan."[40]

Criticism of this situation often takes on a moral tone. This is nothing new. For example, in the play "Odna" ("Alone") by Aleshin, which appeared a few years ago, the communist engineer Platonov—who stands for the non-conformists who would like to humanize the régime—refuses to deliver a piece of equipment which is not in perfect working order, although the ministry has accepted it, and although the delay in delivery loses him, and his fellow-workers, important bonuses; the following reply is made to him: "Conscience and all that is all very well, but we are living in a planned economy." At the same time, many of the correspondents who try to find a solution to this problem seem to be more concerned with clearing the producers from the charge of immorality. The following writer tries to explain the reason for the generally poor quality of Soviet machinery compared with similar products abroad:

> In foreign factories, workers and engineers try to do good work because they are driven by the fear of dismissal and unemployment. We have replaced this "inhuman" incentive by the idea of work based not on fear but on conscience. Why then do we still have poor-quality production, and why are we unable to do anything about it? First and foremost, because there is no material responsibility.

This is true; a worker who turns out bad work will not be penalized in any way for it.[41]

[38] *Izvestia*, 4th December 1961.
[39] A sheepskin coat unbuttoned, *Izvestia*, 1st April 1962.
[40] DANILOVSKY and NADEZHDIN, *Izvestia*, 9th January 1962.
[41] KH. IZAKSON, head of an agricultural machinery designing office, *Izvestia*, 12th October 1961.

Some examples from the field of transport serve to illustrate the absurdity of the situations in which workers can find themselves as a result of the indicators used. The following correspondent was also replying to engineer Antonov. "For some thirty years", he writes, "transport plans have been expressed in tons and ton-kilometres, and every year it has been customary to raise the plan indicator systematically for each lorry. The result is that, in a certain Moscow transport enterprise, customers are served until the 20th of the month. After that date, the lorries are simply sent off to distant towns with some load or other in order to mark up ton-kilometres, regardless of whether the journey is necessary or not. Nor does anyone mind about the number of bricks broken in transit, the main object being to fulfil the plan."[42]

The examples quoted by Antonov, the aircraft engineer, who was a deputy to the Supreme Soviet and whose article gave rise to some of the foregoing discussions, are also somewhat hair-raising. In Moscow he had witnessed the sight of two women workers unloading a lorry-load of bricks for use on a housing site in such a way that roughly 30% of the bricks were broken. Upon enquiry, he had found out that the women were paid by the hour, and the lorry-driver according to the tonnage unloaded and the distance covered, and that they were all under orders to hurry so as to fulfil the plan. "I am sure that the women were irritated by this stupidly organized schedule which forced them to act against the dictates of their conscience and our code, and that is why they looked rather sad as they worked." Likewise in restaurants, he said, "Work should be measured not according to the cost of preparing a dish, but according to the number of customers served". Thus even in restaurants—where the slowness of service and the lack of interest in the customer are well known—the index of gross output turns up. It is some consolation to the traveller who has eaten in Moscow's restaurants, and walked her streets, to note that the things which have irritated him are also the subject of official criticism.[43]

The newspaper *Izvestia*, for its part, conducted an enquiry into the ports of Leningrad, Riga and Odessa. This revealed great

[42] Plan indicators must be revised, *Izvestia*, 23rd December 1961.
[43] O. ANTONOV, For all and for oneself, *Izvestia*, 22nd November 1961.

slowness in unloading, illogicalities such as the unloading of copra for a factory in Leningrad at the port of Riga, despite the existing congestion there, an extraordinarily high rate of loss due to the waiting period for Soviet boats (the dockers had worked out that "it would be enough to pay for two liners"), to say nothing of the compensation which had to be paid to foreign boats. The Ministry for External Trade, the Ministry for the Mercantile Marine, the railways, etc., naturally pass the buck when it comes to taking the blame. However, according to the reports, "the port of Leningrad is one of the biggest in the country, it handles millions of tons of goods of various types every year, and 80% of all its operations are mechanized". The newspaper states that these are the averages used by the Ministry for the Mercantile Marine and the economic planning organs. But it also reveals that in fact almost half of this traffic is accounted for by sand coming from the Gulf of Finland nearby. The sand could be taken on by coastwise shipping; "but the port must show an increased gross average traffic. The sand 'makes' the plan, and also creates an illusion of advanced mechanization." In fact if one excludes the sand, the traffic is reduced by 40%, and the figure for total mechanization falls to 30%.

"One thing is clear. There must be a radical reform in the existing system for the organization and planning of transport!" But the newspaper's reports reveal once more how difficult it is to achieve reforms, for, one year previously, the introduction of a "direct progressive" system of payment for work in Odessa had led to a drop of 15% in productivity, and the same anomaly had also occurred elsewhere.[44]

Yet another article criticizes the system of bonus payments by results as being an obstacle to modernization in industry, since directors and workers are unwilling to study and manufacture new models, which may cause a slow-down in the production programme—an old complaint. By turning out long-established, or even old-fashioned models, the producers find it easier to fulfil or exceed their production quotas, and thus to obtain their bonuses.

> Our country has lost hundreds of millions of roubles as a result of this policy . . . The planning system is so bad that the USSR is at the

[44] Anomalies in statistical averages, *Izvestia*, 3rd January 1962.

moment short of essential goods, such as socks, underclothes and shoes, while the shops are crammed with articles which are so ugly and of such poor quality that no one will ever buy them."[45]

How is this situation to be remedied? At first sight, it might seem that the surest way would be not to complicate the system of indicators and bonuses still further, but to streamline it. There could be a reduction in the number of indicators used, bonuses would have less importance, or would be awarded less automatically; in a workshop it is relatively simple to distinguish between good and bad workers and it ought to be possible to find out which are the most efficient factories without becoming entangled in complicated regulations. But in practice no such solution seems open to the Soviet planners. In a capitalist economy there are always several incentives at work; in addition to the system of payment by results, there is also the spur of individual profits and competition, as far as the enterprise is concerned and, for the workers, the fear of missing promotion or being dismissed. But in the Soviet economy, where taste and love of good workmanship do not seem to be any more highly developed than they are elsewhere, there is very little incentive to turn out good work in the absence of any "material interest"; judging from official statements, lack of conscientiousness, irresponsibility and indifference are commonplace features of the working scene.[46]

One may argue about the supposed immorality of capitalist incentives; or one may dismiss the problem with the conclusion that those who wish to live in accordance with moral principles will always be able to find room for them. It may also be argued that "human nature" is not really capable of progress, and is fated to prove the undoing of any system such as the Soviet

---

[45] *Pravda*, 4th October 1962.

[46] The foregoing observations are not intended to belittle the many manifestations of "socialist emulation", or the undoubtedly authentic instances of selfless devotion to duty on the part of certain workers, especially the young people who in recent years have responded to the appeal made to them to help in the development of the eastern territories; but the striking thing is that these manifestations of work enthusiasm, which are loudly acclaimed by Soviet propaganda, usually coincide with the "campaigns" for the achievement of particular objectives which are a distinguishing feature of Soviet life. However, what counts is the average situation.

economy which presupposes in men a virtue which they do not possess; or again, that the fault always lies in the institutions rather than in the people. Whatever one's view, the fact remains that the majority of the solutions at present put forward in the USSR still tend towards even more detailed "plan indicators". For example, O. Antonov suggested introducing a system of new, more progressive indicators "which would enable performance to be assessed in such a way as to encourage every worker to put his best moral qualities into his work".[47] Another correspondent suggests that enterprises producing consumer goods should have an interest not only in the production but also in the sale of their products to the consumer.[48] The same correspondent demands that those in charge of the planning organizations should be responsible for the results of planning.[49]

In March 1961 a conference, mentioned earlier in these pages, was held in Moscow to discuss reforms in planning methods; taking part in it were representatives from scientific and administrative bodies, from the sovnarkhozy and from enterprises— among them several of the officials whom I had interviewed— and one of the aims of the conference was in fact to examine this question of "plan indicators". The conference was preceded by publication of an article by A. Efimov, the director of the Institute of Economic Research attached to the State Economic Scientific Council.[50] Commenting on the various indicators which can be used as an incentive to enterprises in fulfilling the plan, he criticized, firstly, those indicators based on output by weight, or gross overall output, and not strictly on the value of sales. He then expressed a preference, in addition to the traditional technical norms, for composite indices reflecting reductions in selling prices, productivity and the cost of the machinery used, in other words all the factors which may have a bearing on the volume of an enterprise's profits; he seemed reluctant, however, to deal with profits as such, which can vary as between sectors or types of production according to the number of conditioning factors.

[47] *Op. cit.*
[48] *Izvestia*, 1st April 1962.
[49] *Izvestia*, 7th March 1962.
[50] A. Efimov, Tasks in perfecting the planning of the national economy, *Kommunist*, No. 4, March 1961.

Another problem is that of deciding whether a greater reward should be available for over-fulfilment of the main objectives of the plan than for fulfilment of all the physical output or productivity plans. The answer is in the negative. Rewards must be so calculated that fulfilment of the various plan objectives rates higher than over-fulfilment of only some of these. According to statements made to me in 1961, and with the exception of a small number of priority products, over-fulfilment of plans is in any case forbidden, in theory; all the same, it is clear that this principle is not applied very strictly, since public announcements are still quite frequently made that some enterprise or branch of industry has exceeded its annual plan.

Yet another problem: on what basis should the performance of an enterprise be assessed? On the previous year's results, on the objectives of the current plan, or according to some other factor? Traditionally, in the USSR the plan itself has always been the criterion. But this has the obvious drawback that directors of enterprises and their personnel have a direct interest in ensuring that the plan contains only easy objectives, which in turn leads them, in their dealings with their superior authorities, to present the activities of the enterprise in the light which suits them best for this purpose. From the director's point of view, the ideal plan seemed to be one fixed at about 105% of the previous year's results, so that it could conveniently be exceeded without the risk of a marked increase in objectives for the next year.

It is certain that, in this respect, there will have to be widespread changes in the near future. It may be of some interest here to recall a discussion which I had with professors and students at the University of Warsaw, shortly after my visit to the USSR.

After recalling that, since 1958, the practice of linking bonuses with over-fulfilment of plan objectives had been discontinued in Poland, because of its harmful effects, and that the criterion now in use was the preceding year's results, Professor Oskar Lange told me that, without, of course, wishing to make any personal forecasts, he would not be surprised if a similar practice were adopted some day in the USSR.

In the autumn of 1962, there was wide discussion in the Soviet press following the publication of an article by E. Liberman, professor at the Technical Economic Institute of

Kharkov.[51] Professor Liberman had put forward the revolutionary proposal that "the current plan should be freed of its function as a criterion for determining the amount of the bonus" and that the bonus paid to an enterprise should be related to the profits of the enterprise. (More precisely, the amount of the bonus would be a declining proportion of the amount of profit, that is of the relationship between profit and fixed and working capital; the amount of retained profit would itself be an average between the planned rate of profit and the actual rate.) In this way, the author argued, enterprises would no longer have an interest in minimizing the plan, calling for unnecessary investments and building up useless reserves, as was too frequently the case, but would instead have an incentive to maximize production while reducing production costs. The bonus would naturally be awarded only if production targets had been reached with the required product assortment.

Of the many comments which appeared in *Pravda* and elsewhere in the weeks following Professor Liberman's article, the majority reacted favourably to the proposals put forward. Only a very few considered a cut in production costs or an increase in gross output to be defensible as indicators. Some suggested indicators which, though different, were inspired by similar ideas (over a hundred suggestions had already been discussed in the weekly *Ekonomicheskaya Gazeta*). The actual method of calculating bonuses proposed by Liberman seemed to come in for a good deal of discussion. In fact he pointed out that, of two enterprises making the same profit, the one with the larger capital, whose rate of profit would consequently be lower, would receive the larger bonus; such a reform would tend, therefore, to encourage an unnecessary expansion of capital. Many commentators did not fail to point out — as did Professor Liberman himself — that one of the prerequisites for putting these proposals into effect would be a proper price system. For this and other reasons, officials of the Institute of Economic Research attached to Gose-

[51] E. LIBERMAN, Plan, profit and bonus, *Pravda*, 9th September 1962. Cf. *La Documentation française, URSS*, special issue: Une polémique autour de la prime à l'effort de production dans la planification socialiste, 25th November 1962. Also see B. KERBLAY, *op. cit;* A. NOVE, *op. cit;* E. ZALESKI, *op. cit;* A. ZAUBERMAN, Liberman's rules of the game for Soviet industry, *Slavic Review*, December 1963.

konomsoviet — whose opinion may be regarded as carrying particular weight — had considered that one single indicator would be difficult to operate, and had expressed a preference for "a system of multiple indicators which, without being too numerous, would still give as detailed and complete a picture as possible of the economic activities of the enterprise". In a system of this kind, considerable weight would be given to the rate of return and productivity.[52]

In any event, whatever reforms are made in the basis for calculating bonuses, it is difficult to imagine that they would go so far as to omit all reference to plan objectives. Bearing in mind the mass of returns which have to be made at regular intervals to the various authorities — I saw some of these returns, still uncompleted, on the desk of the chief planning officer of one large enterprise — one realizes that any change in the basis for calculation and checking of bonuses which would reduce and simplify the amount of paper-work involved would be a great step forward.

Nevertheless, great importance must attach to the fact that a reform which could not fail to have the most widespread repercussions has been the subject of an open discussion in the USSR. If a criterion as simple as that of profit, or rate of profit, were to be adopted, the provisions for the reduction of output costs in enterprise plans would become meaningless. The enterprise would of necessity acquire a much greater degree of autonomy. In particular, contracts between enterprises would assume a much greater importance in relation to the supply plans. Moreover, it would seem that this is the direction in which matters are developing. Thus, one of the main recommendations made by Academician Nemchinov, when he entered the discussion, was that contracts between enterprises *(zakazy)* should have a greater importance *vis-á-vis* planning objectives *(zadanie)*, thus establishing reciprocal obligations, which would be legally binding, between the enterprises themselves, and between them and the planning organs.[53]

The real question raised by Liberman's proposals, and one which is underlined both by A. Nove and A. Zauberman, relates

[52] *Pravda*, 30th September 1962.
[53] V. NEMCHINOV, Socialist economic administration and planning of production, *Kommunist*, No. 5, 1964.

in fact to the survival of centralized planning as such. Do these proposals not in fact imply the abandonment of state controls and the administrative allocation of products and materials? How then will the authorities ensure that there is no contradiction between the objectives arrived at by the planners, according to their own methods, and those which enterprises will seek to implement using profit as their criterion? Man cannot serve two masters, as the scriptures say, a comparison which — if we substitute plan and profit for God and Mammon — is perhaps not so far-fetched as it might appear at first sight.

At all events, there will no doubt continue to be objections to the straightforward use of profit as a criterion for some time to come. One of the main obstacles is the imperfect nature of the price system, which we shall be discussing in a later chapter, and which tends to turn profit-making into something of a lottery. Yet another obstacle is the difficulty of relating enterprise profits to a total value of capital of which they did not previously have to calculate the pay-off. Precisely on this point, the recommendations by Academician Nemchinov referred to above are of significance. He is in favour of doing away with the notion of capital as being provided for enterprises free of charge, and suggests to begin with that profit norms be calculated not as a percentage of costs (as is generally the case at present) but as a percentage of existing capital.

Efforts in this respect recently seemed to be taking a new turn. There was a proposal that gross output — the much criticized *valovaya produktsia* — should be replaced by a concept closely akin to what is known in the West as value added, and which is described in the USSR as "normed processing value" *(normativnaya stoimost obrabotki)*. This is in effect gross output, minus purchases of raw materials and intermediate products and — oddly enough at first sight — profit. V. Lagutkin, whose article on this type of indicator appeared prominently in *Kommunist*, following on the article by V. Nemchinov from which we have quoted, explained that it had first been introduced in 1963, notably in the Tatar republic, and then in 1964 in the sovnarkhozy of the central Volga. The article, however, does not explain in precisely what way the principle was applied.[54]

[54] V. LAGUTKIN, Plan indicators stimulate greater efficiency in production, *Kommunist*, No. 5, March 1964.

It may well be that, in the future, such an indicator, which corresponds indeed to an economic reality[55], will be given a role of some importance. In the USSR too, there are doubtless operating the same forces which, in Western countries — where indirect taxation continues to play an important or dominant role as a complement to, or a substitute for, direct taxation — have led to the replacement of turnover tax by a tax on value added (this is the case both in France and now in several other countries following the French model). A great many of the objections to gross output *(valovaya produktsia)* are in fact removed by an indicator of this kind which, moreover, unlike the profit index, does not have the disadvantage of creating an impossible contradiction between the micro-economic and macro-economic levels, and is itself closer to the famous "net product" which economists have long used as a criterion.

---

[55] See on this indicator the commentaries of MALYSHEV (*Izvestia*, No. 32, 1964) and the reply by A. SIDOROV (*Izvestia*, 9th April 1964).

CHAPTER VIII

REGIONAL ECONOMIC POLICY

IN THE foregoing chapters, we have at various times touched upon certain of the regional aspects of planning; thus, we have discussed the place of the various territorial echelons in plan elaboration, the general features of the plans adopted at these levels and the effects of implementation of the "territorial principle" in the administration of industry and construction. We must now turn our attention to the criteria used in solving problems connected with the location of industry, and to other regional aspects of planning.

We shall be examining not only the theoretical principles involved, but also those that are applied in practice. In the USSR, as in other countries, specific concern with a viable regional policy and a rational distribution of industry is in fact a recent development. However, the day-to-day operation of the economic system has had certain more or less conscious effects on the distribution of industry, and these must not be overlooked.

Regional problems are not a minor aspect of planning. Nowadays, it seems to be generally agreed in most countries, whatever their political régime, that a policy for the location of industry is one of the essential elements in any policy for stimulating economic development. A knowledge of Soviet methods in this context is necessary to a better understanding of the special features and the success, or lack of success, of the "Soviet development model"; at a time when many nations, whatever their size or degree of development, are engaged in the effort to stimulate and co-ordinate their economic growth both at national and regional levels, such knowledge is surely of the greatest relevance.

However, the information which I have gathered on this as yet little known subject, which was the specific purpose of my visit in 1961, is still incomplete, and many of the opinions expressed are to some extent based on conjecture. To be in a position to speak more authoritatively, not only would I have had to travel much more extensively in the USSR than I in fact did, but above all I would have needed the opportunity to assemble much more detailed information on the various phases of plan elaboration and decision-making with regard to some given region, which was perhaps asking too much. As for published information in this field, it is still not always as fully detailed as one might wish.

BASIC PRINCIPLES: UTILIZATION OF LOCAL RESOURCES

We should first recall the principles governing the location of industry, and the policies to which they may give rise, in Western economic systems, and more specifically in the case of a country like France, although the scale is, of course, much smaller than in the USSR. The basic principle is that, whether the enterprise be public or private, freedom of decision lies with the entrepreneurs; in theory the latter will tend to locate their undertakings in places which favour maximum production at minimum costs, and such decisions will also, in general, be the most advantageous ones from the point of view of the common good. However, it is usually recognized nowadays that there may sometimes be a conflict between individual interests and the common interest, and this provides the justification for State intervention.

The State's first concern is to ensure, in connection with the various services, that there is, insofar as possible, a proper relationship between the prices paid by the users and the charges falling on the community, to ensure that the decisions made by entrepreneurs are the correct ones. This concern with realistic prices is in itself a justification for many instances of State intervention, especially from the development point of view (for example, the anticipation of future developments in calculating costs), but State responsibility extends still further. Theory recognizes in fact that free competition is not necessarily the ideal solution, particularly because of the existence of tendencies towards monopolistic practices and the fact that it is difficult for individual agents to take a sufficiently long-term view when making their decisions. This kind of situation may call for a special effort, directed towards certain zones or regions, in order to counteract any harmful effects arising from unco-ordinated

decision-making, as well as a general effort in respect of information, forecasting and co-ordination, within the framework of
a policy for stimulating economic growth. And lastly, it is essential that the infrastructures for encouraging future developments
should stem from a regional planning policy, which is undoubtedly indispensable, and which relates the distribution of population and industry to the size and structure of towns and
regions.

These considerations lead to the adoption of a policy of intervention by the State, while maintaining intact the principle of
autonomy for multiple centres of decision. There is certainly a
temptation toward a more precise central direction in this field,
but this is restrained not only from lack of an adequate enforce-
ment mechanism but also from consciousness of the lack of an
adequate conceptual framework. On a purely theoretical level,
it seems that it should be possible to perfect some system of
equations which would take account of all relevant factors, and
would permit the simultaneous determination of all optimal locations and transport links for all sectors. However, because of
the very great complexity of the phenomena involved, it has not
so far been possible to devise any perfectly practicable models
either for industry as a whole, or even for any one sector, except
at the cost of very great simplification, nor does it seem probable
that this can be done in the immediate future.

It is certainly not to be expected that Soviet economists should
subscribe to such principles as those described above, since more
or less by definition they reject the premises on which these principles are based. However, it is not only that they reject the concept of the entrepreneur's decision as being the optimal one;
when seeking a criterion for the location of industry, it appears
that they reject the validity of almost any calculation based on
the rate of return.

This does not, of course, imply that no attention is paid to the
question of costs in the USSR; on the contrary, the specialist
press and the reviews provide a great deal of information on comparative costs in enterprises manufacturing the same products
but situated in different parts of the USSR, or on the costs of
working various deposits which it is proposed to develop. But
the purpose of these comparisons seems much more frequently
to be to castigate backward enterprises, or to justify decisions

which have already been made, rather than to influence future developments.

Before attempting to determine, in the light of personal observation, what are the criteria which are in fact used, we might usefully recall what has been written recently on the subject by some Soviet experts.

S. Tokarev and P. Alampiev, officials who were attached, respectively, to Gosekonomsoviet and to the Institute of Economic Research, have a major criticism to make of the way in which planning of the location of industry (generally described as the "distribution of productive forces") was carried out in the USSR in earlier years, in that it was conceived within the framework of economic administration by sector. The result was that decisions relating to the location of enterprises were made from the narrow standpoint of particular sectors of industry, without any reference to inter-enterprise links or to the "territorial principle" which is now in operation. The authors add that there was also a desire, on the part of those in charge of economic organizations, to give undue preference to the highly populated and developed regions of European Russia, and that insufficient attention was paid to the development of natural resources in the new eastern territories.[1]

However, it is more than likely that the authors were particularly anxious to draw a parallel between the principles underlying the location of industry and the methods of industrial administration which were, as we know, reformed in 1957, and also to justify the new drive towards the eastern regions as envisaged within the framework of the seven-year plan. Above all, it should not be thought that sectoral choices of location meant that sites were chosen and that, after they had been selected, production was then arranged in such a way as to minimize output and transport costs; such a consideration does not seem to have been very much in evidence, at least not in this way. What is undoubtedly true is that decisions were made in a rather haphazard fashion, with individual ministries or administrations deciding, at a given moment, and on a more or less *ad hoc* basis, that it might be a

---

[1] S. TOKAREV and P. ALAMPIEV, Problems of improving the territorial organization of the economy and economic regionalization, *Plan. Khoz.*, No. 7, 1961.

good idea if they built a factory on the outskirts of this or that large town.

Academician Nemchinov, an authority in this field as in several others, has tried for his part to define the economic criteria for a rational distribution of industry. His approach to the problem is a normative one, in that he is concerned not so much with describing what is done, as with putting forward principles which ought to serve as a guide. Incidentally, it should be noted that his analysis is fairly close to the line followed at present by certain Western experts; he begins by emphasizing that, in addition to the time factor, the space factor must also play an important part in the building up of a complete economic theory, and then goes on to point out the unequal geographical distribution of the factors of production, and the existence of forces tending toward concentration, finally remarking that there is, however, a reverse tendency toward the progressive development of all parts of a territory which, with new technical advances, may well prove to be the dominant trend in the future.

The three main criteria which he puts forward in this connection are as follows. The first is, "within the framework of the territorial organization of production" to ensure minimum cost per unit of production. The second is the drive for "multiple and integral" utilization of regional resources of manpower and raw materials. And lastly, the third relates to the republics, and is aimed at ensuring that proper use is made of their resources both in their own interests, and in those of the Union as a whole.[2]

There is no doubt that these are the principles by which the Soviet leadership would wish the conduct of regional policy to be inspired. The question is, however, to what extent such principles can in practice influence decisions. Judging from the interviews which I had at various levels of the Soviet economic administration, it seemed to me that considerations of costs (Nemchinov's first principle) in fact played a much less important part than utilization of local resources, particularly raw materials.

In the end it would appear that maximum utilization of local resources is what constitutes a rational basis for decision-making. All the available information shows that the factors which carry

---

[2] V. S. NEMCHINOV, Theoretical problems relating to the rational distribution of productive forces, *Vopr. Ekon.*, No. 6, 1961.

most weight are the existence of local supplies of raw materials, and the possibility of exploiting them and thereby building up basic industries and industrial complexes.

Naturally, the cost of developing these resources is not overlooked. The great resources of the eastern regions, which have as yet scarcely been tapped, can also be exploited very cheaply, but this is only a secondary consideration.

The first task of the various territorial authorities appears to be the creation of their own fuel and power base, utilizing available local resources. This is one of the questions on which there must be co-operation between the oblast authorities, who have a general jurisdiction over all industrial activities in their territory, and the sovnarkhoz, which is concerned only with heavy industry. The aim is firstly to organize geological surveys, and then to call on the specialist "project-making institutes" to draw up specific development projects. From the point of view of local authorities, the overriding objective seems to be that of encouraging the setting up of "combines" and industrial complexes based on local materials.

In the same way, co-ordination of the development of local resources is the primary task of the "co-ordinating councils" which were set up in 1962 in the seventeen large economic regions. Finally, at all-Union level, exploitation of the resources of the various regions or territories seems for long to have been the main, or one of the main objectives, and looks like continuing to be so in an increasing degree.

An example of the extent to which costs are still only a secondary consideration in the making of development decisions is to be found in a speech by J. V. Spiridonov, then first secretary of the Leningrad obkom, at the plenum of the Central Committee on the 6th March 1962.[3] He reported that a proposal by the Leningrad obkom and the local sovnarkhoz to produce ammonia from local shale deposits had been turned down by Gosplan and the State committee for the chemical industry, on the grounds that the cost per ton of ammonia produced in this way would be higher than if it were produced by natural gas (which is now being used in the Leningrad region). Spiridonov disagreed with this point of view. In fact the north-west produces some 400 million cubic

[3] *Pravda*, 7th March 1962.

metres of bituminous gas per annum. It was therefore "of no importance to the national economy to enquire what use would be made of this gas, which is relatively dearer than natural gas, and whether it was meant for use in industry or agriculture". And he went on to say, apparently without being contradicted: "We do not suppose that anyone either from Gosplan or from the Committee for the chemical industry is thinking of closing down the Slantzy combine (shale) at least within the next ten years, or even longer, simply because our national economy has found a cheaper source of fuel." And indeed, what justification is there for using production costs as a criterion in the case of a manufacturing industry, if the same standard is not applied in the case of raw materials? Logically, under the present system, it would seem obvious that the proposals made by the Leningrad sovnarkhoz must be agreed in the end.

The importance attached to the existence of local resources and the development potential which they represent does in fact emerge very clearly from the analysis made by Academician Nemchinov, who says "the regional economy can be defined as a specialized complex, utilizing local resources in raw materials and manpower with maximum efficiency, with the object of satisfying local needs and increasing the contribution made by each region to the national economy".[4] Thus there are two principles which seem to be advocated, and which are complementary rather than contradictory, in other words utilization of resources and satisfaction of local needs. They correspond to the two other principles which, as we have seen, appear to play a very important part in the choice of general objectives in Soviet planning: study of production possibilities, on the one hand, and estimate of consumption norms on the other. As in the previous instance, the most important consideration here seems to be utilization of the available resources.

It might be argued that optimum implementation of a policy of allocating productive resources by reference to profitability (which is the underlying principle of a market economy), or of a policy of maximum utilization of resources (the underlying principle of the Soviet economy) should in the end produce approximately similar results. But since no system, in the light of its own criteria, can be

---

[4] *Op. cit.*

considered as giving rise to an optimum pattern of distribution, it must be said that the initial divergence of viewpoint leads in the end to very different decisions and distribution patterns. Several of the officials whom I met seemed well aware of this difference; speaking of the development of important natural resources, or of the setting-up of combines in the eastern regions of the Soviet Union, they freely admitted that these would not have been justifiable, and may still not be justifiable, on grounds of profitability alone.

THE BUILDING UP OF REGIONAL COMPLEXES

In the USSR, so it is said, great importance is attached to the rational location of new enterprises in conformity with an overall State plan. Given the vast distances involved, this factor is of prime importance "since mistakes or defects in the choice of regions and locations for new enterprises will inevitably give rise to very high transport costs, and cross-haulage of raw materials, fuel and finished products", to say nothing of the other losses which result from slowness of transport. Similarly, "when planning the geographical location of new enterprises, great care is taken to situate them as near as possible to sources of raw materials, fuel and power ... (and) to the regions where they will be utilized."[5]

In the interviews which I had with Dr. Feigin, the head of the "Distribution of productive forces" section of the Institute of Economics of the Academy of Sciences of the USSR, and several of his co-workers, one of the most frequent themes was the preoccupation with an adequate source of power for each region. Thus, they particularly underlined the advantages accruing from development of the great resources of natural gas which had been

[5] I. G. FEIGIN, *Geography of the national economy of the Soviet Union*, report to the XVIIIth International Geographical Congress, 1956. See also article by the same author, La répartition des forces productives de l'URSS, in *Les Régions économiques en URSS*, a collection of Soviet articles in French translation, *ISEA*, G, No. 5, March 1959. See also the impressive volume *Osobennosti i faktory razmeshchenia otraslei narodnovo khozyaistva SSSR (Special Characteristics and Factors in the Location of Branches of the National Economy of the USSR)*, 695 pp., 1960, and also another joint work, *Problems of the Distribution of Productive Forces during the Period of Construction*, Institute of Economics of the Academy of Sciences of the USSR, 336 pp., Gosplanizdat, 1960.

discovered during recent years or were already being worked, such as those in the Saratov region of the Volga, and in Stavropol in the North Caucasus — both now carried to Moscow by pipeline — and in Chebelinka in the Ukraine near Kharkov, or those discovered or rediscovered in 1959 at Gazli near Bokhara in Central Asia. The great "central black earth region" (Bryansk, Kursk) which lies between Moscow and the Ukraine, which is poor in natural resources and, as the officials at the Institute put it, was formerly regarded as a "non-perspective" region, is now covered by these gas pipelines and as a result will be transformed in the future.

It is, however, striking to note that, even at the present time, when many areas are assured of a plentiful supply of natural gas, the authorities, in their anxiety to ensure local fuel supplies, are still extensively working the high-cost lignite of the Moscow basin, and the rich peat deposits to the east and south-east, as well as the shale mentioned earlier on. Although there is occasional criticism of this policy, the criticism does not so far seem to have had much effect.

Another factor which also appears to be regarded as a prerequisite for balanced development is the supply of metal, based on local production. This was the reason for the building of steel-works at Cherepovets and Rustavi. The former are situated about 300 miles east of Leningrad, on the Volga–Baltic waterway, and get their coal mainly from Vorkuta in the Arctic circle, over 1000 miles away, and their iron ore from equally distant parts;[6] the Rustavi works, in Georgia, are also very far from their sources of raw materials; production costs in both these works are said to be very high. In the central part of Russia, which we mentioned above, low-grade ore is now being taken from the ore deposits at Kursk (the high-grade deposits at Krivoi Rog are rapidly running out) and this will feed the new steel-works at Novo-Lipetsk.

There is no need to go into detail here about power and raw materials problems in the Urals and the Asiatic regions of the

---

[6] Oddly enough, Academician Nemchinov appears to justify the building of this factory on grounds of the availability of scrap metal; but on the one hand, the factory is at a considerable distance from either Leningrad or Moscow, and on the other hand, under present technical conditions, scrap metal can be used in steel-works, but not in blast furnaces *(op. cit.)*.

USSR, since there is ample documentation on this elsewhere.[7] Suffice it to say that the main problems most frequently discussed in connection with these regions are closely related to the development of fuel and mineral resources: for example, the dislocation of the Ural–Kuznetsk combine by the granting of autonomy to its two constituents; the opening up of mining in the coal fields of Karaganda and of open-cast mining, with very low extraction costs, in eastern Siberia; the bringing into use of the iron-ore deposits at Kustanai, in western Kazakhstan, which are designed to supply the iron-works of the Urals and the steel-works which are in course of construction at Karaganda, and the iron-ore deposits of central and eastern Siberia (the Angara-Ilim and the Angara-Pit basins) which will be sufficient to supply Kuznetsk and the future steel-works of the "third base of the iron and steel industry" (the Ukraine and the Urals being regarded as the first two); and lastly, the construction of giant hydro-electric power-stations, notably on the Angara and the Yenisei rivers, and of several smaller ones on the Irtysh, and the setting up of electro-metallurgical and electro-technical industries fairly near at hand. In Central Asia the foundations of a common basis of power supplies have been laid with the opening up of vast deposits of natural gas, and will be reinforced as a result of major hydroelectric and irrigation projects, such as the Nurek Dam, which will involve three of the four republics making up this large region.

On what basis are decisions about the development of these vast natural resources made? After examining investment in the hydroelectric industry in eastern Siberia, the American author J. P. Hardt came to the conclusion that the Soviet authorities were and still are prepared "to construct hydroelectric stations far in advance of industrial needs, even if this meant slowing down the overall industrial growth rate".[8] The very low cost of

[7] Cf. particularly, Le développement du bassin du Kuznetsk, ISEA, G, No. 8, April 1960, and the article by H. CHAMBRE, Kuzbass et troisième base sidérurgique, Cahiers du monde russe et soviétique, July–December 1960, also studies at present in progress at the ISEA on Kazakhstan.

[8] J. P. HARDT, Investment policy in the Soviet electric-power industry, Value and Plan (ed. G. GROSSMAN), p. 302; cf. same author, report to the Joint Economic Committee, Congress of the United States, "Comparison of the United States and Soviet economies", October–November 1959, 615 pp.

the power produced by the hydroelectric stations or the open-cast mines of eastern Siberia is naturally quoted as the main justification for undertaking the development of these resources; but given the remoteness of these regions, it is not at all certain that an overall study of the working costs and profits involved would have led to the making of these decisions at the time when they were actually made. This interpretation is borne out by all Soviet writers on the subject. "The hydroelectric power-station which is being built at Bratsk will not have the estimated demand for its electricity for some time yet, and will have to export power to considerable distances," writes S. Slavin, for example.[9] The same situation had already been noted after the completion of the first power-station on the Angara, at Irkutsk, where five years elapsed before work was begun on the main factories which were to take its electricity.[10]

However, although the building of giant power-stations has sometimes been criticized, it is not on these grounds but simply on the grounds of what is thought to be their excessive cost — the press quoted certain statements by N. S. Khrushchev to this effect — although other officials, such as V. I. Novikov, who was chairman of Gosplan at the time, did approve of their construction; however that may be, it should be noted that the 1960–80 plan made further provision for large dams of this kind.

Soviet specialists in this field, who frequently appear to be geographers by training, rather than economists, tend nowadays to describe their subject as the science of "regional complexes of productive forces".[11] The work of these specialists seems to be not only to identify and define these regional complexes, but also to plan and foster their development.

In his work on regional classification, Professor Shaushkin has used the analysis made by Professor Kolosovski[12] who broke

---

[9] S. SLAVIN, Projects and planning for the development of the new territories, *Plan Khoz.*, No. 6, p. 28, 1962.

[10] *Plan. Khoz.*, No. 5, 1961.

[11] Cf. Prof. J. G. SHAUSHKIN (of the University of Moscow), "Large regional complexes of productive forces in the Soviet Union", report to the joint congress of the Association of regional Science and the International Geographical Association, The Hague, September, 1961.

[12] N. N. KOLOSOVSKI, Territorial productive complexes in Soviet economic geography, 1947. An English translation of this article appeared in the Sum-

down industry as a whole into a certain number of separate cycles, according to the nature of the fuel employed (ferrous metal-working, non-ferrous metals, oil and chemicals, hydro-electric power and the electro-technical industries, industries concerned with the processing of wood and of agricultural products, and the intensive use of water in agriculture). Taking this analysis as a basis, Professor Shaushkin classifies the regional complexes under five main headings and tries to trace the broad outlines of their development. It seems difficult, however, to arrive at any very specific conclusions from work based on this type of analysis.

The problem of the definition of economic regions presents much the same difficulties in the USSR as in other countries, and we shall not go into it in detail in the present context. Would it be better to take "complex" regions (in other words, regions with a diversified economic pattern) as being the most practical framework for action and co-ordination? Similarly, by what standards should one determine the specialized activities of a given region, and what part should these standards play in defining development objectives for a region? Soviet economists seem to be well aware of all the problems, and to realize at the same time that it is not always possible to find a ready answer in every case.

One of the objectives to which they seem to attach great importance is the building up of a machinery industry in each of the large regions. We are reminded that many large machine factories have been built not only in the Ukraine, in Byelorussia and in the central and western regions of the RSFSR, but also along the Volga (Gorki, Kazan, Saratov, Stalingrad), in the Urals (Sverdlovsk, Chelyabinsk, Nizhni-Tagil), in Siberia (Omsk, Novosibirsk, Krasnoyarsk, Irkutsk, Ulan-Udei), in the far eastern regions, in Kazakhstan and in the Central Asian and Transcaucasian republics. The full extent of this ambition for the

Nowadays, it would be difficult to find in the Soviet Union a republic or region which does not have its modern machine-building enterprises. This is the most significant pointer to the level of industrial development in all economic regions of the Union, including the republics and regions of formerly backward national minorities.[13]

mer 1961 issue of the *Journal of Regional Science*, published by the University of Pennsylvania.

[13] FEIGIN, *op. cit.*

building up of regional complexes is apparent in the pride taken in the economic development of the Ukraine since the pre-revolutionary period. Prior to 1914 this region, which was rich in iron and coal, was already a big metal producer, but had relatively few manufacturing industries; these were mainly concentrated at that time in the outskirts of St. Petersburg and Moscow, and in the Moscow industrial centre. Efforts were therefore made to build up bit by bit a strong engineering industry, with particular emphasis on machinery construction; by virtue of the fact that the Ukraine and the south of the USSR were the richest agricultural lands in the country, there was a notable development in the tractor and agricultural machinery industries.

At the same time, there is hardly any need to speak in terms of the transition from capitalism to socialism in seeking to explain such a development. It is not so very different from what has taken place in other countries, or other regions, and in any case it is by no means complete. Thus, in 1961 the Ukraine was still producing more pig-iron than the Russian republic (26·4 as against 22·8 million tons) but markedly less crude steel or rolled products (23·1 as against 30·0 million tons of the latter) which shows that the Ukraine is still an exporter of metal.[14] Moreover, although the engineering industries have been developed in the Ukraine — which, it should be remembered, covers an area of 232,000 square miles, and in 1959 had 42 million inhabitants, thus being fairly comparable to France — there are other industries which are non-existent, such as the motor industry, for example: in 1961, the RSFSR produced 508,000 motor-cars and lorries, while the Ukraine produced only 20,000.

As for the other republics and the various large national territories of the USSR, of which we shall be speaking later on, there are indeed serious grounds for doubt about the nature of the economic independence and unity which they do in fact enjoy under the "regional complex" theory. With regard to the newly developed eastern territories of the RSFSR, in Siberia and the Urals, the lack of regional co-ordination, of which we have given abundant examples here, and which has been so frequently criticized, has given rise to many cases of disparity in development as between the extractive and the manufacturing industries.[15]

[14] *SSSR v. tsyfrakh*, pp. 132 *et. seq.*, 1961.
[15] *Plan. Khoz.*, No. 5, 1961.

Soviet authors themselves give numerous examples of imperfect co-ordination at regional level and of inadequate development of regional complexes. For example, in *Problems of distribution*, from which we quoted earlier on, Shokin points out that the chemical processing of natural gas, with the possible exception of the production of nitrogenous fertilizers, would be better carried out on the spot, rather than at the consumer end, which is seldom the case at present; similarly, Shorski makes the point that not sufficient attention has been paid to the opportunities for agricultural expansion in the development plans for the eastern regions.[16] O. Ivashchenko, the chairman of the economic committee of the council of nationalities of the Supreme Soviet, referred to the principle of seeking an effective reconciliation of the interests of individual republics and the interests of the State as a whole, and went on to instance numerous cases of delay in the industrialization of republics which were in no way short of natural resources.[17]

A group of correspondents in the Perm region raised the question of wood manufactures, which it was thought would be better carried out in the timber-producing areas; in this instance it was pointed out that five-sixths of the timber dispatched from the region was at present floated down the Kama and the Volga, and that the 1959–65 plan even provided for a considerable increase in this traffic; however, as a result of the building of dams and reservoirs on the Volga, the time for these journeys had been doubled, the river was frozen for longer spells, and there was increased danger in timber-floating operations; in the long run, it would be necessary to process the timber on the spot, and dispatch it by boat, but so far no plans had been made for doing this.[18]

In practice, the problems of distribution of industry are still to a great extent treated individually, sector by sector; the main body of work on the subject, like the great collective study published by the Academy of Sciences of the USSR,[19] still uses this approach to problems of industrial location in which, as the

---

[16] *Op. cit.*
[17] *Izvestia*, 7th March 1962.
[18] *Pravda*, 24th April 1962.
[19] *Osobennosti . . ., op. cit.*

introduction to the above work points out, much still remains to be done.

However, the difficulty of finding a rational solution to these problems in the Soviet context was made clear to me during a discussion with one of the officials of the "distribution of productive forces" section of the Institute of Economics, on problems relating to the location of cement-works. Cement, which is in fairly widespread use, is a low-cost commodity, whose principle raw material (lime) is to be found in many places. But it is also a product in which considerable reductions in costs can be effected as the size of the factory increases.[20] A correct decision about the number and size of cement-works to be built must take into account both costs of production and costs of transport, so as to ensure that the community's needs are satisfied at minimum cost. In a capitalist economy, the solution which presents itself at this stage is no doubt not optimal, but the device used — namely competition — although it may involve losses, does come somewhere near to the optimum, when it is effectively applied and certain of the drawbacks of a monopolistic situation are avoided. It seemed to me that my Soviet colleagues were perfectly well aware of the problem, but so far had not found the right answer, either in theory — how would one weigh the various factors involved? — or in practice.

THE IMPORTANCE OF DEMOGRAPHIC FACTORS IN REGIONAL POLICY

Even in countries with a rapid rate of growth, there is a limit to the new sources of raw materials to be developed and the basic industries to be created around them. Certainly in European Russia, as in western Europe, the place of origin of raw materials, which in the long term exerts a considerable influence on the distribution of industry, plays a relatively small part in the immediate process of decision-making. New developments as such do not account for the biggest changes in the economic map. Of far greater practical importance, if one is to judge by the number of

---

[20] In factories with a capacity of less than 200,000 tons per annum, the cost of a ton of cement in 1957 was 164 (average for the USSR as a whole = 100) whereas, in factories with a capacity of more than 800,000 tons, the cost fell to less than 75. *Op. cit.*, p. 350.

areas and workers affected, are questions of location of manufacturing industries, and the setting up or development of service industries. In choice of locality the availability of communications, the size of the population (which represents a market as well as a source of manpower) and the existence of important industrial and intellectual centres plays a considerable part in the USSR, as in other countries. It was therefore interesting to see how these different factors were taken into account in policy-making with regard to the distribution of industry, and in particular what role was played by demographic factors.

Firstly, these factors may come into play at regional level in determining certain needs of the population. As we know, responsibility for satisfying these needs is a matter not for the sovnarkhozy, but primarily for the oblast and, at a higher level, the republican authorities. The central administrations are concerned with determining needs in the different regions. Thus, it was announced that the Dietetics Institute of the Academy of Sciences of the USSR had drawn up rational food consumption norms for the Soviet people, in accordance with the different needs of the various republics. However, one of the objects of these norms was to effect a greater future degree of standardization in local eating habits, which are sometimes widely divergent. For instance, in future, milk consumption per head of the population in the most favoured republic should not exceed that of the least favoured republic by more than 40%, whereas the present figure is 150%.

Demographic data also play an important part as factors in production decisions. In order to clarify this point, I repeatedly asked, in the course of my interviews, what weight was given to demographic factors in the preparation of plans at regional level. Mostly, the answer was that these factors were not regarded as essential, and this was stated in much more definite terms than when the same question was put to all-Union organs. To my great surprise, as a Western economist, I found myself being informed that the question of determining whether there was a movement of population into, or out of, a given zone or region, or whether the availability of work was sufficient to take account of the expected increase in the working population, was no concern of the local authorities; these matters were dealt with, so I was informed, at all-Union level.

Similarly, the question of determining whether a given region had a lower, or higher, average standard of living than neighbouring regions, was regarded as a matter of no consequence. The argument was, either that the standard of living in a particular zone or region was on a par with that of its neighbours, or with the national average, which is obviously not always the case, or else that the really important factor was much more the level of output of a given product per head of the population, which seems just as surprising.

It is not suggested, of course, that questions of employment or living standards play no part at all in the study of regional economic problems; any such suggestion would no doubt meet with strenuous denials. But it does seem that such considerations play a part only in the final stages, and not at the outset of planning. To look at the problem from another angle, emigration to the new rapidly developing regions, about which we shall be speaking later on, is being very much encouraged, but it does not seem, or no longer seems, to be organized with reference to the regions providing the emigrants.

Nevertheless, it seems that local demand may sometimes be a factor of some importance in the decision to set up a factory on a given site. I met with an example of this in the course of a visit to the Economic Research Institute of Gosplan of the RSFSR. When there was question of building a large computer factory, which was to be part of a scientific centre at Penza, which has a university and is about 400 miles from Moscow on the road to Kuibyshev, the local soviet, which had had wind of the proposal, asked to have the factory in their town. Although there were other towns in the running, Penza was in fact finally chosen, their own initiative having probably been the deciding factor. In a case like this, the question of transport and sources of raw materials was obviously a very minor consideration. However, what was here described as local demand was no doubt a fairly accurate reflection of the influence of the local soviet and its power to intervene. Many other countries as well as the USSR can certainly provide similar examples of this kind of local intervention.

As for long-term demographic studies of the type which have been attempted in recent years, particularly in France, where rightly or wrongly they form a key part of regional policy, it would appear that nothing of this sort has been undertaken in the USSR, either in administrative organizations or in research institutes, or in the few monographs on regional questions which have appeared in recent years.

THE BALANCE BETWEEN TOWN AND COUNTRY:
EXAMPLE OF THE UKRAINE

One of the results of the growth of industrialization was that, after 1917, the majority of the principal towns, which had been the traditional regional centres, found themselves acquiring new industries. There are scarcely any regions nowadays, at least in the European part of the USSR, which can be said to be more or less exclusively rural, or so one is told when one puts this question.

At the council for the study of productive forces (SOPS) I was told that all regions of European Russia could now be regarded as more or less adequately industrialized. In response to further questioning, it was admitted that there might be one possible exception, namely the Kostroma region, on the upper Volga, north-east of Moscow. This region suffers from a shortage of natural resources, and there is said to be rapid migration of the agricultural population. The authorities were therefore anxious to set up a machinery factory there in the fairly near future. The Kursk region, between Moscow and Kharkov, was up till recently another purely agricultural region where it was felt that "something ought to be done"; the decision to develop the huge deposits of low-grade ore in the Kursk area, which will supply new steel-works in the centre of European Russia, should help to solve this problem.

I was also told at the Economics Institute of the Academy of Sciences of the Ukraine that local demand for new industrial establishments could play some part in the making of decisions. In cases where it was thought that there was a need for a new factory, the chairmen of the municipality or other officials of the township would normally put the matter not to the local sovnarkhoz but to the republican Gosplan.

Broadly speaking, the balance between town and country in the Ukraine, so I was told, could be regarded as more or less satisfactory, and there were now no regions in the republic which were too exclusively agricultural. Several instances were quoted of towns with a population of around 35–50,000, lying outside the most highly developed regions, where there had been scarcely any industry twenty years ago, and which now have three or four large factories apiece. It is certainly true that visitors travelling along the permitted routes nowadays will see evidence of factories in most of the large towns they pass through.

However, it may be desirable to try to assess the real extent of this industrialization. There is indeed a striking contrast between urban zones and rural zones. Thus in 1956 the Ukraine had 5 towns of over 500,000 inhabitants, and 24 of over 100,000 inhabitants, which is not less than in France. Certain zones are very highly urbanized, particularly in the Donetz basin, the Stalino oblast (province), now Donetsk, where according to official figures[21] the urban population is 82% of the total population, and in the Lugansk oblast. But in 15 of the 26 oblasts of the Ukraine — each of them equal to 3 or 4 French *départements* — in other words the great majority, less than 25% of the population is situated in the towns, which is a very small proportion. And in all, the urban population of the Ukraine in 1961 was only 48% of the total,[22] which despite differences of definition is noticeably less than in France.

Nor does this discrepancy show any signs of lessening. It can indeed be shown, from the statistical yearbook for the Ukraine, that industry has increased rather less rapidly in regions with a preponderantly rural population than in others. On an average, the nine most highly urbanized oblasts showed an increase in industrial output between the years 1940–55 which was 46% greater than that of the other oblasts; in the period 1950–55, there was still a difference of 20% in the same direction.[23] The relative backwardness of the less urbanized regions tends to increase,

[21] Population of *settlements* with more than 3000 inhabitants.

[22] Here, population of *towns* of over 3000 inhabitants.

[23] SOURCE: *Narodnoie Gospodarstvo ukrainskoi RSR*, Statistical Handbook, pp. 7 and 31, Kiev, 1957. The 9 urban oblasts in question are those of Voroshilovgrad–Lugansk, Dniepropetrovsk, Zaporozhe, Crimea, Lvov, Odessa, Stalino–Donetsk, Kharkov and the city of Kiev. Indices reported (unweighted averages) 283/225 (1940–55) and 206/188 (1950–55). The proportion of urban population in 1956 was 57% in the first group, 20% in the second group, and an average of 40% for the Ukraine.

and the difference is by no means negligible. Certainly in the case of the Ukraine up till 1955, it would appear that official optimism about a dominant trend toward industrial dispersion is not justified.[24]

However, it must be pointed out that if a similar calculation is made, not about the 26 oblasts, but about the 14 sovnarkhozy functioning in the Ukraine in 1962, the difference which we have just noted disappears; in fact a sovnarkhoz frequently includes within its area a large town and certain predominantly rural areas where the rate of industrial growth is slower. It is, therefore, within the area of a sovnarkhoz, whose population averages around 2–3 million, that industry continues to be concentrated.

Generally speaking, one can scarcely say that there is a tendency to industrial dispersion in the USSR, and the contrast between the most favoured areas and the others, in other words between those which are predominantly industrial and those which are predominantly rural, remains very marked. Among factors contributing to this disparity between town and country, one should mention the lower density of population, even in the Ukraine, and also the severity of the climate and the inadequacy of communications. All in all, the fusion of agricultural, industrial and other activities is much less complete than it is in many parts of western Europe; one need only call to mind, for example, the alpine and subalpine areas, where this pattern of development is very advanced.

New projects are usually related to the construction of large factories. In connection with the textile industry, for instance, I had learned about the construction of new "complexes" in the Ukraine for the production of linen, wool and cotton, situated respectively at Rovno and Zhitomir, Chernigov and Kherson, and each employing several thousand workers. The theory seems to be that large factories of this kind should only be set up in towns which already have a sizeable population, seemingly at least 30,000 and preferably more, and towns which are the seat of a sovnarkhoz seem to be particularly favoured. Towns with a population of less than 20,000 should, in principle, be limited to local industries only.

---

[24] See previous quotation from Academician Nemchinov, p. 176.

As for the big cities, the role assigned to them seems to be to produce high-quality goods and also occasionally to serve as testing grounds for new processes or manufactures. This is the aim in the case of Kiev, the traditional capital of the Ukraine (except in the period from 1917 to 1934, when its place was taken by Kharkov); there was formerly very little industry here, but it now possesses several important ones (synthetic fabrics, mechanical engineering). It is also particularly true of Leningrad, where prior to 1917, 35% of all machinery production of the USSR was concentrated;[25] it has an intellectual and scientific tradition second to none in the USSR, and continues to play an *avant garde* role in many spheres of activity.

Another principle which the authorities try to put into practice, and which corresponds fairly closely to the efforts made in other countries to deal with similar problems, is that of building up diversified industrial complexes, in order to make the best use of existing labour potential. Efforts are being made, for example, to set up hosiery factories in and around the mining towns of the Donbass, with a view to providing work for the women. Although women in the USSR do heavy work which they would not be employed on elsewhere, they still do not carry out all the jobs that men do; in the tractor factory at Kharkov, for instance, there were a lot of women workers in the foundry, a hard enough job it would seem, but none on the electric furnaces.

Great attention is paid, both at enterprise and at regional level, to all indices relating to the degree of vocational training and the cultural level of the workers. It must be admitted that far less attention seems to be paid to this point in Western countries, where greater importance is usually attached to the employment pattern by sector of activity, and to the standard of living in the area, than to the actual composition of the working population by socio-professional group, and the degree of education. It seems to be a matter of personal pride in the USSR for the director of a factory to be able to point to the number of workers who have had a higher education, or are attending evening classes; a citizen of a particular town, in the same way, is proud of the

---

[25] O. A. KONSTANTINOV, Restriction of the growth of towns as a factor in rational location of industry, report to the XVIIIth International Geographical Conference, edition of the Academy of Sciences of the USSR, 1956.

number of institutes of higher education which his town can boast, and likes to make favourable comparisons with the other big towns in the Union (my Kharkov guide was prepared to give best only to Moscow and Leningrad in this respect); a citizen of a republic, like the Georgian I met, for example, is proud to be able to say that the number of persons having received higher education in his republic is not only greater than in neighbouring republics but also greater than the all-Union average.[26]

The officials whom I met in Kiev had also quoted the following as another example of the principles applied in matters of regional development. When a factory is being built or enlarged, there is a norm for "social investments" (housing, public services, etc.) which are supposed to represent 35% of total investment. (It must be assumed that this refers only to investments directly necessary for the development of an industry, and not to all social investments incurred by urban growth.) In fact they had told me this norm was rarely implemented, probably because of the need for giving priority to productive investments, in order to fulfil the plan. The above examples, and particularly the one relating to building problems in Kharkov,[27] make it clear indeed that this is one domain in which Soviet planning is still far from being able to fulfil all its promises.

The achievement of a satisfactory balance between town and country, to which we alluded earlier on, is subordinated to the need for progress in agriculture. As we know, Soviet agriculture is still remarkably inefficient. This situation, which is nowadays openly admitted in the USSR, is sometimes put down to the social circumstances affecting agriculture in the Soviet Union.

> The kolkhozy, said N. S. Khrushchev in September 1959, are large-scale collective farms resulting from the voluntary amalgamation of peasant holdings. In consequence the number of persons working in a given kolkhoz does not represent the minimum required for cultivation of the land, harvesting and the raising of livestock and poultry, but the number actually attached to that particular kolkhoz. For one could not

---

[26] In respect of the number of students per 1000 of the population, Georgia does in fact take the lead among the 15 republics (13·4), followed by the RSFSR (12·3) the all-Union average being only 11·1 per 1000. *Nar. Khoz.*, pp. 44, 197 and 769, 1960.

[27] See page 129.

countenance a situation in which some members of the collective were able to work, while others were deprived of that right.[28]

Whatever the truth about the origins of this situation, or about the supposedly "voluntary" nature of collectivization — and coming from one who has in other connections so freely denounced Stalin's misdeeds the expression might be regarded as a slip of the tongue — the fact remains that kolkhoz members are often under-employed or wrongly employed. A. Voronin underlines even more clearly "the existence of ample labour resources in the kolkhozy... The kolkhozy have a surplus labour force, not only in winter, but even during the periods of intensive cultivation".

There should henceforth be a change in this situation, since it has been announced that the increase in productivity should enable a reduction of at least 15% to be made in the agricultural population during the seven-year plan. It is interesting to note the aim, as stated, that the labour force thus freed from agriculture should preferably be directed towards industrial enterprises directly serving the collective sector. In various parts of the country, there already exist interkolkhoz organizations engaged not only in the manufacture and supply of various products needed in agriculture, but also even in the production of building materials, including in at least two cases the production of cement. There is probably a degree of muddle involved, since the need for these enterprises may have arisen from poor organization of the supply arrangements[29] and they may not always meet the highest standards of efficiency. A need has been expressed for directing the activities of these co-operative organizations preferably towards stockpiling, the processing of agricultural products and the provision of fertilizers and other supplies, in order, as the draft Party programme puts it, to "build up an agro-industrial association in which agriculture will be organically linked with the industrial processing of its products".[30]

Nevertheless, all the examples which have been quoted, here or elsewhere, demonstrate the backwardness of agriculture both in

[28] Quoted by A. VORONIN, Combining agricultural and industrial production in the countryside, *Vopr. Ekon.* No. 10, 1961.

[29] There are numerous examples in Chapter VII.

[30] A. VORONIN, *op. cit.*

relation to the degree of mechanization and to links with other sectors of the economy, as compared with other countries. One of the most well-worn tenets of Marxism is that "revolutionary elements will do away with the old division of labour, along with the separation of town and country";[31] there could hardly be a domain in which the divergence between doctrine and reality is more marked.

CHANGES IN THE GEOGRAPHICAL DISTRIBUTION OF INDUSTRY

In the USSR, as in other countries, changes occur in the distribution pattern of industry. In Russia these are due not so much to urban growth, which is very marked, as to changes in the balance between the various regions.

Within European Russia itself, the changes which have occurred appear relatively slight. For example, in the Ukraine, the predominance of the traditional urban zones, that is, the Donetz basin in particular, and the cities of Kharkov, Kiev and Odessa, remains unchanged. However, certain other towns have undergone very rapid growth. This is especially true of Dnepropetrovsk, whose population has more than quadrupled in the course of the last few decades, and of Zaporozhe on the Dnieper, both of which towns are the site of very important steelworks. Their growth is in fact in line with the movement of the iron and steel industry away from the coal-basin; the towns on the Dnieper and Krivoi Rog (where the ore mines are) now produce 51 % of the steel in the Ukraine, as compared with only 29 % in 1913.

However, looking at the USSR as a whole, the most striking changes in its geographical structure are those resulting from the rapid growth of population and industry in the eastern regions, i.e. the Urals, western and eastern Siberia, the far eastern territories, Kazakhstan, and, to a much smaller extent, Central Asia. For a long time, exploitation of the vast potentialities of these regions was hampered by the great severity of climatic conditions and the difficulty of communications. Development of these areas has, especially of recent years, become one of the Soviet government's main tasks.

[31] *Anti-Dühring, op. cit.*, p. 327.

The existence of almost untapped resources in the eastern regions (including in particular 89% of total solid fuel resources and 86% of total hydroelectric resources in the entire Union) has certainly been an important factor in influencing the direction which the Soviet economy has taken. From another point of view, however, one can hardly fail to see in this vast effort a further instalment of the Russian people's drive for colonization and expansion which began in the 17th century and which, under the guise of the building of socialism, now leads them to establish themselves firmly in lands which are not those from which they originally sprang.

Since 1913, the share of the eastern regions (i.e. the Urals, western and eastern Siberia, the maritime area, Kazakhstan and the four Central Asian republics) in the population and industrial production of the USSR as a whole, has developed as follows (in per cent):

TABLE IV

Location of Industrial Production in the USSR from 1913 to 1961

	1913	1940	1958	1961
Population		25		30
Total industry	21	29	more than a third	
Coal		36	46	49 (1965 : Plan)
Steel	21	32	45	48 1965 : Plan)
Electricity		22	40	46 (1965 : Plan)
Oil	—	4	31	40 (1960)
Cement	7	15	31	33 (1960)
Timber		39	45	44 (1960)
Cotton cloth		4	8	11 (1965 : Plan)

This table, based on official figures, shows that over a long period development of the eastern regions was markedly greater than that of the rest of the USSR.

However, development of these regions was not always uniformly more rapid than in the rest of the country, as the spectacular successes which have been achieved, particularly in basic industries, might have led one to suppose. In fact, work on major projects often fell behind schedule in relation to plan objectives, and had to be offset by a speeding up of the rate of investment in those regions which were already developed. Furthermore, industrial development in the eastern regions was mainly directed toward heavy industry, the extraction of raw materials and the production of fuel and power. In the eastern regions as a whole, light industries are still relatively underdeveloped.

The impetus given to heavy industry was largely due to the war, which led to the transfer east of 1200 large new industrial enterprises[32] from regions which had either been overrun or were threatened, and to the building of a total of 2250 large new enterprises.[33] The years which followed the war, and were devoted to reconstruction in the European part of the USSR, merely served to stabilize the lead acquired by the east during the war. Thus, from 1945 to 1950, and again from 1950 to 1955, the growth in capacity and production of power-stations in the eastern regions was slightly lower than in the western regions of the USSR. In respect of steel, the share of the eastern regions, which rose in the period 1940–45 from 32 to 74% of the total for the USSR, because of war losses in the European part of the USSR, has been going down ever since: 53% in 1950, 45% in 1958, 44% in 1959. According to the provisions of the seven-year plan, it is only now that the rate of growth in steel output in the eastern regions should once more become relatively greater; but this forecast is in part dependent on the completion of entirely new factories at Karaganda and Taishet, and for this reason might not be wholly realized.

The eastern regions are widely diversified in nature. They include, firstly, the Urals, which is a relatively highly populated area (19 million inhabitants in 1951) and whose development does in fact go back to olden days; it will be remembered that it was here that Peter the Great and his successors established charcoal foundries, associated with the name of Demidov, which for the greater part of the eighteenth century were the first in Europe, in advance even of England.[34] Siberia, on the other hand,

---

[32] S. G. PROCIUK, The territorial pattern of Industrialization in the USSR. A case study in location of Industry, *Soviet Studies*, pp. 69–95, July 1961.

[33] FEIGIN, *op. cit.*

[34] S. C. STRUMILIN, The problem of the origins of capitalism in Russia, *Voprosy Istorii*, No. 9, 1961. "In the middle of the 18th century," according

is virtually a new land. The development of western Siberia, centred around the town of Novosibirsk and the Kuznetsk basin, in fact dates back to the period between 1928 and 1941, whereas the development of the vast expanses of eastern Siberia and the far eastern region, which have a particularly rigorous climate and are still very sparsely populated, has really only just begun. The same is true of Kazakhstan, where the Russians (Great, Little and White) who comprised 52% of the population in 1959, now largely outnumber the Kazakhs.[35] And lastly Central Asia, the seat of very ancient civilizations, is still very much a world apart.[36]

There is considerable variation in the growth rates in these various regions. Those with the highest growth rates are neither the most remote, nor the ones that were previously the most backward.

If we examine the growth rates for industrial output[37] by large region from 1940 to 1955, it will be seen that western Siberia heads the list (index 563, taking 1940 as 100), followed by the Urals (515) and Kazakhstan (421); on the other hand, with the exception of Kirgizia (381), the Central Asian republics and the far eastern region (indices from 250 to 300) show a rate of growth which is markedly below the average for the USSR (which is shown as having reached a rate of 320). From 1955 to 1960, the same trend was accentuated, so that from 1940 to 1960, the growth rate for industrial output in Tadzhikistan and in Uzbekistan was 20% below the all-Union average, while Turkmenistan was 35% behind.[38] Analysis of growth rates by oblast (province) shows that the highest rates are in the Urals region, and the region sometimes known as the South Urals (which straddles the European and Asian parts of the USSR). Heading the list for the USSR as a whole in industrial growth between 1940 and 1955 are the 4 oblasts of Kuibyshev, the Tatar republic (Volga region), Bashkiria (Urals) and Novosibirsk (western Siberia), closely followed by the oblast of Omsk.[39]

to M. Dobb. "the output of iron in Russia was several times higher than in Britain, and Russia competed with Sweden as an exporter of iron." DOBB, *op. cit.*, p. 56.

[35] *Nar. Khoz.* 1960, p. 18.

[36] See later, p. 204. *et seq.*

[37] An analysis of Soviet indices will be found in the conclusion, p. 274.

[38] *Nar. Khoz.* p. 227, 1960; and industrial statistical yearbook.

[39] See S. G. PROCIUK, *op. cit.*

The development of the virgin lands of north Kazakhstan and south-west Siberia, and the major industrial projects envisaged by the 1959–65 seven-year plan, or subsequent plans, are intended to bring about a new and rapid growth in the eastern regions of the USSR, notably in Kazakhstan and eastern Siberia. But no doubt many difficulties still lie ahead in regions such as these, which are at present so thinly populated, and subject to such rigorous conditions.

The opening up of these eastern regions involves an incessant movement of population from the European parts of the USSR, mainly from Central Russia (the central black earth region) and from Byelorussia and the Ukraine. It was estimated that, under the seven-year plan, at least 6 million workers would move to the eastern territories of the USSR;[40] 60% of the labour force leaving their native region would go to the eastern regions.[41]

The people with whom I had had the opportunity of discussing these migrations were always careful to point out that they were voluntary, and that there was now no forcible movement of population. However, although this is no doubt true so far as the workers are concerned, it must be remembered that students on completion of their training are posted for service in these areas—just as civil servants in other countries may be subject to compulsory postings—and this can produce tense situations of the kind depicted from time to time in films (for example, the faint-hearted student who lets his fiancée set out alone for some distant outpost, etc.).

In addition, there was the decree by the Praesidium of the Supreme Soviet of the USSR, dated 4th May 1961, concerning "the struggle against those who shirk socially useful work", and which provided for the "deportation" of the "parasites" and drunks who hang around the big cities, especially Moscow, by sending them to labour camps in Siberia (agricultural, construction or lumber camps). A correspondent from *Krokodil* visited the camp at Yeniseisk (Krasnoyarsk province) where numbers of these "parasites" had been assembled. Not much seemed to have been achieved in the way of re-education, since it is scarcely to

[40] V. S. NEMCHINOV, *Vopr. Ekon.*, June 1961.
[41] KORZINKIN, I. MATROZOVA, N. SHISHKIN, On the redistribution of manpower and its allocation to the newly-developing regions of the USSR, *Sotsialisticheski Trud*, No. 6, 1961.

be expected that the seasonal work provided for the deportees would teach them to lead a regular working life (in this connection, *Izvestia* reported the sorry story of a twenty-year-old orphan girl, living at Kiev, who had been sentenced to two years' deportation under the same decree, and had in fact been denounced by neighbours anxious to appropriate her room).[42]

In the absence of compulsion, the main incentive to migration in this way is provided by wages which, in Siberia, the far eastern regions[43] and the far north seem to be on the average about a third higher than elsewhere. However, these wages do not appear to entail a proportionately higher living standard than elsewhere. In fact living conditions in the eastern territories appear to be very difficult. The intake of new workers is far in advance of the housing programme, so that the amount of living space available per worker falls short of the average for the USSR, low though that is, by 5% in eastern Siberia, 10% in western Siberia and 25% in Kazakhstan; the volume of retail trade (State and co-operative trading) in these three regions is from a third to a quarter lower than in the central region (Moscow). The scarcity of supplies makes cultivation of the private plot a necessity, which in turn hinders production. There are many problems connected with the recruitment of trained personnel.[44]

Another feature of these migrations is "socialist emulation" mainly among the young, which inspires them to join "work brigades" and to form the nucleus of new villages or new enterprises. One need only read the reports of the young communists' congresses, which centre on the "battle for production", if one is in any doubt about the importance of the role assigned to the young and their leaders in achieving the objectives fixed by the Soviet authorities. But here again many problems arise, and there is some resistance, as a study of certain works of fiction will show.[45] Some of these have depicted the difficult conditions under which these young people, part-volunteer, part-conscript, lived

---

[42] Reforming the parasites in exile: Camp in Siberia, *Krokodil*, 20th January 1962; *Izvestia*, 21st February 1962.

[43] On the subject of labour costs in Sakhalin, see the speech by Leonov at the XXIInd Congress (*Pravda*, 31st October 1961).

[44] KORZINKIN, etc., *op. cit.*

[45] For example, whether to go to Siberia, or live on the black market in Leningrad, which is the theme of the play *White Nights of Leningrad*.

when, totally unprepared for their job, they found themselves
drafted to some of the big Siberian construction sites.[46]

ATTEMPTS AT DECENTRALIZATION

Migration to the eastern regions is only one aspect of the movements of population which are taking place in the USSR. As in
other countries, the pull of the big urban centres is very strong.
The main beneficiaries are Leningrad (3·3 million inhabitants)
the former capital, which is still a great scientific and intellectual
centre and much sought after as a place to live in, and above all
Moscow. The latter city, which is now the real seat of power, has
increased from 1·8 million inhabitants in 1913 to 6·4 million in
1964, and now covers an area of about 330 square miles.

In relation to the population of the country as a whole, the
population of the two metropolises may not seem unduly large,
compared with the situation in other countries, where there is
sometimes a tendency for cities to become grossly overgrown.
However, the need for some move towards decentralization has
long been felt in the USSR. One of the reasons for this was no
doubt the slow rate of house building, which persisted until about
1950, and which meant that newcomers could only be housed
by overcrowding of the existing population.

In so far as industry was concerned, there had already been a
decree before the war which forbade the construction of new
factories, or any sizeable expansion of old factories, in a certain
number of large towns. This law was suspended during the war,
but reintroduced in 1952, and at present applies to twelve towns
(Moscow, Leningrad, Kiev, Baku, Gorki, Kharkov, Sverdlovsk,
etc.) in other words, to all the big cities. Upon my enquiring, in
1961, if the law were strictly enforced, I had detected a certain
hesitation, or even a grin, of the kind that would be readily
understood by anyone, anywhere, who has ever had anything
to do with the implementation of an avowed policy of decentralization. However, some authors have no hesitation in affirming,
on the strength of this decree, that "the increase in the working

---

[46] See A. KUZNETSOV, *Zvezda v tumani, op. at.*

population of these towns will be in excess of further manpower requirements",[47] a statement which does not seem to take any account either of the declining birth-rate in the big cities, although all the indications appear to point this way,[48] or of the considerable practical difficulty, even in a "socialist" country, of putting an effective stop on demands by enterprises. It should be noted that, from January 1959 to January 1962, although the population of Moscow did in fact rise by only 4·2%, that is less than the average for the USSR as a whole (5·4%), the rise in the population of Leningrad was on a par with the national average, and the increase in the other big cities mentioned was considerably above average (from 6 to 11%).[49]

Nevertheless, it is no doubt thanks to this policy that the growth of Moscow has been kept within bounds in recent years. Efforts have indeed been made to move a certain number of industries, such as chemicals, tanneries, etc., outside of the town. Some examples relating to the motor-car industry were likewise quoted, earlier on in this book.

The attempt at geographical decentralization is not confined to industry. The wider powers conferred on the republics, the creation of the sovnarkhozy, the setting up of the co-ordinating and planning commissions at the level of large economic regions and oblasts, can all be regarded as a very considerable effort at decentralization or deconcentration of the apparatus of decision-making. However, in comparison with Western countries with a liberal tradition and a federal structure, there is no question that much of the decision-making power in the USSR is still concentrated in the capital.

In the intellectual field, and the field of research, the concentration of activities in and around Moscow and Leningrad, although not perhaps quite so great as that which exists in France around Paris, is still very marked. Efforts have recently been made to arrest this tendency. Thus a Siberian branch of the Academy of Sciences was set up some years ago at Novosibirsk; one of its main activities is the operation of a computing laboratory for research into the use of mathematical techniques in economics. I was also informed during my visit that the work of the important

[47] KORZINKIN, etc., *op. cit.*
[48] See earlier, Chapter II.
[49] *SSSR v. tsyfrakh*, pp. 29–31, 1961.

Institute of Metallurgical Research *(Gipromez)*, which was formerly situated in Moscow, had been shared out among several centres near the iron and steel works of the Urals, the Ukraine and Kazakhstan; a part of the Institute of Research on Cellulose and Paper *(Giprobum)*, formerly in Leningrad, was likewise transferred to Irkutsk, near the site of new factories engaged in this sector of production. The minister for Agriculture received orders to set up his headquarters at a sovkhoz in the country, and the press from time to time reports "invitations" along the same lines which have been issued to some category or other of Soviet citizens.

However, there are opposing trends too. For example, the French Coal Industries Mission[50] had noted that the biggest research institute concerned with the coal industry, which was formerly located at Kharkov, and had been destroyed during the occupation, had been rebuilt on a site some 12 miles from Moscow where it was due for completion in 1959.

All of these transfers must have involved considerable movement of officials and technicians away from the capital cities. But it is difficult to keep a check on such movements, and it is clear that, in the USSR as elsewhere, the reverse tendency toward centralization is powerful, and not easily restrained. As a rule, despite statements to the contrary, members of the intelligentsia and already established residents, as well as their families, seem very anxious to maintain their foothold in Moscow and Leningrad, and are reluctant to move as suggested; moreover, the population as a whole are very conscious of the attractions of the big city.

There was a discussion at the XXIInd Congress about the places where writers chose to live. E. A. Furtseva, the Minister for Culture, had denounced those writers whose choice of residence cut them off from the real life of the workers. She had disclosed that 4000 of the 5200 Soviet writers lived in the capital cities of the republics; that 1700 of the 2700 Russian writers were living in Moscow and Leningrad, all the 220 Armenian writers, save 15, were living in Erevan, and 105 of the 116 Latvian writers were in Riga,[51] proportions which, at least judging from the example of the French, could hardly be regarded as excessive.

[50] Voyage en URSS de la mission des Charbonnages de France, *Annales des Mines*, pp. 677–762.

[51] Writers here understood as being members of the writers' unions.

> Ought we, added the minister, to launch a campaign to move writers
> and artists from the industrial centres out to the countryside? Our writ-
> ers' and artists' unions should not seek to concentrate their members
> in the capitals of the republics. The young members should be rooted
> in the places where they began their artistic careers.

But on the same platform three days later the writer Sholokhov told comrade Furtseva that she might as well give up, as
foredoomed to failure, any hopes of persuading writers to live any
closer to the people they write about.[52]

Many enquiries have revealed how frequently in fact youthful
personnel, who had been sent to work in small towns in the
countryside, drifted back to the city after three or four years.[53]

At any rate, the Soviet authorities seem to be very conscious of
this *de facto* inequality between the capital cities and the provinces—a phenomenon which is not peculiar to Russia—and they
are very anxious to combat it, if not to eliminate it.

In the effort to plan the development of large cities, a place
must naturally be found for the building of satellite towns which
in Russia of course, will be known as "sputnik" towns. The Soviet
planners seem interested in British experiments with new towns,
particularly the satellite towns encircling London, and other
similar experiments abroad. It was decided to build a sputnik
town some 35 miles from Moscow, on the road to Leningrad
(Kryukovo), but it seemed that in 1961 work had not yet begun.
I had also been informed that it was the aim, in planning urban
development, to locate a number of large enterprises near new
housing developments, so as to create more or less self-contained
living and working units: here again, research seems to be on
much the same lines as that carried out by town-planners in other
countries.

THE SOVIET ROAD TO DEVELOPMENT: THE EXAMPLE OF
CENTRAL ASIA

Some indications have already been given of the way in which
the economy of various regions of the USSR has developed since

[52] *Pravda*, 22nd and 25th October 1961.

[53] "A job in the front line or at home," comments by a number of correspondents, *Izvestia*, 9th February 1962; on student problems, see also previously, Chapter I.

the Soviet government came to power. It may be worthwhile to restate these earlier points confining our attention to one particular region which does not belong to the dominant Slav group. There is no need to re-affirm the relevance of such an analysis, at a time when all the developing countries, even if they do not seek to emulate the Soviet experience, do at least take it into account. The region we have chosen is Central Asia (the republics of Uzbekistan, Kirgizia, Tadzhikistan and Turkmenistan) which, if one adds the republic of Kazakhstan, more or less corresponds to the former Russian Turkestan.

The notes which follow must perforce be brief, and are in no way a substitute for the detailed study on the subject which has yet to be written. However, we are able to draw on a most valuable study made by the secretariat of the United Nations' Economic Commission for Europe, which sent a mission to Central Asia some years ago.[54]

The total population of Central Asia (known as Middle Asia in Russian) has developed, since 1897, as follows (in millions):

TABLE V.

Population of the USSR and of Central Asia from 1897 to 1962

	1897	1939	1955	1959	1962
Central Asia	5·6	10·5	12·1	13·7	15·1
USSR	126	191	198	209	220
Central Asia as a % of USSR	4·5%	5·4%	6·1%	6·6%	6·9%

The growth in population is thus markedly more rapid than that of the USSR as a whole.

This is due in the first place to a higher birth-rate than in the rest of the USSR, the difference increasing with the passage of time.

---

[54] *ECE Bulletin* (Geneva), vol. 9, no. 3, pp. 55–85, November 1957. Except where otherwise stated, the information which follows on 1956 and preceding years is all taken from this source.

TABLE VI.

Birth-rates in the USSR and in Central Asia in 1940,
1951 and 1956 (per 1000)

	1940	1951	1956
Central Asia	33·8	37·4	36·6
USSR	31·7	26·8	25·0

It is also the result of immigration from the rest of the USSR. From 1926 to 1939, the non-Asiatic population of Central Asia rose from 9 to 20% of the total (2.1 million); this influx was mainly directed towards the towns, the urban population having increased, between those two dates, by 1 million inhabitants, while movement of the indigenous rural population, according to the ECE study, remained negligible over the same period. Since then, the non-Asiatic population seems to have remained stable, at a total of 2·5 million, according to the 1959 census, in other words 18·4% of the population (in Kirgizia, the proportion is as high as 37%).

Judging from all accounts by travellers, the Russian element in Tashkent forms a very large part of the population and in particular, fills most of the industrial posts.

The situation revealed by these figures is reminiscent of that which obtained, some thirty years ago in North Africa. There too, the European immigrants gradually came to represent an appreciable proportion, or even, at a given moment, the majority of the population of several large towns, where their arrival brought about a rapid increase in development. The sequel, in the case of North Africa, is well known; the slowing down of immigration and the ever-increasing gap between the natural rate of growth of the European and the indigenous population led to a progressive reversal of the relationship between the size of the two populations, and the mass exodus of the rural populace to the big towns upset the balance there even more violently.

Of course, it must be realized that the Russian and Ukrainian elements form a much higher proportion of the population of Central Asia than was ever the case with the French and European elements in North Africa, and also that the contrast between the birth rates of the two groups seems to be much less marked here than it was there. Nevertheless, when one has two populations living alongside one another with little or no tendency to assimilation (there are very few mixed marriages recorded in Central Asia) there is a certain logic of numbers which, short of the elimination of one of the two ethnic groups, it is difficult to escape.

The economic situation, in other words the state of employment and production relationships, is of course, another equally fundamental factor in the evolution of a particular region.

The study made by ECE shows that from 1897 (the date of the last census taken in Tsarist times) till 1940, the rate of industrial growth in Central Asia was markedly slower than in the rest of the USSR. On the other hand, from 1940 to 1955, the growth in industrial employment was much more rapid; however, if one takes into account the virtual disappearance of the craftsman sector, which was formerly very highly developed and produced high-quality articles, the proportion of the population employed in industry and handicrafts was still lower in 1955 than it had been at the end of the last century.

TABLE VII.

Employment in Industry and Handicrafts Expressed in Percentages of the Total Population in 1897, 1940 and 1955

	1897	1940	1955
Industry and mines (millions)	0·1	0 2	0·5
Handicrafts (millions)	0·2	—	—
Total (as a percentage of total population)	4·8%	2·7%	4·2%

"In Samarkand, the centre of the craft traditions of Central Asia, the number of craftsmen is now less than 4000, and it is vegetables which have pride of place in its legendary bazaar." Thus, it would appear, the experience of Central Asia is similar to that of India and other backward countries with an ancient tradition, for whom the industrial revolution has in fact meant a reduction in the proportion of the population employed in industry and handicrafts.

At the beginning of the nineteenth century, Central Asia imported crude metals from Russia and exported finished products, and regularly showed a favourable balance of trade. It was not until after about 1865 that the colonial-type trade pattern began to emerge, with Turkestan exporting mainly raw materials (cotton and sugar). After the Soviet régime was established, not only was there no reversal of this trend, but the situation even became worse.

"In effect, the industrialization of Central Asia was mainly accomplished after 1950." However, although there has been a more rapid increase in employment since then, output and productivity are still increasing at a noticeably slower rate than in the USSR as a whole; again according to the ECE report, in the period from 1940 to 1950 productivity rose by 3% per annum in the USSR, but by only 1% in Central Asia, the corresponding figures for the period from 1950 to 1955 being 9% and 3% respectively; industrial employment in Central Asia was 2·6% of the total for the USSR in 1950 and in 1955, so that the share of Central Asia in the gross industrial output of the USSR fell, between these two dates, from 2·4% to 2·2%. Since 1955 Central Asia has continued to show a slow rate of growth and the 1961 output expressed as an index over 1955 was as follows: Turkmenistan (132) Uzbekistan (153), Tadzhikistan (170) and Kirgizia (176), these being below the average for the USSR (178).[55] According to the official figures, the industrial output of Central Asia per head of the population is less than a third of average output for the USSR.

The ECE study further notes that it was only after the war that employment in the heavy industries of Central Asia ceased to be confined to Russians and other non-indigenous workers. In the textile factory at Tashkent, for example, the number of Uzbeks employed in 1956 was 11% (as compared with 0 in 1934), in the agricultural machinery factory they represented 25% of the workers, while they were in the majority in the silk mills.

[55] *SSSR v. tsyfrakh* and *Nar. Khoz.*; from 1955 to 1960, industrial employment in Central Asia fell from 2·7 to 2·6% of the total for the USSR. However, with the exception of Turkmenistan, between 1961 and 1963, industrial production in all the Central Asian republics increased as much or more than the average for the USSR.

The main industrial output of Central Asia is in raw materials: oil (5% of Soviet production in 1961) in Turkmenistan, coal (1·7%), a small production of iron and refined lead; however, production of electricity (9·6 milliard kWh or 2·9% of Soviet production in 1961) and of cement (3·5%) may be regarded as fairly considerable, and point to a certain degree of industrial development. The engineering industries still lag behind, however: 1% of total Soviet production in 1956, according to ECE; it is unlikely that the subsequent increase has substantially altered this proportion. Again, a study of the major industrial projects announced for the eastern regions under the seven-year plan reveals that almost none of them involves Central Asia, and that it is still Siberia, Kazakhstan or the Urals which are affected. As for the extensive natural gas deposits near Bokhara, whose production is supposed to increase from 1·2 (1961) to 18 milliard cubic metres by 1965, although it was doubtless stated that some of this was to be used by the local chemical industries, very few details have been given, and the emphasis seems to be mainly on the construction of two large gas pipe-lines leading to the two principal industrial towns in the Urals, Sverdlovsk and Chelyabinsk.[56]

Thus it would seem that recent developments have not substantially altered the situation as described in the ECE study. "During the coming years," this survey stated, "it will be difficult to avoid a violent contrast between the employment situation in Central Asia and the other regions of the Union." Why then is Russian immigration to Central Asia being encouraged, when the amount of land cultivated per head of the population is already significantly smaller than it is elsewhere? The answer, we are told, is partly in order to forestall separatist tendencies, partly to prevent a rural exodus which would jeopardize cotton policy, and, lastly, to deal with the problem of employing women, the traditional labour force in the textile or light industries, in a Moslem country.[57] These observations are all the more interesting in view of the care which we know is taken by the ECE secretariat, the only European economic organization in which both East and West are represented, to avoid political bias.

[56] See previously the section on "Changes in the geographical distribution of industry".

[57] *Op. cit.*, p. 61.

The principal feature of the Central Asian economy is its dependence on cotton. In the period from 1913 to 1955, the amount of cotton grown increased over fivefold, while production of grain went down by a quarter; this specialization in cotton was made possible by trade with neighbouring republics, and especially by the building of the "Turksib" which opened up communications between Central Asia and Kazakhstan and western Siberia; 54% of the land irrigated (which increased in the same period from 2·2 to 3·8 million hectares) is devoted to cotton-growing, as compared with only 10% in 1913; a third of all the nitrogenous fertilizers produced in the USSR are used in cotton-growing. Yields are consequently very high. Central Asia provides 85% of the cotton used in the entire USSR (as compared with 50% in 1913).

It should, however, be noted that, since 1958, there seems to have been a slight lessening of the emphasis on cotton, and maize and fodder plants have assumed greater importance in crop-rotation.

But although cotton provides a certain amount of agricultural industry (oil-works, cotton-picking) spinning and weaving are for the most part carried on outside Central Asia. 90% of its cotton is exported in the raw state. Although the population of Central Asia is nearly 7% of the total population of the USSR, its production of cotton cloth, despite a monopoly of the raw material in question, is barely 5% of the all-Union total. Traditionally associated with the central Russian region (Ivanovo, Vladimir, the Moscow region), the cotton industry is in fact expanding much more rapidly in new regions such as the Ukraine or Siberia, rather than in Uzbekistan. In this instance there seems to be little evidence of the "regional complex" theory at work.

The ECE study notes in passing that, in order to stimulate cotton production, very high bonuses have been paid since 1955 to enterprises which overfulfil their plan, or obtain high yields per hectare; but, because of high revenues resulting from this bonus system, the accumulation of manpower in kolkhozy which have a high yield has had the net effect of increasing the cost of cotton production and reducing output per worker. Although yields per hectare are high, productivity is low.

However, the important thing for Central Asia is the high price of raw cotton, which means that, despite its low rate of industrial development, the country is assured of a relatively high standard of living. The members of the ECE mission estimated that the average living standard in Central Asia in 1956 was about 20–25% lower than the average for the USSR; consumption of cotton textiles, per head, about 13% lower; consumption of radios, tobacco and other luxury items, about 30% lower; the amount of living space per head (7 square yards) was even lower than the all-Union average, which was then about 9 square yards, but living standards in the kolkhozy were thought to be higher than in the rest of the USSR. According to ECE, this difference is less than that existing between many of the richest and poorest regions in western European countries; in addition, although there is undeniably a difference in living standards between the Asiatic and non-Asiatic populations, the contrast is not so very great, and is certainly less marked than is sometimes the case in other countries where European and other races live alongside one another. Moreover, the standard of living in Central Asia is unquestionably much higher than in the neighbouring Asiatic countries. More recent reports have confirmed that the earnings of kolkhoz members in Central Asia, including the income from the private plot, were at least equal to the earnings of industrial workers in Central Asia or Russia, and were considerably greater than those of kolkhoz members in other regions, and that the income of sovkhoz workers was even higher.

An enormous effort has been made in education and public health. In 1955, with 5·7 hospital beds per 1000 inhabitants, Central Asia was not very far short of the USSR average (6·5) although rather far behind a country such as France (10·9). The number of secondary schools was on a par with that of countries in the West, and the number of students apparently much higher (8·5 per 1000 inhabitants, as compared with an average of 9·3 for the USSR and 4·2 in France).

The ECE report also recalls that for thirty years it was the all-Union Gosplan which drew up the State investment plans for Central Asia, and that decisions were made by the government, through the appropriate ministries, except in the case of minor projects, where decisions were the responsibility of the republican governments. Between 1955 and 1957 there was some transfer of responsibilities to the councils of ministers and, in

1957, to the new sovnarkhozy; however, "by retaining the right of supervision over turnover tax, profits and prices, the all-Union government did in fact retain the power to direct investment to a particular region." As a result, the amount of investment per head was in fact only two-thirds of what it was for the USSR as a whole; taking only State investments, it will even be seen that total investment per head in Uzbekistan in 1960 was only 41% of the USSR average; however, one must take into account kolkhoz investments, which are noticeably higher in the cotton-growing region.[58]

Thus, the following conclusions may be drawn from the ECE study. First of all, it notes that "although a very considerable amount of work has been done on industrial development since the establishment of the Soviet régime, the economy of Central Asia is still none the less heavily dependent on production of raw materials, and, insofar as the degree of industrialization is concerned, the disparity between this region and the rest of the USSR, despite changes, has increased since the war". And in addition "if the relatively high income derived from cotton-growing in Central Asia is not the result of fairly high productivity but is due to the fact that prices for this commodity are more favourable than they are for others, then obviously the position of Central Asia is still intrinsically weak". The report ends on the following note:

> The cultural revolution which is already reaching central Asia is therefore one of the factors in its long-term economic development, for which the prospects are favourable despite the difficulties which will assuredly arise when the numerous post-war age-groups find their way onto the labour market.[59]

All available information on subsequent developments merely bears out the truth of these observations.

The foregoing analysis may be supplemented by comments from travellers whose work affords them a regular opportunity of following developments in this part of the world. There seems to be total segregation of the races and, according to these reports, which are confirmed by the findings of Soviet ethnologists, this is more marked nowadays than it was formerly. Mixed marriages are extremely rare, the rarest of all being marriages

[58] *Nar. Khoz.*, 1960, p. 599.
[59] *Op. cit.*, pp. 71, 80, 85.

between Moslem women and Russian men; it would appear to be the women who are reluctant. (It should be noted that this problem does not emerge clearly in the Soviet statistics, which sometimes confuse these particular mixed marriages with marriages between other ethnic groups.) It seems that circumcision is also generally practised among the Moslems, even in Party members' families, and that this tends to be a political rather than a religious manifestation (that is, an affirmation of one's membership of the Moslem community).

In the political context the Russian group is unquestionably dominant, and there has been a policy of "splitting up the nationalities"; the formation of five republics (including Kazakhstan), of which four have a closely related Turkic background, has effectively put a stop to any efforts at pan-Turkic or pan-Turanian realignment. But although Russian cadres are both numerous and ubiquitous (one finds them, for example, occupying posts as accountants or secretaries in the kolkhozy or in Party organizations)[60] there are also plenty of local cadres and officials, and they are the ones who, apparently, occupy positions of authority. A considerable effort seems to have been made to encourage recruitment and training among the people, and to raise standards of education, including higher education; this has been done on the spot, wherever possible, and on an *ad hoc* basis if no other means are available, and it appears to have been done unreservedly, with no ulterior motive. In this way, investment in human welfare seems to be the Soviet régime's first and most striking solution to the problem of the so-called underdeveloped countries. The local authorities appear to be very conscious of this, and certain of them were reported as having remarked to visitors from the uncommitted countries: "Politically we are controlled from the centre, but we are the winners in the long run, because independence is meaningless unless you have the means to exercise it, in other words trained personnel." Furthermore, since the standard of living in Central Asia seems to be more or less comparable (or even, for some people, superior) to what it is in Central Russia, it could be argued that the dominant Russian group has to a great extent made sacrifices on behalf of the group which it dominates.

[60] See previously, p. 39.

In the light of these considerations, we may ask ourselves whether Soviet policy with regard to the non-Russian races of the Union can justifiably be described as colonialist. This is a frequently debated question in certain Western circles. It was even the subject of a conference and a publication by the Munich Institute for the study of the USSR.[61] In this publication, which there is no reason not to quote here, the majority of the contributors, as one might expect, reply to this question in the affirmative. In the political context they instance the liquidation of certain ethnic groups accused of disloyalty during the war (Crimean Tatars, Volga Germans), the virtual dominance of the great-Russian group, the suppression of all genuine self-determination tendencies during the first years of the Soviet régime; in the economic context, they point out, as has already been done in these pages, that many of the non-Russian territories are in fact highly specialized in the production of raw materials, very little of which they themselves turn into manufactured products; that investments per head of the population in the RSFSR and Kazakhstan (where they do in fact benefit the Russians) are very much higher than in the other republics, and that, largely owing to the effect of the turnover tax (which is said to be lower in the RSFSR than in the other republics), they are in fact covered to a great extent by payments from the other republics.[62]

However, certain of the participants in this conference—who can scarcely be accused of being Sovietophiles—adopted a different attitude. As one of them said, "if colonialism is an attempt by the parent state to exploit the subject races, to the detriment of the latter..., then there is nothing that we can describe as 'Soviet colonialism'". "The principal aim of the ruling group in the parent state, in other words the Communist Party, is not economic exploitation of the subject peoples' sources of wealth, but rather the destruction of these sources, in order to create the conditions necessary for the forcible transplantation of communism." And indeed, the peasants of Kostroma, Vologda or Penza, who still live very poorly, cannot be said to have grown

[61] An issue on Soviet colonialism in theory and practice, *Studies on the Soviet Union*, Institute for the Study of the USSR, Munich, Vol. I, No. 2, 1961.

[62] See in particular comments by A. Adamovich, P. Fedenko and Baymirza Hayit.

rich at the expense of the non-Russian peoples who live under Soviet domination. The author here quoted, who was living in Lithuania in 1940, remarks that the Soviets, when they arrived in his country "did not want Lithuanian butter, or bread, or lard. All they wanted was to introduce communism ... The first thing they did, and which was obviously to their own disadvantage, was to destroy completely everything that was necessary to our well-being."[63] It can indeed be argued that the standard of living in this particular part of the USSR is actually not higher, or is indeed still lower, than it was twenty-five years ago, and that no one is any the better for it. Another speaker, in the same vein, goes even further. Undoubtedly, he says, the objective and subjective criteria of colonialism (discrimination with regard to the natives, on the one hand, and economic exploitation on the other) do not exist in the Soviet Union, nor can one speak of "Russianism". But there is a dialectic development of Western-type colonialism which does in fact operate in favour of those formerly colonized:

> An examination of the history of Western colonialism proves that although, subjectively, it gave rise to economic exploitation, objectively it could not fail to lead to the gradual emancipation of the colonial peoples. This was a historical necessity [. . .] The Soviet peoples would assuredly prefer colonialism in this guise to their present lot. Unfortunately, in the Soviet Union, we are concerned with a solution to the problem of nationalism which leaves the non-Russian nationalities with no hope for the future [. . .] In the future communist society [. . .] what is expected of every nationality is that it should be merged into a toiling mass without national identity which will be known as the Soviet people.[64]

Leaving aside the commentary, there does seem to be some justification for this interpretation, particularly in view of the anti-nationalist tendencies which became apparent during and after the XXIInd Congress, such as, for example, the denunciation of bourgeois nationalist tendencies, the almost total absence of remarks about "great nation chauvinism", and affirmations about the primacy of the Russian language.[65]

[63] J. MACKIEWICS, Soviet optimism, nationalism and colonialism, *op. cit.*
[64] A. BILINKY, Colonialism or genocide, *op. cit.*
[65] See earlier, Chapter II.

What conclusion are we to draw about the USSR's policy for regional economic development and, in more general terms, about the economic utilization of the territory of the Union?

The first question which arises is whether *the geographical distribution of industry which obtains under the Soviet system is a rational one* and whether, at a given moment, it is likely to approach what could be regarded as an economic optimum.

The answer, as we have seen, must on the whole be in the negative. Of all possible distributions for a given production at a given moment, the distribution which one finds in the Soviet Union is assuredly not the one which is most conducive to minimizing costs or, to take only one element in the latter, to cutting down transport requirements. The enormous size of the goods traffic involved in the USSR, in relation to an output which is still relatively small, is in itself an indication of this; in 1954 the total of ton-kilometres recorded for rail transports was higher than the equivalent figure for the USA. Neither the size of the country, nor the slowness in developing other forms of transport, are sufficient justification for this state of affairs; indeed, the conclusion should perhaps be that economic integration is carried further than is necessary.

During the past few years, and particularly since the creation of the sovnarkhozy, there has been marked progress. Nevertheless, the rationalization of location, trade and specialization, insofar as it can be measured, is still undoubtedly less efficient than in the market economies, despite the imperfections of the latter.

But the question of the immediate optimum is by no means the only one, or even the most important one, which arises. Taking the long-term view, one asks *which is the system most conducive to economic growth in the various regions*, especially those which are the most backward to begin with and, in the end, what system of distribution of industry is most conducive to the growth of the economy as a whole?

In this respect, the Soviet experience certainly appears in a much more favourable light than was the case before. Almost every territory, every region, every large town, has now acquired industries, including those which were formerly underdeveloped. One need only look at the republics of Transcaucasia or Central Asia, all of which now possess the bases for modern industry and, for the most part, a partially or wholly modernized agriculture and a well-developed educational system, and compare them with the countries lying on the southern frontiers of the USSR.

Or again, one may ask whether a solution to the regional problems of the so-called "developed" countries, many of whom have to combat excessive concentration and to stimulate growth in their most backward areas, might not more easily be found within the framework of a system characterized by centralization of the powers of decision. Is there not some advantage in the minor attention paid to the immediate rate of return in the course of deciding new investment projects, which is a distinguishing feature of the Soviet economy, and the emphasis placed, by contrast, on human investment? In fact one of the drawbacks of *laissez-faire* economies is that the multiplicity of decision-making units does not allow the various economic agencies to make sufficiently long-term calculations in arriving at their decisions, which is the reason for the steps at present being taken in many countries in matters relating to the distribution of industry.

One of the articles of faith of the Marxist-Leninist creed is that "the characteristic feature of world capitalism is the law of unequal economic and political development which widens the contradictions and accentuates the competitive struggle between States".[66] This part of communist doctrine, leaving aside its purely political aspect, in other words that which has a bearing on the relationships between States, has been relatively less elaborated than certain others. If, without necessarily subscribing to it for that reason, there can be said to be some truth in it, that truth is best borne out by the point we have just made.

Nevertheless, it could not be said that on this count the Soviet system is superior, or entirely satisfactory.

In the first place, the market economy system seems to have a built-in corrective to its own imperfections, which may operate either spontaneously, or through the adoption of "policies for regional development", and in the light of recent experience it can be said that this is done with a fair degree of efficiency.

Moreover, the Soviet economy as such is subject to all the sources of immediate imperfection which we have mentioned, and these undoubtedly have an effect on its growth. In seeking to achieve

[66] Report on the draft programme of the CPSU (18th October 1961).

a greater degree of rationality, it may itself come up against problems of geographical concentration which, as we have seen, call
in turn for a policy of decentralization which it is not always
easy to put into practice.

Nor is distribution of the State's major industries and of urban
activities the only consideration. The other question which one
must try to answer is whether, within a given region, the Soviet
economic system succeeds in creating a balance in industry which
is favourable to the general economic growth. In particular, can
the balance between town and country be regarded as satisfactory? So far, it would not appear that their efforts in this direction have been outstandingly successful. Even in areas which are
fertile and fairly well populated, a marked contrast can be observed
between the towns and the countryside. Industrial growth (apart
from the small service industries at present encouraged in the kolkhozy) has been confined mainly to the fairly large towns; communications are difficult, and so far urban development seems
to have had only a limited effect on the surrounding countryside.

It must also be said, with due allowance for the inadequacy of
information on the subject, that the foregoing observations would
not lead one to concur with the statements of Soviet propagandists, and with the numerous observers who repeat them, doubtless in all good faith, when they affirm that the Soviet socialist
formula provides a complete and definitive solution to the problem of nationalities and the political and economic development
of multi-racial societies. This is assuredly a domain in which the
Soviet régime can point with some pride to its achievements;
but at the same time it cannot be denied that all difficulties, contradictions and uncertainties about the future are still a long way
from being resolved.

One further word must be added about the "Soviet plan for
the transformation of nature" which one sometimes hears discussed, particularly outside the Soviet Union, and which supposedly contains a special formula for the economic improvement
of backward countries. It is hard to see in what way the economic
projects which might come under this heading are in fact different
from those that may be undertaken elsewhere. The diversion of
the waters of the Northern Dvina into the Kama and Volga
which will increase the volume of water going to the power
stations of the Volga and will partially alleviate the gradual dry

ing-up of the Caspian Sea; the planting of forest belts in arid or semi-arid regions; the building of canals, dams and "seas" (or large lakes) on rivers, the development of irrigation and, at present, the diversion southward of the upper reaches of the great watercourses of western Siberia towards the desert regions of Central Asia, may all be far-reaching projects, although some of them, which were planned during the Stalin period, have now either been abandoned or considerably reduced in scale. But in the event none of these schemes is in any way more striking, or more revolutionary in terms of the transformation of nature, than projects which are being carried out in many other parts of the world. As for changing the climate, there is no reason to suppose that this is any more of a reality in Russia than it is anywhere else.

CHAPTER IX

ECONOMIC EQUILIBRIUM AND THE SEARCH FOR OPTIMIZATION

THE problem of the efficient utilization of resources is one of those which receive most attention from Western economists studying the Soviet economy. This is undoubtedly one of the basic problems, if not indeed the basic one, of economics, which is commonly described as the science of the utilization of scarce resources.

In this connection Western economists usually adopt a very critical attitude towards the Soviet economy; whatever the advantages or disadvantages of a planned economy in other respects, they are of the opinion that, on this point, the system as it operates in the USSR has undeniable weaknesses. Contrary to the usual Soviet assertions about the "anarchic" nature of capitalist economies, they believe that it is the planned economy which lacks the laws which would enable it to make proper use of economic calculation, and that the planned economy is therefore less efficient.

Our conclusions will not differ very much from the view held by the majority of those economists; in this respect they are on very solid ground. However, the search for maximum economic efficiency is a problem whose implications are wider than is sometimes realized. It is not only a question of deciding whether enterprises and economic agencies, by following the rules of their own rationality, can combine to achieve optimum distribution of the resources utilized in respect of the economy as a whole; there is also the equally important question of determining to what extent the economic system favours the efficient utilization of all the potential resources available.

It must be recognized, as the majority of Western economists following Keynes do in fact recognize nowadays, that there are two distinct economic problems: the problem of optimum allocation of resources, and the problem of full employment,[1] the latter being identifiable, within the context of a dynamic analysis, with the problem of growth rate of an economy with a given structure. Now it can be argued—and the main body of evidence tends to confirm this as a working hypothesis— it can be argued, I would repeat, that capitalist or market-type economies are on a theoretical level superior to planned economies of the Soviet type on this first count, but are probably inferior in respect of the second.

Both of these problems must be examined. We shall deal firstly with the mechanism of growth. The study of the second problem, that is, of the way in which the Soviet economy endeavours to increase its efficiency, will involve examination of a series of questions including enterprise accounting, the system of prices and values, investment criteria and the application of mathematical methods in economics. Throughout this analysis, frequent references will be made to the behaviour of capitalist or market economies.

THE DYNAMICS OF GROWTH IN A SOCIALIST ECONOMY

In the capitalist or market economies, there has of recent years been a tendency to pay less attention to the study of trade cycles, as the memory of the great pre-war booms and slumps has receded. However, these are by no means a thing of the past; since 1945 the United States, in common with every one of the western European countries, has experienced at least three complete cycles, each including a more or less marked phase of economic recession or stagnation. For example, in France, since the year 1948, in which production returned to pre-war level, there have been six years in which industrial output exceeded that of the previous year by about 10% or more, and five years during which progress, by comparison with the preceding year, was on the contrary either slight or nil, the average rate of growth being about 6 or 7%.

There is no need, in the present context, to discuss the question of whether major fluctuations in the capitalist economies are now a thing of the past, and whether such fluctuations as may

---

[1] L. L. KLEIN, *The Keynesian Revolution*, p. 56, Macmillan, London, 1950.

occur in the future will, thanks to improved methods in economic planning and administration, be more readily controllable as
time goes on. It must, however, be admitted that so far, in economies of the Soviet type, no such general pattern of trade cycles
has been noticeable, despite the existence of numerous particular fluctuations.

One explanation which certain Western economists like to put
forward is that, in practice, the Soviet economy functions like
a war economy, in which, owing to the State's requirements, all
products are in short supply, and in which fluctuations of the
kind experienced by market economies cannot therefore develop.
Nevertheless, if a siege-economy of this type can turn into a durable régime and show evidence of growth not only in the means of
production but also in consumption—and this would seem to be
unquestionable—its nature is thereby transformed. It would
therefore be worth while examining the mechanism of its growth
or, in Marxist terms, its "expanded reproduction", by comparing
it with the growth mechanism of market economies.

The characteristic of all dynamic models which may be used to
describe an economy of the capitalist type is that they can give
rise only to unstable situations, in the sense that any divergence
in respect of the rate of progress required to ensure equilibrium is
cumulative. Thus, to take for example the model suggested by
R. F. Harrod,[2] if at a given moment the rate of growth is greater
than the equilibrium rate, the investment rate will not tend to go
down, which would re-establish the balance, but will on the contrary tend to rise, because of business confidence in continuing
growth; the result of this will be a boom, which is of necessity temporary, since the disequilibrium thus created must ultimately be
corrected. Two dangers thus threaten the economy. One of them
is that described by Keynes himself, where the interest rate determined by the liquidity preference is too high, thus engendering a
durable state of under-employment. The other is an inflationary
situation in a time of full employment, when investment tends to
exceed savings, thus bringing about pressure on prices, and an
artificial rate of growth which it will not be possible to maintain.

The measures recommended in this context, which are roughly
those employed in Western countries, are to attempt to maintain

[2] *Towards a Dynamic Economy*, London, Macmillan, 1949, particularly
pp. 71–2.

equilibrium, rather than to force the rate of progress, since any such efforts would probably be doomed to failure. However, the effort to achieve equilibrium may involve emphasis on some independent factor or variable, as a result of which not only will equilibrium be re-established, but it may also be possible to speed up the rate of growth. This, for example, is the sense in which French indicative planning can be said to have influenced the expansion of the economy, by encouraging a rising growth rate on which business expectations were based.

In socialist or planned economies, the situation appears to be different from the one we have been describing in that savings and investment decisions and long-term business expectations come into play simultaneously, and cannot in practice be differentiated one from the other. The rate of accumulation, which it is one of the first tasks of the Soviet government and planning authorities to determine, and which seems to remain at a fairly stable level over a long period, can therefore be fixed at the desired level without risk of affecting any economic balance which by definition must be reached—or at least is always susceptible of being reached provided the correct physical and financial balances have been observed in the plan—without interference from these "series of fluctuations due to the propensity of a private enterprise economy to exaggerate its response, either way, to the chances and changes of history".[3]

It is not suggested that the financing of investments and the maintenance of economic equilibrium in a planned economy present no problems, or are always achieved. But in terms of theory they are remarkably simple, the adjustment of disposable incomes and of production of consumer goods to one another appearing almost as the basic point of departure.

It would appear that even this—which is far from being always attained in practice—is not an essential prerequisite. Indeed it is interesting to learn that there exist, in the book-keeping of Soviet banks, two completely separate kinds of accounts. The first of these relates to the payment of wages or to savings bank deposits; they alone represent monetary circulation and can give rise to cash payments. On the credit side, these are the deposits

[3] J. ROBINSON, *The Rate of Interest and Other Essays*, Conclusion, p. 142, London, Macmillan, 1952.

made by trading enterprises, which have sold goods to individuals; on the debit side, the disbursements consist of sums made available by banks to enterprises for the payment of wages. The second kind of accounts are utilized by enterprises to buy goods; they too are decided in advance in the financial plans; however, they cannot give rise to any circulation of money. This practice is not without its parallel in the West, as there exist in Italy commercial accounts which cannot lead to any circulation of money, but in the Soviet Union the distinction is more clear cut.

The advantage of this practice is that it facilitates the planning of individual expenditures, the maintenance of financial equilibrium and the struggle against inflation. One of the officials whom I met in Moscow, a specialist in public finance with considerable experience of Western economies, underlined this point. Any unplanned increase in the credits granted to enterprises would not be reflected by an increase in savings and in private consumption; the two circuits of production and consumption can be kept more or less separate, and a disparity in the one will have almost no repercussions on the other. As we know, this is a frequent occurrence in market economies were, by reason of reactions in the enterprise sector, which in turn have repercussions in the household sector, an excess of credits, even when completely covered from the point of view of banking technique, gives rise to one of the classic cases of inflation.

GROWTH MECHANISM: THE EFFECTS OF TECHNICAL PROGRESS

The foregoing observations on growth should be amplified somewhat, and in order to do this, it might be advisable to take one particular aspect of growth, which is itself of basic importance, and to examine its effect on the economy as a whole. The factor to be chosen for this purpose is technical progress and innovation, which economists nowadays agree is one of the prime movers of economic progress.

Technical progress is nowadays the determinant. The implementation of technical progress and the changes in market conditions which are caused thereby are the factors which encourage investment and promote expansion. Whether an entrepreneur is more inclined toward saving or toward consumption, whether or not he wishes to extend his business activities, changing technical conditions force him to almost constant and ever more rapid reorganization of his business, usually in the direction of expansion.

The normal and usual result of technical progress is to bring about a reduction in costs. The problem is to determine what repercussions the reduction in costs has on the economy as a whole. In this respect there seems to be a considerable divergence between the two economic systems.

The main difference seems to arise from the different methods by which investments are financed. In the Soviet economy, investment funds are provided for the enterprise free of charge, mainly out of the State budget, and do not figure either in the accounts of the enterprise or in calculations of costs. On the other hand, in countries whose economies are characterized by private ownership of the means of production, enterprises must themselves bear the cost of their investments. They must make provision for the paying off of past investments and for the payment of interest on loans, and must set aside profits to finance future investment; these considerations must therefore be taken into account in the fixing of selling prices.

In both systems there have, of course, been changes in practice over the past few years; but there is no reason to suppose that this major divergence between the two systems in the methods of financing investments is in any way likely to become less marked.

In the Soviet economy, an increasing proportion of investment is nowadays covered by enterprise "profits", which may be defined, as they are elsewhere, as being the difference between receipts and costs of production. According to the provisions of the budget, the resources of enterprises and economic organizations were supposed to cover about 31% of total investments in 1960, and nearly 40% in 1963; in respect of the industrial sector alone, the proportion was 42% for 1959 and 46% for 1960.[4] Not included in this total were unplanned investments which in 1959 reached

---

[4] E. ZALESKI, Le budget et la situation économique en URSS, Tables III and IV, *Statistiques et études financières*, Paris, 1960, and, *idem, The Soviet Budget and Finances in 1963*, occasional papers, The Thomas Jefferson Center for Studies in Political Economy, University of Virginia, 1964. Cf. also J. MARCZEWSKI, Le rôle du profit dans la planification de type soviétique, in *L'Economie soviétique en 1957*, Institut de Sociologie Solvay, Brussels, 1957,

a total of 17% of all investments, but were mainly concerned with private house building and the kolkhozy, only a very small fraction being related to industry.

In respect of large factories, however, the share of investment covered by enterprise funds appears to be noticeably smaller. According to the information given to me by the head of the planning section of the tractor factory at Kharkov, investments at the factory were financed at the rate of roughly two-thirds from non-repayable State funds, about 20% from enterprise funds and, for the rest, about 15% by short-term credits from Gosbank, repayable in two or three years, the interest rate being 2%. It is noted that in this instance profits were about 10%, or rather more than the norm (which is about 5% for factories of this type) but that the greater part of these profits was utilized not for financing productive investments but for the payment of bonuses and other social or cultural expenditures.

Not only are enterprise investments financed predominantly from budgetary allocations, but enterprise profits as such are rather different in the USSR from what is understood by the term in other countries. Normally, they in fact revert to the State, and only a certain proportion is retained by the enterprise. In any case, the enterprise is not free to dispose of this part of its profits as it thinks fit, but must obey the orders issued to it in this respect. In addition it must not be overlooked that the enterprise itself does not decide on its investments, either on the basis of its financial results, or on any other basis; such decisions are governed by the plan. If the enterprise's own resources are not sufficient to cover the investments planned, supplementary funds have to be allocated. Instances in which investments have had to be postponed, because enterprise profits did not reach the estimated figure and cases in which enterprises may receive interest-bearing loans in order to carry out unplanned investments, are of marginal interest only: in fact the finance law of 1961 limited the powers of directors of enterprises in respect of "unplanned" investments, and all sources of decentralized investments were reduced by half with effect from 1st January 1962[4a].

Conversely, a fairly large proportion of investment in western European countries is now, as we know, financed by or with the

[4a] Cf. E. ZALESKI, *op. cit.*; B. KERBLAY, *op. cit.*

help of the public authorities; this proportion may be nearly as much as a half, of total investments, though it is smaller in most of the industrial sectors. This is the case not only in France, but in several neighbouring countries as well. However, it is also known that these figures are the consequence of grouping together, with investments made by public authorities out of budgetary allocations, all kinds of other expenditures. Among the latter there may figure investments by nationalized enterprises, which, however, are generally subject to the same conditions as private enterprises and can only benefit from budgetary allocations in exceptional circumstances; and loans and subsidies made by the State or by public bodies to private enterprises, for the purpose of helping them to finance their investments, and sometimes granted on conditions which differ little from those obtaining in the market (these loans may, moreover, have their counterpart in loans raised on the capital market).

Having made these points clear, we must now return to our original question: How do the two different systems react to the reduction in costs which results from technical progress? In a planned economy, it is held that a reduction in costs should normally bring about a reduction in selling prices. In principle this is held to be true both in the case of producer goods and consumer goods.

In a paper written some years ago, the Polish economist Oskar Lange—who is peculiarly fortunate in having an expert knowledge both of the market economies and the planned economies—justified in the following way the policy of reducing the prices of consumer goods:

> All increases in productivity—whether arising during the process of manufacturing consumer goods or during the process of manufacturing producer goods—bring about a reduction in the cost of production of consumer goods. If prices of consumer goods are maintained at their former level, the profits of the producing enterprises go up, as does the proportion of the national income withdrawn from distribution to individuals. What is required is either an increase in the rate of accumulation and the provision of public services, and consequently a change in physical objectives, or—if these rates are to be maintained at their previous levels—an increase in the output of consumer goods. In the latter case, prices of consumer goods must be reduced so as to enable the public to buy the increased production.
>
> An alternative solution might be to increase money wages, thus enabling the workers to buy increased amounts of consumer goods at

> the old prices. However, in this case the only ones to benefit from the increase in productivity would be the workers in the nationalized sector . . . If the prices of consumer goods are reduced, the benefits of increased productivity are automatically extended in the same way to the workers and the peasants. For this reason, socialist countries follow a policy of systematically reducing the price of consumer goods with the gradual rise in productivity.[5]

One might add that the objective has never been to increase real income in exact proportion to the rise in productivity. An increase in consumption is always systematically slower in the USSR and other planned economies as compared with national income, so as to maintain and increase the rate of growth by expanding the "accumulation fund".

In practice, during the period from 1947 to 1954, there were numerous sizeable reductions in the prices of consumer goods in the USSR to something approaching pre-war price levels. However, since 1954 price reductions have been less marked, and have been nullified by movements in the opposite direction, so that on the whole the general level of prices has remained more or less unchanged for several years now. There was also, as we know, a large rise in prices in June 1962 for the majority of foodstuffs on the official market, which was accompanied by a similar movement on the kolkhoz market, and the small number of price reductions which were announced at the same time did little to offset this.

There were a number of reasons for this change in practice. In the first place, it was necessary to reorganize the wage scale by gradually raising the wages of the lowest paid workers, so as to correct what had for long been excessive wage differentials. In the same way the increase in the price of foodstuffs was explained by the need for increasing the very small return obtained by kolkhoz members from the sale of their produce to the State shops (without interfering with the taxes which are paid to the State in the process). In the case of producer goods, all price reductions were likewise halted, so that almost all production of producer goods is now profitable for the enterprises concerned (with a very small number of exceptions, notably in the case of coal-mining

[5] O. LANGE, Les fondements de la planification économique, *ISEA*, G, No. 2, January 1957.

during the past few years). Even a few years ago, this was not always the case, since many commodities were being sold below cost.

It could also be that the halting of the downward trend in prices is a temporary measure, brought about by the need for making the adjustments described above; indeed, it would appear that the intention still is to continue with the policy of seeking further reductions in prices.[6] In any case it will be noted that the "planned reduction of costs", which continues to figure as one of the obligations of enterprises, should in principle be easily achieved since, as we said before, investment funds are virtually free of charge to enterprises. Moreover, if there is a reduction in costs, it might seem more logical to take advantage of this by lowering selling prices accordingly, rather than raising wages.

In Western economies, the above reaction would not be feasible, since enterprises must themselves bear the cost of their investments. In practice, and especially since the end of the last war, it is only in exceptional cases that increases in productivity have been reflected by a reduction in prices to the consumer.

More often, there is a chain reaction which develops as follows: the increase in productivity resulting from the effects of previous investments, or of technical progress, is reflected not by a fall in selling prices but by a rise in enterprise profits and reserves. Enterprises in fact consider it essential to build up such reserves in order to allow for expansion and to provide for future investment. The wage-earners in their turn, since they are well aware of these increased profits, put pressure on the enterprises to be given a share in the benefits accruing from the increase in productivity, at a time when the employers are either not so well placed to resist their demands, or are less inclined to do so. The higher wages thus distributed bring about a general increase in consumption and push up prices.

However, expansion encourages both the consumers and the State to anticipate on the increase in their income, while the entrepreneurs anticipate increased demand by stepping up their investments, which they are able to do owing to boom conditions. This dual pressure accelerates the inflationary movement, which in the end threatens the stability of the currency, the budgetary

[6] See further on the section on prices, p. 241.

balance and the balance of payments. At a given moment, it becomes necessary to put a brake on this unhealthy expansion by means of monetary and financial restrictive measures. The cycle is thus complete.

Are enterprises in a capitalist economy not at a disadvantage in having to cover the cost of their investments? Obviously, in a market economy system, where capital depreciation and interest on loans figure in the calculation of selling prices, it is possible to express the total real cost of a given commodity to the community. The resulting allocation of the factors of production—leaving aside the problem of the level of interest—may come close to the optimum, in contrast with the situation in a planned economy, where reliable investment criteria so far appear to have been lacking. But the counterpart seems to be a certain instability and rigidity. In the first place, let us take the case of the most dynamic industries, where the elasticity of demand is greatest, and where productivity is liable to increase at the most rapid rate, because of the long production runs favoured by mass production. These industries also figure among those whose need for investment and fresh capital, including the floating funds made necessary by the increase in production and the organization of sales, is the greatest. The burden of these investments is such that it often has the effect of making it impossible for enterprises, owing to the threat to their finances, to reduce their prices as demand expands. This explains the slow growth or accident-proneness of new industries despite the existence of all the conditions which would favour rapid expansion.

In the less favoured industries, where demand is relatively inelastic, any additional production is liable, on the other hand, to bring about a fall in prices; or alternatively, since the introduction of modern equipment almost always leads to an increase in output, it may be necessary to scrap equipment before it is entirely obsolete, in order to keep output from rising too sharply. In either case, the gain in production is liable to be wholly absorbed by financial commitments, since total profit or the rate of profit are smaller than they were before.

Doubtless, in the classical economic models, this fall in profit dictates changes in the behaviour of producers, which restore output to a level at which prices and profits once more become adequate. But in practice various other factors may operate against mobility of the means of production, and thus may prevent or delay modernization.[7]

In general, the fact that enterprises are obliged to make provision for future expansion which may either develop slowly, or even not at all in the case of the less favoured industries, may lead to the building up of excessive reserves, or reserves which will simply be distributed among the directors; at the same time, other concerns which might be capable of expanding will be unable to do so for lack of the necessary resources.

In addition, in sectors where self-financed investments are the rule, as is often the case, investments tend to be of the "induced" type, in other words they are greatly dependent on the financial situation of enterprises, and therefore on the present state of the market. This is not necessarily the result of imperfect forecasting on the part of enterprises who have been over-influenced by short-term considerations; in practice lack of available capital frequently slows down the implementation of investment programmes. In consequence there is a tendency for economic fluctuations to be accentuated. It would appear that this tends to limit considerably the effectiveness of plans at national level, however rational these plans may be.[8]

Thus, the actual behaviour of enterprises in a market economy has to be related not only to an investment policy, but also to a theory of the firm.[9] This is a long way from the "theoretical" simplicity of the growth models in a planned economy which we discussed earlier on. In a market economy, the equilibrium achieved is precarious. It is known that, while preliminary work on the fourth French plan was in progress, consideration was given to three average annual rates of expansion of the gross national product (3%, 4·5% and 6%) but eventually it had to be admitted that internal and external equilibrium could not be maintained if the rate of 6% were adopted.

The points made above were intended to show that the planned, or "socialist" economy, enjoys an important advantage in the manner in which the mechanism of growth operates. However,

---

[7] See lecture by M. Denizet, of the economic and financial research section of the Ministry of Finance, Paris, 1957.

[8] P. Dieterlen, *Revue économique*, p. 962, November 1959.

[9] An allusion to the possibility of a divorce between these two approaches is made in P. Massé, *Le Choix des investissements*, p. 36 Dunod, Paris, 1959.

it must be noted that this is only one of the factors which can actually affect growth. Furthermore, it cannot be denied — and I shall not attempt to deny here — that methods of economic control based on the projection of national accounts and their various aggregates, which are increasingly used in non-socialist economies, now permit a reasonably close approach to the objective of achieving growth in equilibrium, and it can hardly be doubted that there will be further progress in this direction.

Furthermore, it must be added that despite the simplicity of the mechanism of a planned economy, in practice, so far as the Soviet economy is concerned, equilibrium is very rarely reached. Thus, as we have already amply demonstrated, the result of the priority accorded to certain sectors is that other sectors are more or less constantly sacrificed, and become subject to fairly serious fluctuations and disequilibria which may have repercussions from one sector to another. Moreover, it would appear that a proper balance between the incomes of the population and the supply of consumer goods is almost impossible to achieve. Because of the continuing lack of consumer goods, particularly foodstuffs which are available to the public, the Soviet Union has, during the past few decades, been subject to an almost constant inflationary situation due to excessive money payments, which the authorities have sought to counteract by measures which are sometimes completely arbitrary, such as the twenty-year moratorium on loans which was decreed in 1957. Moreover, a detailed study of Soviet economic growth reveals that it is less regular than might appear at first sight. Indeed it may well be that with the growth of the economy and the raising of levels of consumption these various disparities, far from being evened out, will tend to be aggravated and will affect the overall growth of the economy to an even more marked degree than has so far been the case.

It must also be added, in connection with the reform in the management of enterprises, that the trend may now be to put a stop to the practice of "free capital" for enterprises, which is so much the core of the above analysis. As shown in Chapter VII, proposals to this effect were made during the course of 1964.

We can now leave aside the question of growth mechanism, and turn once more to the immediate problem of the efficient utilization of resources. This problem may be examined under two distinct heads: firstly, the allocation of resources in current production, and secondly, the choice of investments.

The attitude of most Western economists, who follow the teachings of the nineteenth-century marginalist school in this respect, is that an optimum allocation of resources is achieved within the framework of free competition. And indeed, if the economist's criterion is satisfaction of the freely-expressed needs of the consumer, which, in aggregate and dynamic terms, is represented by the growth of the national income, then it can be demonstrated mathematically that the free activity of the various economic agencies through the interaction of demand, prices and profits, results in the best possible utilization of resources; for many economists, especially the present-day exponents of the "social rate of return" theory, the question is even one of definition.

In practice, although few Western economists, apart from the Marxists, have questioned the validity of the liberal "theorem", experience has led some of them to make a certain number of reservations about it; these may vary according to the individual viewpoint of the author in question, but some measure of agreement is gradually being reached.

The first of these reservations, and one which is made even by the most orthodox among the liberals, such as A. Marshall, is that the savings effected by the existence of large-scale units of production are such that it is possible to envisage a system of economic organization which would be more efficient than that obtaining under a system of free competition; none the less, there is a way out, which consists of seeking to widen the market to a continental or world scale, which today gives liberalism renewed opportunities. Another reservation of considerable significance relates to the fact that *laissez-faire* and free competition are not synonymous; *laissez-faire* in practice leads to imperfect or monopolistic competition, which has been the subject of much theorizing since 1933; it then becomes necessary to ensure the establishment or the re-establishment of the conditions and price relationships of competition, or if this is not wholly possible, to ensure at least that economic calculations are based on a situation equivalent to that to which free competition would have given rise.

The study of problems of industrial location[10] leads to still more reservations; the non-equivalence of *laissez-faire* and free competition, the lack of mobility of the various factors of production, and imperfect foresight, lead in practice to an imperfect utilization of regional resources, which gives rise in turn to government action. On a macro-economic level, the lack of foresight of the various economic units calls for a collective effort to provide economic intelligence and co-ordination; the French type of flexible planning is but one of the possible ways of doing this. Finally, it is sufficient merely to recall the problems of growth and the difficulty of maintaining equilibrium in a free enterprise economy, which we have already discussed.

It may be held that despite the foregoing reservations, which provide the justification for various kinds of State intervention, the principle of optimum allocation of resources within the fluid conditions of a perfectly competitive market remains valid. None the less, many Western economists, who themselves follow the mainstream of classical economic thought, have shown considerable interest in the theoretical possibilities of a planned collectivist economy. It is generally agreed that the first to follow this particular line of enquiry was the Italian economist E. Barone (*The Minister of Production in a Collectivist Economy*, 1908); the most notable of his successors have been L. von Mises (*Economic Calculation in a Socialist Community*, 1920), O. Lange and A. P. Lerner (*The Economics of Control*, 1946). Barone had predicted that a socialist economy "would be forced to re-instate all the old value categories". Von Mises observed that those in charge of a planned economy would find themselves faced with the problem of resolving an infinite number of simultaneous equations which, in a market economy system, were resolved automatically by the interaction of prices and competition; he had therefore no hesitation in affirming that a wholly planned economy was totally impracticable.

---

[10] See previously, Chapter VIII.

The trend of Western discussion on the conditions in which a planned economy might be operated may be summed up by saying that it "has underlined the fact that a rational allocation of resources in a socialist economy might be possible if the costs of the factors of production were experimentally fixed in such a way as to ensure that for all purposes demand may be equal to the available resources".[11]

Soviet economists have paid little attention to these conclusions; indeed they have in fact completely ignored them. Contrary to the theory advanced by von Mises, the Soviet economy is proof that a planned economy can work; but it can scarcely be denied that the results have been obtained at some cost or, in other words, that the Soviet economy still does not function efficiently. For some years now, Soviet economists themselves have been willing to admit their shortcomings in this respect. They have even recognized that, in contrast to the capitalist economy with its so-called "market" or "profit" law, the Soviet economy has no specific quantifiable law which governs its operation. Among the many comments on this point, we quote the following: "The principal economic law of socialism and the law of planned development were formulated in general terms, which did not include any sufficiently precise quantitative criterion for selecting those particular variants of plans and projects which would conform most closely to the laws in question." It should be noted that P. Mstislavski, from whom we quote, does not himself consider it in any way necessary to invoke the "law of value", as many of his colleagues tend to do at present, and maintains that, provided they are properly elaborated, an effort of which he himself is wholeheartedly in favour, the "laws" of socialism should be perfectly capable of providing the "regulator" which the economy needs; but his admission, following as it does on many others, that no such regulator yet exists, merely serves to underline the point.[12]

The lack of efficiency which we have been discussing has nothing to do with the difficulties of achieving correct balances and ensuring a proper allocation of supplies to the sectors where

[11] N. SPULBER, *The Soviet Economy, Structure, Principles, Problems*, p. 206, Norton, 1962.

[12] P. MSTISLAVSKI, Quantitative expression of economic relationships and mechanisms, *Vopr. Ekon.*, No. 2, 1961.

they are needed; all these problems we have already discussed at length in the earlier chapters of this book. Even if the mechanics of planning functioned correctly, and the plans were perfectly balanced and implemented, without any of the adjustments, shortages and muddle which are denounced even in the most official statements, the Soviet economy would probably still be inefficient, in the technical sense of the word. Indeed, in the absence of any good criterion by which results can be judged, there is nothing to guarantee that the allocation of products for particular uses, and the use of factors of production in a given proportion for producing a given output, are those which reflect optimal choice.

This lack of rationality in the Soviet economy may be observed both at micro-economic level (that of enterprises) and at macro-economic level, and both in relation to current resource allocation and to investment decisions. In the following paragraphs we shall try to demonstrate the point, while making due allowance for the considerable efforts which are at present being made in the USSR to correct this particular shortcoming.

THE INADEQUACIES OF ENTERPRISE ACCOUNTING

At micro-economic or enterprise level, there are two points to be made:

1. In the Soviet economy, choices about the factors of production to be used for a given product are based, not on the minimum cost of production for the enterprise, but on the provisions of the plan, which may be a very different matter.

2. When consideration is given to some cost factor, this is based, so far as the enterprise is concerned, on a very imperfect system of accounting and, at national economic level, on a price system which itself reflects very imperfectly the costs of production as they are calculated by enterprises.

So far as the first of these statements is concerned, little more need be said at this stage. As a consequence of the priority given to growth and to the achievement of the production targets laid down in the plans, insufficient attention is paid to costs of production. Our discussion of "success indicators" has shown what absurdities may arise not only in the choice of what is produced, but also in the way in which it is produced. This is laid down in detailed fashion in the production and supply plans, and enterprises are obliged to follow instructions, without being given the opportunity of finding out if there is any more efficient method of producing the same result. In consequence, as many Soviet economists have readily admitted, it becomes difficult to introduce new techniques, even when these would lead to a higher rate of return; enterprises which produce capital goods have no incentive to produce more efficient machinery, from which they themselves will reap no special benefit; and it may well be that the enterprises which use these capital goods are reluctant to go over to new techniques, and new types of equipment, which may require a fairly long period of adjustment and cause a temporary fall in output; in this connection certain measures have been proposed (for example, changes in the bonus system, the setting up of a fund for the adoption of new techniques).[13] Many Soviet novels, which perhaps provide the most vivid and penetrating glimpses of factory life, have taken as their theme the struggle between the conscientious and talented inventors or innovators, and a rigid system run by die-hards whose minds are befogged by plan indicators, and who are opposed to the adoption of new methods or techniques.[14]

However, while it is true to say that the question of costs of production is only of secondary importance in the USSR, it would be untrue to say that it receives no attention at all. Enterprise plans do in fact generally contain indicators relating to the lowering of consumption of raw materials per unit of output and the lowering of costs of production. Calculations of costs also figure in a great many economic and technical studies.

But we must take a look at the method by which these production costs are calculated. As is usually the case in the Soviet economy, there tends to be more emphasis on indices expressed in physical quantities, rather than in value. The reason for this is to be found not only in the primacy accorded to production engineers

[13] See L. M. GATOVSKI, *Communication au colloque franco-soviétique*, Paris, October 1960, and Problems of economic stimulation of technical progress, *Vopr. Ekon.*, No. 5, 1960.

[14] See, for example, DUDINTSEV, *Not by Bread Alone*, English translation, Hutchinson, London, 1957; D. GRANIN, *Les Chercheurs*, and G. NIKOLAYEVA, *L'ingénieur Bakhirev*, French translation, Les Editeurs français réunis.

in Soviet industry, in preference to economists or accountants, but also in the absence of proper criteria by which the various factors entering into production costs might be reliably weighed. I had an example of this during a visit which I paid to a large footwear factory in Leningrad. My guides had been at pains to point out that the leather used in the manufacture of the shoe uppers was an expensive raw material, which the staff were encouraged to use as economically as possible. In fact great care seemed to be taken in the cutting of the individual skins, which are never of a standard shape. But the care thus taken involved a considerable expenditure of time. In a market economy, a simple calculation of costs would no doubt have made it possible for the entrepreneur to determine whether it was more profitable for him to economize in raw materials or in labour. In the Soviet economy these two concepts still seem to exist on more or less separate planes.

Money accounting is also extensively utilized in enterprise administration. But as R. W. Campbell has pointed out, their calculations have serious shortcomings, which do not appear to be of the same order as those which may arise in Western systems of accounting. The main defects in accounting appear to be as follows: incorrect valuation of basic capital, and the fixing of excessively low rates of depreciation, even though the latter are a highly imperfect measure of capital consumption; very rudimentary cost calculations in respect of joint products, and in consequence a very arbitrary evaluation of the cost of each product; and inadequate breakdown of the various expenditures, so that it is not usually possible to calculate the cost of each phase of production.[15] In addition, as we know, no interest charge is as a rule included in the calculation of costs.

Each of these factors may give rise to faulty estimates of costs and in consequence to very faulty decisions. Thus the inadequacy of depreciation allowances has meant that the misleadingly low costs of production of oil, gas, or electric as against steam traction, which are often cited to justify the emphasis now being placed on fuels hitherto neglected in the USSR as against coal, in fact fail to reflect the profitability and real cost of these changes to

[15] R. W. CAMPBELL, Soviet accounting and economic decisions, *Value and Plan*, 1960.

the national economy. The inadequacy of cost estimates in the case of joint products implies that particularly scarce products are not those which are dearest to produce, given the structure of demand. This is so in the case of oil products, for which the price structure is similar to that of America, despite the fact that the demand for light oils is relatively very small in the USSR. Enterprise specialization and coordination, which were discussed in an earlier chapter, are difficult to organize, as neither profitability nor real cost for the enterprise are known with sufficient precision.[16]

It is of some interest to note the very different part played by depreciation in capitalist economies and in the Soviet economy. In the market system, the depreciation fund is at the disposal of the enterprise; it is therefore in the enterprise's interest that this fund should be as high as possible, so as to reduce the amount of profit on which tax is payable — except possibly in cases where they wish to borrow on the stock exchange. In the USSR, on the other hand, depreciation funds are held by the State, except for that part laid aside for major repairs. This being so, it is to the advantage of the enterprise to keep the depreciation fund low and profits high, since a part of these profits can be used for the direct benefit of staff and directors in the form of bonuses and social funds; but this does not encourage them to calculate exactly the amount of capital consumed.

Given the present state of the Soviet economy, an effort to improve accounting would probably have a limited effect only. The part played by accounting does in fact vary between the two systems. In a market economy, the indications provided by costs and financial results play a decisive role in determining resource allocation and enterprise policy. In a socialist economy these indications may assist the supervisory authorities to assess the efficiency of enterprise administration; but they play only an indirect part in decisions relating to the allocation of resources and to production policy if only because interest on fixed capital does not figure in calculations of costs. It is the plan which determines the direction of enterprise activity, in accordance with its

---

[16] *Ibid.;* see also R. W. CAMPBELL, Accounting for cost control in the Soviet Economy, *Review of Economics and Statistics*, February 1958, and *idem, Accounting in Soviet planning and management*, Harvard University Press, 1963.

own methods. Factors relating to accounting, costs, profitability, are mainly the concern of the central economic institutions, whose duty it is to provide certain general guiding lines which affect the plan, and thus eventually have a bearing on enterprise policy.

Naturally, the information reaching these economic organizations must of necessity be incomplete, and it takes some time before the effect of any changes which they deem advisable can be felt. This is probably the reason why top-level policy decisions intended to correct shortcomings in economic practice so often appear both drastic and long overdue. Things would be different if enterprises were free to decide for themselves within the context of general policy indications from above, how best to draw up their own plans. From time to time, proposals have been made along these lines, and were particularly in evidence at the time of the reforms introduced by the November 1962 plenum.[17] If by any chance a move in this direction were to be made — and this would mean a radical change in Soviet planning — it is obvious that accounting would have to play a much more important part. All the recent proposals which have been put forward tend to confirm this. For example, Academician Nemchinov suggested that, when submitting alternative growth plans to their superior authorities, enterprises should also submit calculations of their costs for the various products, and variations of their costs and total receipts covering the alternative assumptions.[17a]

In the event, it is clear that some attempt has been made in the USSR to bring accounting more into line with economic realities. This is reflected in the discussions which have been going on for some years now as to whether or not depreciation should include the so-called "moral desuetude" *(moralny iznos)* of capital, which is otherwise known as obsolescence. In the USSR this is a problem which primarily concerns the central organs whose duty it is to determine the norms for depreciation. As a result of the rapid advance in technique which has become evident in the USSR, as it has in other countries, and above all because of the need which the Soviet Union now feels to expand productivity in view of technological advances, there is a tendency to scrap equipment before it is entirely worn out; but as

[17] See, for example, the article by BERMAN, director of a machine-tool factory in Moscow, in *Pravda*, 30th November 1962.
[17a] V. NEMCHINOV, *Kommunist*, No. 5, 1964.

we know, investments made in the USSR were for a long time in fact "extensive" in character, that is they were concentrated much more on extension of existing capacity, than on renewals, and equipment was frequently retained to the full limit of its life.

Another problem therefore arises, one which was to some extent already reflected in a remark made by N. S. Khrushchev during a visit to a factory in Pittsburgh in 1959: "These are very old machines! I thought you capitalists spent your time scrapping practically new machines!" Nowadays it seems to be accepted that, alongside ordinary depreciation, in the sense of the wearing out of equipment, which was formerly the only factor taken into account in official norms, allowance must also be made for technical depreciation, so that out-of-date equipment can be replaced more speedily. This particular concept is freely recognized as having been borrowed from the market economies.[18]

THE PROBLEM OF VALUE AND PRICES

Even assuming that enterprise accounting functioned efficiently, and that the information thus provided were properly used so as to assist in determining not only the policy of the individual enterprise but also the course of general economic policy, there would still be a major obstacle to the achievement of a state of optimal resource utilization in the Soviet economy. In fact there would have to be in the USSR a price system which would reflect accurately the degree of scarcity and the actual cost of production of the various commodities, and so far this is still lacking.

This is a point which is unfailingly made by all Western economists who study the Soviet economy. Thus, according to the French economists' mission, there are two factors which make it unlikely that the problem of optimum resource allocation can be solved under the present Soviet planning system: in the first place, there is the clumsiness of present planning methods, which makes it impossible to study effectively more than a few growth

[18] See discussion on this subject in Chapter III. Cf. A. EFIMOV, New principles relating to capital depreciation, *Vopr. Ekon*, No. 9, 1959; cf. also A. BUZAN, How depreciation is defined under socialism, *Vestnik Statistiki*, No. 10, 1959.

hypotheses, or even possibly more than one; and in the second place, there is the mechanism of price fixing, which is not such as to ensure that a given price is an accurate reflection of the burden falling on the community during the planning period.[19]

Before looking at the way in which prices are fixed in the USSR, we may wish to ascertain what their usefulness is in an economy which is more or less wholly planned. This question has already been touched upon in connection with the use of the concepts of money and marketing; some further indications are now required, particularly in respect of consumer goods.

One of the officials whom I interviewed in 1961 put the matter very clearly when he said that, in market economies, both supply and demand are elastic in relation to prices, whereas in a planned economy, there is elasticity of demand only; supply, which is determined beforehand by the planning organs, has no elasticity in relation to prices. In these conditions the main purpose of price manipulations can only be to ensure a normal turnover of goods which have already been produced.

In fact it will be seen that the price of certain goods which are in short supply (such as motor-cars, for example) remains fairly high. Conversely, in the case of articles such as aluminium or light metalware, for which there is now very little demand since better quality articles are now available to the public, prices were considerably reduced some time ago, though not, it appears, sufficiently so to ensure a demand for these articles.

In the Soviet economy, it would appear that consumer demand plays no part in influencing production policy, except insofar as it is taken into account by the planners when fixing their "consumption norms". Nevertheless, there is and there always has been in the USSR a channel through which consumer reactions can to a certain extent make themselves felt; this is provided by the press, and by meetings of trade unions, the Party, local soviets and various other organizations, where observations, suggestions and criticisms from the consumers about the availability and quality of goods and services can always find expression. Some importance must be attached to this channel although, as there is every reason to suppose, the remarks and criticisms which are made are not entirely spontaneous and are mainly inspired

[19] *ISEA*, G, No. 7, p. 67, 1959.

from above, with the aim of encouraging the lower echelons to criticize the intermediate echelons.

During recent years, as the amount and quality of goods available to the public has gradually improved, trade organizations have not been slow to learn of the existence of unsold stocks or consumer complaints, and this information nowadays finds its way back to the producers fairly rapidly. For some years now, it has become the custom to hold an annual conference of sales agents in the major factories engaged in producing consumer goods, at the time when the new season's models are being chosen. There is a whole organization, which we can only mention briefly here, for the very short-term planning (45 days) of retail trade, which enables information to be exchanged between sellers and producers and vice versa.[19a]

In respect of goods other than consumer goods, the main role of prices is, as we have seen, to provide a means of supervision, and a means of assessing the efficiency of enterprise management, rather than to influence decisions about what should be produced or how it should be produced. However, in practice prices do provide some guidance on this point, both at enterprise level and at the level of the economy as a whole.[20]

The discussions which have been going on in recent years have thrown some light on the function which prices are expected to fulfil. It was thought that prices should be fixed in such a way as to enable enterprises to cover their expenses and to make what was held to be a "normal" profit; similarly, the State which levies a turnover tax and takes its share of the profits should have available the revenue which it needs. Prices should now also facilitate the application of modern methods of calculating the rate of return, and of solving planning problems.

> Prices which have a sound economic basis are essential in the organization of planning, in determining the effectiveness of economic measures, and in applying the principle of material incentive in a coherent manner.
>
> The result of the present price-fixing mechanism is that prices do not reflect real changes in the expenditure of socially necessary labour, and it

[19a] On this question see also Postscript.

[20] See G. GROSSMAN, Industrial prices in the USSR, *American Economic Review*, May 1959; A. NOVE, *The Soviet Economy, an Introduction*, ch. IV, Allen & Unwin, London, 1961.

is consequently impossible to introduce cost accounting, and economic administrations have no incentive to make effective use of working or fixed capital.[21]

In what way precisely were Soviet prices defective? What can be said about prices for this or that product? In fact there are almost as many answers as there are products. The various comparisons made by foreign economists or technicians between prices noted in the USSR and other countries have revealed variations in the rates of exchange which may be as much as one to six, or even more. However, broadly speaking, it would appear that some years ago, Soviet prices were, and still are at present, under-valued in the case of producer goods, and over-valued in the case of consumer goods. It would seem that Soviet economists themselves had come to more or less the same conclusion, judging at least from a discussion which went on during 1957–8 in the pages of the reviews *Voprosy Ekonomiki* and *Planovoe Khozyaistvo*, and which ended by saying "the general level of prices for producer goods is lower than their total value, and that of consumer goods is more or less equal to total value;" certain of those who took part in the discussion had, however, maintained that prices for consumer goods were higher than their value, and that prices for producer goods were either lower or on a par with their value.[22]

Discussions on price reforms which have been going on during recent years have been dominated by the question of whether the "law of value" did hold in a socialist economy. What in fact is the point at issue? The debate has been summed up by saying that the discussion on the law of value had a bearing on "the importance of economic laws in general in relation to decisions based on political considerations".[23] In fact if one keeps within the strict terms of Marxist analysis, the conclusion must be that in a socialist society which has reached a state of freedom with regard to social necessities, there can be no room for "commodities" or for objective economic laws. In his famous publication entitled *Economic Problems of Socialism*, Stalin himself had already

[21] S. PERVUSHIN, The law of value and prices in a socialist economy, *Plan. Khoz.*, No. 7, 1961.

[22] A. SMIRNOV, How to allow for differences between price and value in making the balance of the national economy, *Vestnik Statistiki*, No. 10, 1959.

[23] A. NOVE, *The Soviet Economy*, p. 268.

moved some way away from this doctrine, although still maintaining that in the State sector there was no "commodity production" and that the only role assigned to prices was one of supervision and convenience.

Since then, the great majority of Soviet economists have retreated from the earlier position, and admitted that the "law of value" has an undeniable place in a socialist economy.[24] But the theoretical and practical problems of price-fixing still remain unsolved. As S. Pervushin has said, "no satisfactory solution has yet been found to the problem of the application of the law of value and of the categories of value in a socialist economy. Certain economists and philosophers have not yet discarded the metaphysical approach in their interpretation of the law of value."[25] By law of value, we must understand the Marxist law — in which Marx himself followed the theories of Ricardo — according to which the basis of value is the amount of human labour involved, exclusive of any payment for capital or any profit to the entrepreneur (the famous "surplus value"). However, prices based on labour-value are in practice too low to be practicable, for in a socialist economy as well as a capitalist economy, funds must be accumulated in order to finance further development.

In practice, although agreement seems to have been reached nowadays on the need for applying the law of value and fixing prices which will correspond as closely as possible to costs, as these are determined by the accounts of an average enterprise, there is still some controversy about methods of implementing this principle. In fact some divergence between prices and value must be accepted if only in order to facilitate accumulation (saving) since an increasing proportion is at present retained by enterprises for re-investment, while the rest is taken by the State.

Would it be better, as Strumilin has suggested, for the divergence between prices and value to be the same in all sectors, and for profits to be directly proportionate to expenditure of labour—a step which could be accompanied by a reform in the system of taxation by increasing taxes on profits as opposed to the present turnover tax? Or would it be more practicable for profit norms to be calculated as a fixed proportion of the capital invested,

---

[24] On this question, see earlier, Chapter III, The "Laws" of Socialism.
[25] *Op. cit.*

a suggestion which has been put forward by certain economists who are less concerned with the optimal solution implicit in
the first of these proposals, and rather more anxious about reactions from directors of enterprises, for whom a fairer opportunity
for profit-making will provide an incentive to good management?
Or again, might it be better to provide for accumulation almost
entirely out of State funds, in order to avoid having to raise prices of commodities in sectors where investment is heavy, and to
leave enterprises with only a fairly small, fixed proportion of these
funds? The latter solution, which is very little different from the
situation actually existing some years ago, was one put forward
by several of the officials whom I met.

But none of the solutions thus outlined takes proper account of
the degree of scarcity of the various goods and the services which
they may effectively provide. However, according to V. Novozhilov, the mathematical economist, this is a prime necessity;
prices must be fixed in such a way as to facilitate economic calculation, so that the effort to minimize enterprise costs will lead
to a minimization of costs for the entire economy. This principle
would apply, for example, to prices of new types of machinery
which are highly productive but still in short supply, and conversely to prices of machinery which is already obsolete.[26] However, it is not at all certain that these theories, which have aroused strong criticism,[27] are likely to be put into practice, although
Academician Nemchinov did make an effort to reconcile the
various hypotheses.

The above discussion, which has taken up a considerable
amount of space in the pages of Soviet journals in recent years,
and which we have only briefly summarized,[28] is probably of not
much practical importance. Even now, there may still be considerable variation between selling prices and costs, and rates of
profit seem to vary considerably from product to product, which

[26] See the article in reply by V. Novozhilov, Calculating expenditure in a
socialist economy, *Vopr. Ekon.*, No. 2, 1961.

[27] See A. Boyarski, "On the use of mathematics in economics," in the
same issue of *Vopr. Ekon.*

[28] For a fuller account, see particularly R. Bordaz, *La nouvelle économie
soviétique*, pp. 190–217, Grasset, 1960; A. Zauberman, The Soviet debate
on the law of value and price formation, in *Value and Plan, op. cit.;* A. Nove,
op. cit.

limits the practical significance of theoretical exercises on the determination of profit norms.

Nevertheless, it seems clear that during recent years prices have tended to come more into line with costs, although this is due more to the lowering of costs (which is said to average about 1–3% per annum) than to adjustments in selling prices. It is stated that under the present price structure, all branches of heavy industry, with the single exception of the mining industry, are able to show a profit.

However, it is certain that a further adjustment in prices will be required, most probably taking the form of an overall adjustment; this had even been envisaged for 1962. According to an authority such as L. M. Gatovski, the editor of *Voprosy Ekonomiki*, when I spoke with him, it was possible that widespread reductions in the prices of consumer goods, similar to those current up till about 1954, would again take place in the coming years. This would be one method, perhaps not the only one or the most important one but nevertheless a useful one, of bringing some of the benefits of increased productivity to the public, and also a means of keeping up pressure on enterprises by reminding them that their costs must be brought down; in years gone by, it was argued that this policy could not be followed while there was still a primary need for adjusting prices, first of all, so that all enterprises would be in a position to make profits, and, later, for adjusting wages. From all sources there is continuing evidence and continuing criticism of the imperfections of the price system.[28a] During the year 1964, an important reform in prices was again announced, which was due to come into force at the end of the year.

CALCULATIONS OF RATE OF RETURN AND INVESTMENT CHOICES

Both from the point of view of the distribution of the production effort among the various industrial sectors, and of the choice of the best projects within a given sector, the calculations on which economic decisions are based seem to have been long neglected in the USSR. It is not suggested that projects were

[28a] Cf. S. STOLYAROY and Z. SMIRNOVA, The analysis of price structure, *Vestnik Statistiki*, No. 1, 1963.

decided upon without method, but the decisions which were taken when, for example, a choice had to be made between two projects, or two alternative versions of the same project, were often, it seems, based on essentially technical criteria. In building blast-furnaces, for instance, the important considerations seem to be the ratio of coke consumption, the annual output of pig-iron per cubic metre of the effective volume of the blast-furnace, or again the volume of transport required per unit of production, and the requirements in manpower.

Economic considerations were not entirely absent, but since the main objective was that of achieving the maximum rate of growth, and since capital was in short supply, the Soviet authorities were forced to concentrate on obtaining the greatest possible increase in productive capacity with the minimum of investment. Since at the same time an effort was being made to introduce advanced techniques, this could mean, in practical terms, that investment in the principal production processes, for example, was encouraged at the expense of investment in subsidiary processes (for example, materials handling), even if production costs increased as a result, so that production could be expanded as much as possible with available capital resources.

In the past few years, the disadvantages of this approach have become clear, and a great effort has been made to determine and to introduce economic co-efficients by which economic efficiency may be assessed. As one of the delegates to the XXIst Congress of the CPSU (February 1959) remarked: "We make great efforts to produce the greatest possible amount of steel per square meter of a Siemens Martin furnace. Why should we not make the same effort to derive the maximum profit from every rouble invested?"[29]

[29] CHERNYAVSKI, An attempt at defining investment efficiency in the steel industry, *Vopr. Ekon.*, No. 7, 1957; see also the work of the conference at Moscow in June 1958 on Determination of the economic efficiency of investment in new techniques in the national economy of the USSR, *Vopr. Ekon.* No. 9, 1958, French translation published in "Critères des choix de l'investissement en URSS", *ISEA*, G, No. 6; articles by A. EFIMOV and V. KRASOVSKI, "On the planning of indicators of the economic effectiveness of investments in the national economy of the USSR", and by T. KHACHATUROV, Methodology of the determination of the economic effectiveness of investments, *Plan. Khoz.*, No. 8, 1959; the handbook *Model Method for Determining Effectiveness in the Introduction of Equipment* (ed. T. KHACHATUROV), Institute of Economics of the Academy of Sciences, 1960; B. SMEKHOV, Calculating investment efficiency, *Plan. Khoz.*, No. 5, 1961.

Nevertheless, it seems unlikely that these efforts will lead to the formulation of a single, relatively simple criterion which would correspond to the calculations for rate of return on investments as used in Western countries; however, the foregoing observation does not take into account the fact that, in practice, several methods of calculation are used in the West, for example the total discounted cash flow—bénéfice total actualisé—or the total or marginal rate of return, to take only the most developed ones, to say nothing of the considerable influence of interest rates or the various other working hypotheses employed.[30] All this was freely admitted by the various experts whom I interviewed in 1961, such as T. Khachaturov, corresponding member of the Academy of Sciences, and head of the "Investment efficiency" division of the Institute of Economics, and several of his colleagues; some of them went so far as to say that in the West the basic assumption of profitability was "automatic", which was perhaps going a bit far.

In the USSR it appears essential, in any case, that a series of different criteria should be employed, and that a choice should be made among the different results yielded by these criteria, when decisions have to be made about different projects, or about variants of the same project. Nor is it only the inadequacy of the assumptions on which these calculations are based which makes this advisable, as is sometimes the case in other countries.

Nevertheless, it would seem that at present there is a certain uniformity in the concepts used, and some broad agreement at least on the relative importance to be attached to the various possible criteria. I shall note briefly as they were given to me during my interviews[31] some of the criteria or indices which may be used in comparing two or more variants of the same project:

Cost, this being equal to the cost of production divided by total production. Costs of production include current expenditure (wages and raw materials), depreciation (physical depreciation of capital), but not interest on loans;

Labour productivity;
Total investment per unit of production;
Investment recoupment period.

[30] Cf. P. MASSÉ, *op. cit.,* Chapter I.
[31] Particularly by P. Mstislavski, whom I should like to thank for his patience and kindness.

The latter assumes that one is comparing a given project with a variant which will give the same output, and require less investment, while resulting in a higher cost of production. If we take I as total investment and C as cost, in a comparison between solution 1 and solution 4, the recoupment period is as follows:

$$\frac{I_1 - I_4}{C_4 - C_1}.$$

The result of this calculation is expressed in *years*. The converse of the investment recoupment period is sometimes described as the investment efficiency co-efficient;

Investment recoupment period, allowing for additional expenditure governed by the length of the period of construction.

This is an attempt to make allowance for variations in the length of time involved in construction, given the various alternatives, by adding to the investment cost interest for each of the years of the construction period. In these calculations, a rate of 6% is usual.

Mention is sometimes made of other criteria, such as the relation of profit to investments, or various physical coefficients relating to productivity or economy in the use of raw materials.

The latest trend seems to be to judge investments as far as possible as a whole, rather than in isolation, taking into account all the ancillary investments (for example, a mine and the railway which serves it).

Reference to these various criteria can sometimes lead to conflicting results. It would appear that there can be considerable variation, in each individual case, in the degree of importance attached to one or the other. However, it seems that particular attention is paid to the total amount of investment per unit of output, firstly because of the need for fulfilling plan objectives, and secondly because of the scarcity of available capital. Another important criterion is labour productivity, and it appears that this is playing an increasing role.

Just as in other countries, and perhaps even more so, the decisions which are made must not be the result of applying one single criterion, or a definite set of criteria. There are a great number of other factors, most of which may not be expressed mathematically, which must also be taken into account, and this leaves a fair amount of responsibility to the departments involved. In any case the economists and technicians concerned seem to be in no way reluctant to recommend the simultaneous use of several methods of economic calculation, even if these sometimes lead to contradictory results.

The use of these different criteria raises a great number of statistical problems, such as deciding, for example, what should be included in estimates of production or investments. The main problem, however, relates to value and prices. Economic calculations, apart from those expressed in purely physical terms, can in fact have no more significance than the commodity prices on which they are based, and, as we have already pointed out, Soviet prices present serious shortcomings.

It will be noted that the criteria which we have been discussing are in no way aimed at determining whether or not a given investment should be made, or whether productive capacity in a given sector should be increased. This question is assumed to have been settled earlier on within the framework of planning proper. When the question of the efficiency of investment arises, the problem is solely one of choosing between two or more alternatives, either of which will in any case ensure the achievement of predetermined production objectives; if the productive capacity of different projects is not the same, they will be reduced to a common denominator, by comparing, for instance, three production units with a productive capacity of 100 with one unit with a capacity of 300.

However, some authors hold that these criteria, particularly the "investment recoupment period", should sometimes be employed for purposes of comparison of intersectoral choices. For this purpose, it is necessary to fix "normative" periods which must not be exceeded. But it soon becomes apparent that the heavy industries, which we would describe as being highly capital intensive, have recoupment periods which are much longer than those in other industries; however, this is hardly an argument for penalizing the latter. Nevertheless, it has been laid down in principle that normative recoupment periods per industrial sector should not exceed from three to seven years.

It will be seen that the criteria described above take no account of interest on capital, except in the one instance quoted, in connection with the allowance made for variations in the length of construction periods. However, mention is frequently made of the need to take the "time" factor into account, and the question arises of deciding whether this relates solely to the length of time spent in construction, or whether in fact it also includes the burden of additional investment, although this is not expressly stated. On the occasion of the opening of the hydroelectric power-station at Kuibyshev, on the Volga, N. S. Khrushchev used the following argument to justify the priority which was to be accorded in the future to thermal power-stations, although their "cost of production"—that is, current cost of production—was several times higher than that of hydroelectric power-stations:[31a]

> The relatively higher cost per kilowatt-hour in thermal power-stations will be more than offset by the increased labour productivity in all sectors of the national economy arising from maximum use of electricity. As a result, far from incurring losses, we will in fact reap important economic advantages from the speed-up in the building of thermal power stations.

At all events, the increased attention paid to economic accounting has already had an appreciable effect on general economic policy. It has resulted in an increase in "productivity" investments as opposed to the "extensive" type of investment which had previously been favoured, and has been partly responsible for the changes in investment patterns which have developed during the past few years, and which we have already mentioned (for example, the priority given to development of production of oil and gas as opposed to coal, the changeover to electric and diesel engines on the railways, the relative priority given to the construction of thermal rather than hydroelectric power-stations, etc.). However, as we have already indicated, the results of these policies are still affected by weaknesses in the price and accounting systems, as well as by the imperfections inherent in the economic criteria employed.

The officials with whom I discussed this matter had in fact freely admitted that in their opinion certain grave mistakes in investment choices had been made in previous years. Particularly in the field of transport, it appeared that there had been consistent over-estimation of the potentialities of water transport,

[31a] Quoted by B. SMEKHOV, *op. cit.*

and under-estimation of those of rail transport.[32] The building of the Volga—Don Canal, which was completed in 1952, was instanced as one such error.

THE USE OF MATHEMATICAL METHODS AND THE SEARCH FOR OPTIMIZATION

As we know, a certain amount of discussion has gone on between Western economists and their Soviet colleagues concerning the use of mathematical methods in economics. This is a field which was almost entirely neglected for a long time in the Soviet Union. The reason for this lay in Soviet distrust of the marginalists and of the work on economic equilibrium which serves as a basis for econometrics—described as "merely another form of bourgeois apologetics"[33]—and also in the lack of interest taken during the Stalin period in anything other than production measured in purely physical terms, and possibly also in the intellectual backwardness which characterized this period.

In more recent times, however, there has been a gradual change which has become apparent, for example, in the articles appearing on this subject. Hand in hand with the considerable effort which was made to institute research on this question, there was also an effort, which is not without precedent in other contexts, to russify, or sovietize, as it were, this new branch of economic science. It happens that Professor Leontief, who now works at Harvard, and who perfected the *input–output* model which bears his name, had published in the USSR in 1925, while he was a student at Berlin University and still a Soviet citizen, an article on the balance of the national economy of the USSR for 1923–4 (this balance was, as we know, subsequently discontinued until 1950). The Soviet authorities were not slow to point out that the basis

[32] H. HUNTER, *Transport in the USSR*, Harvard University Press, 1957, observes that although the overall objectives of the fifth plan (1951–5) were more or less fulfilled, the estimated increase in water transport, which it was expected would expand much more rapidly than rail transport, did in fact fall far short of the objective, while the increase in rail traffic greatly exceeded plan estimates; this experience seems to have been repeated subsequently.

[33] A. BOYARSKI, On econometrics and the use of mathematics in economic analysis, *Plan. Khoz.*, No. 7, 1959.

for the new method already existed in this early balance.[34] Similarly, it was claimed that the American, G. B. Dantzig, who is generally credited with being the originator of linear programming (1940) was in fact forestalled in this work by Professor Kantorovich of Leningrad, one of the outstanding present-day mathematicians, who had published work of a similar nature in 1939. It might be possible to take these claims more seriously, were it not that the Soviet authorities only became aware of the possibilities of this particular technique after they had been demonstrated by the West. Although I only touched very briefly on these matters during my stay in Moscow, I did nevertheless hear this point of view expressed.

No doubt with a view to naturalizing these new methods and giving them the official imprimatur, "certain comrades," to quote Academician Nemchinov's own words, proposed that they should substitute for econometrics the rather more respectable term "planometrics".

The prospect of a considerable increase in the use of econometrics in the administration of the Soviet economy is one of the possibilities which has excited most interest and curiosity among Western economists and scientists. For one thing, it is impossible not to be struck by the Russian flair and aptitude for mathematics; according to one of our leading technicians, the USSR is one of the world's two great breeding grounds for mathematicians (the other, apparently, being France — or so at least the scientist in question confidently affirmed). Nor can one fail to be impressed by the vast opportunities afforded for the widest possible use of these methods in a planned and centralized economy. What then is the situation at present?

Before attempting a report on what is so far known about this subject, it would be well to bear in mind what seems to be a particularly Soviet approach to important questions, in other words their extreme discretion about what they have not yet succeeded in accomplishing. It may well be that no information has been forthcoming, or will in fact be forthcoming for some time yet about the promising lines of research which are being followed up in the Soviet Union, until such times as a justifiable claim may

---

[34] The point of view of the individual mainly concerned is summed up in the article by W. LEONTIEF (written after a visit to the USSR), The decline and rise of Soviet Economic Science, *Foreign Affairs*, January 1960.

be made that in this, as in other fields, the Soviet Union is on a technical par with the most advanced countries in the world.

Whatever the facts may be, such evidence as there is would appear to indicate that in this respect Soviet achievements are still behind those of certain other countries. None the less, although the research which is at present being carried out and the results so far published would appear to be relatively unimpressive, there is every indication that a great effort is being made in this field at present, and that this is characterized by many of the qualities and distinguishing features which are generally attributed to important Soviet activities, such as concentration of resources and an abundance of facilities, with the accent essentially on the long-term aspect.

The steps which are at present being taken to develop the use of mathematical methods include, among others, the training of personnel, the setting up of specialist institutes, the building of computers and the elaboration of models. Centres in which the use of economic models is studied, and on which information is available, include the Institute for the study of computer methods, the Gosplan econometric centre, the computing laboratory of the Institute of Economics of the Academy of Sciences, the Siberian section of the Academy of Sciences at Novosibirsk, and possibly certain other organizations, such as the laboratory run by V. Novozhilov.

The first question which comes to mind is whether there already exist mathematical models which can be used in determining major plan options, and the levels which must be reached by the principal variables. On this point, Academician Nemchinov gave a purely negative reply in 1960–1: "The majority of the optimal programming methods at present in use in the USSR are only designed for use in solving programming problems at enterprise level. Mathematical methods appropriate to the needs of national economic planning have not yet been worked out."[35] During the interviews which he was kind enough to grant me in 1961, he also expressed the view that planning, which is described as a work of intellectual synthesis, a "social engineering project", so to speak, would never be entirely a job for machines. However, it

[35] V. NEMCHINOV, The use of mathematical methods in economic research and planning, *Vopr. Ekon.*, No. 6, 1960.

should be possible to make use of mathematical calculations in determining the implications of decisions which have been made and in working out alternatives, which would considerably simplify the problem of choices. At all events, it would seem that considerable scope for developments of this kind is to be found in the drawing up of the material balances for the annual plan; as we know, this has from time to time been suggested but, so far as is known, no steps have as yet been taken to implement any such proposals.[36]

Most of the research examples quoted to me by the three or four officials with whom I discussed these questions related in fact to micro-economic or individual problems, as is also the case in Western economies. For instance, I was told about a calculation for the reduction to a minimum of transport of building materials between the factories which produced them and the construction sites in and around Moscow, by means of a linear programme which was prepared every week; they also mentioned the distribution of various kinds of steel manufactures, and of coal and cement from producer to user, and the determination of the size of sheet steel in relation to the needs of the factories using it and the requirements of the factories producing it, with a view to economizing metal. Other exercises were being undertaken on river transport, or on the allocation of work among different factories in the case of complex manufactures. Some of these studies, such as the one relating to the distribution of sheet steel, were said to involve all seventeen major economic regions. Some information has been published on certain of these studies,[37] although little more detail is available than what we have given above; another article also indicated that Gosplan of the republic of Byelorussia, in collaboration with the local scientific insti-

---

[36] The report of the general assembly of the Academy of Sciences of the USSR contains the following observations: "The general assembly expected great things of teachers and specialists in the social sciences. The economists were subjected to violent criticism. Although they have studied a great many economic problems, the main body of research in this field still falls far short of the needs of economic reality. In particular, progress on the application of electronic computing techniques to economic problems has been very slow." (6th February 1962.)

[37] A. I. Katsenelinboigen, The use of mathematical methods in economic research, *Vestnik Akademii Nauk*, No. 9, 1961.

tutes, was working on an optimum transport plan for a certain number of commodities.[38]

Attention is also being given to the construction of models based on tables of inter-industry relations, or input–output tables—sometimes called chessboard tables in the USSR. The statistical yearbook for 1960[39] gives part of a very interesting inter-industry balance (or square table) in 73 sections covering materials production for the year 1959. According to the introductory articles by M. Eidelman, the figures published are only the first quarter of the complete table which is divided into 83 sectors.[40] The material so far published provides the basis for an interesting reconstruction of the "overall social product" of the USSR and its constituent parts which has been undertaken by Philippe Robert.[41] But there is little to indicate exactly what use is made of these exercises in the USSR itself.

Work has also been begun on regional development models. Judging from the information kindly furnished by Academician Nemchinov, these studies mainly relate to the small regions, for example, the republic of Moldavia, the autonomous republic of Karelia, the autonomous Tatar republic (Kazan), and the oblast of Kaliningrad (formerly Koenigsberg). These models are based on a division among 70 export commodities and 30 to 40 import commodities, the rest of the USSR being divided into 16 regions (in the case of the Moldavian model). However, a similar type of study is apparently also being made for the 17 large economic regions of the USSR.

It is said that, unlike the studies of this kind which are carried out in the United States and in western Europe, in which a great deal of the information contained in the tables is the result of sampling or interpolation, the national or regional tables drawn up in the USSR are based on precise economic accounting.[42] However, I should add that, as I understood it, some of the data

---

[38] MALININ, POLONSKI and GIZENSTAT, Problems of the use of mathematical methods and electronic computers in planning, *Vopr. Ekon.*, No. 9, 1961.

[39] *Nar. Khoz.*, pp. 104–144, 1960.

[40] *Vestnik Statistiki*, No. 7, 1961, and *Vopr. Ekon.*, No. 10, 1961.

[41] P. ROBERT, Essai de reconstitution du tableau intersecteur de l'économie soviétique pour 1959, *Revue Economique*, July 1963.

[42] Y. CHERNYAK, An intersector balance for an economic region, *Nauchnye Doklady Vyshei Shkoly, Ekonomicheskie Nauki*, No. 1, 1961.

were derived not from past statistics but from plan estimates, which is certainly no better than a sample: in fact the inter-industry balance mentioned above was based on a sample fifth.

As for the use made of these regional accounts, how much weight should be placed on the statement contained in the report made by Academician Nemchinov to the Geneva Congress in September 1961, when he made a reference to these studies, and said that they could be used to determine optimum location of industry?[43] The statements made to me, some months earlier, by the same man, when he underlined the difficulties attendant upon constructing these models, seemed to me less ambitious. The article by Y. Cherniak on these same studies, also indicates that they provide "abundant information for improving the techniques of economic analysis and resolving specific national economic problems", but the whole context clearly shows that it is a matter of increasing available knowledge about the special features of local economic structure, and not so far of deriving unambiguous answers to concrete questions.[44]

In the course of 1962 there was an increase in the amount of work undertaken on these questions; the Academy of Sciences began publication of a series of volumes and collections of articles under the title of *The Use of Mathematical Methods in Economics*,[45] and two other volumes appeared on the same subject, under the direction of Academician Nemchinov.[46] It is not within the scope of the present work to attempt any review of these important contributions; however, in so far as one can judge, they seem to display a constant preoccupation with practical application, although on the whole there is less sophistication than is to be found in similar studies appearing in the West, especially in the United States, and although the emphasis is still noticeably didactic. However, whether or not there is likely to be a more rapid increase in such practical applications than elsewhere is, of course, another question.

---

[43] First international conference on the use of input-output techniques, United Nations, Geneva, September 1961.

[44] *Op. cit.*

[45] *Primenenie matematicheskikh metodov v ekonomike i planirovanii*, published by the Academy of Sciences, 1962.

[46] *Primenenie matematiki v ekonomicheskikh issledovaniyakh*, Sotsekgiz, 1962. Cf. on this question the study by A. NOWICKI, *ISEA*, L, 12, 1963.

The latest information would appear to indicate that, although a considerable effort is at present being made to establish a system for the collection and transmission of data based on the use of computers,[46a] no synthetic model for testing different variants of the major plan objectives seems to have reached an operational stage.

One difficulty which arises constantly in all exercises of this kind, as it does in the investment context, is that of criteria. In contrast to the market economy, where profitability in theory at least can be regarded as a perfectly clear guiding principle, the planned economy is unable to arrive at a single optimizing criterion. For example, speaking of transport, a subject with which he was very familiar, one of the officials whom I met told me that it was feasible to apply either a physical criterion (reduction of the number of ton-kilometres) or a financial one (reduction of transport costs, taking into consideration the difference in costs of traffic for the various transport links). But if the use of both types of criteria should produce conflicting results, there would be no means of knowing which to select. Broadly speaking, it would seem that preference is mostly given in the USSR to physical criteria, if only because of the difficulty of establishing financial criteria. But only relatively simple problems can be dealt with in this way. It seems correct to say that in the present Soviet economy, there is no right answer to the problem of deciding which criterion to employ, and how to judge among several different criteria which may have to be employed simultaneously. This point need not be elaborated further, in view of the many examples already quoted.

We have not discussed here the problem of the overall economic criterion, or the aims of the Soviet economy. Here again, there is no simple conceptual framework within which this can be expressed, as in the market economy, where the generally accepted criterion is maximization of the national income, measured in prices resulting from the interplay of individual preferences. Nevertheless, one official had some interesting points to make on this subject, although they would probably not have been regarded as entirely satisfactory from the econometrist's

---

[46a] V. NEMCHINOV, Socialist economic administration and the planning of production, *Kommunist*, No. 5, 1964.

angle. After recalling that the aim of socialism was the satisfaction of human needs by means of constantly expanding material production, he advanced the following three principles: (a) the
volume of the national product must be maximal, its growth
being measured over a period of 10 or 15 years; (b) the volume
of consumption must go up, keeping pace as far as possible with
the increase in the national product; (c) the rate of growth must
be maintained.

According to my informant, the object of planning was to
ensure optimal inter-relationship of these three principles and,
more specifically, the optimal inter-relationship of accumulation
and consumption; however, no objective definition of this aim
appears to be possible, and history has shown that these principles may be conflicting. On the other hand, the objection that
production is badly estimated because of the arbitrary nature of
the price system seemed to him ill-founded, since there was a
certain *de facto* relationship between receipts and expenditures.

THE OVERALL EFFICIENCY OF THE ECONOMY

There is a further question, relating not to the effectiveness of
any single investment, but to the effectiveness of all the investments in the Soviet economy. This brings us back to the problem
of growth which we discussed at the beginning of this chapter.
Can it be said that, as a result of the way in which investment has
been directed in the Soviet Union, and of the large proportion of
available resources which has been devoted to investment, growth
has been more rapid than would otherwise have been the case
given more traditional methods?

This is a commonly held belief outside the Soviet Union. It
may even be said to have given rise to the view of the Soviet
economic effort which is most widespread both among the experts and the general public. The rate of growth which has been
achieved is attributed above all to the fact that Soviet citizens,
voluntarily or otherwise, "tightened their belts", or in other
words accepted a lower level of consumption in order to ensure
a high rate of investment; the investment effort, in turn, was directed primarily towards the directly productive sectors, especially
industry and, more specifically, towards heavy industry, that is,

iron and steel and machinery. Conversely, investments which might give rise to a greater degree of comfort or amenity were sacrificed; thus there are a lot of doctors and medical services, a lot of teachers and students, but there are relatively few hospitals, and the schools are overcrowded.

As a result of this investment policy, the growth in the national product, for a given volume of investment, is high, which means that the relationship between capital and output, in other words the "capital/output ratio", or capital coefficient, is low.

Some of the economists who have attempted an overall examination of this ratio did in fact come to the conclusion that it appeared lower than in other countries, and this view was reflected not only in the United States[47] but also in the USSR, where T. Khachaturov wrote on similar lines.[48] The question was also discussed in France, in connection with investment policy in recent years.[49]

How much truth is there in this view? Firstly, there is no doubt that the volume of resources devoted to investment is the prime factor in economic growth, and that economic growth in the USSR is high. But if, on the other hand, the Soviet economy could obtain from a similar volume of investment a rate of growth which is higher than it is elsewhere, by virtue of the particular direction given to these investments, it is clear that many of the reservations or objections which are made about the efficiency of Soviet economic system would lose a great deal of their validity.

In fact the statistical problems attendant upon assessing the capital/output ratio are such that it is difficult to make any confident pronouncement in this domain. Measurement of the growth of the national product or income, which we shall be discussing briefly in the conclusion, is already difficult enough *per se*. Measurement of the relevant volume of investments is possibly even more difficult, given that for such a comparison only net

[47] See study by N. KAPLAN, in *Soviet Economic Growth* (ed. A. BERGSON), Row & Petersen, 1953.

[48] T. KHACHATUROV, The creation of the material and technical basis of communism, and methods of increasing the efficiency of investments, *Vopr. Ekon.*, No. 4, 1961.

[49] J. BERNARD, Investissements et stratégie économique en URSS, *Revue économique*, January 1961.

investment should be considered, after deduction of an amount for depreciation which correctly corresponds to capital consumption and, as we know, the depreciation allowances in the Soviet Union are very low.

Recent studies, particularly in relation to the period of the first five-year plans, have cast some doubt on the view that the effect of the Soviet method is to keep capital expenditure to a minimum. Thus, Granick has shown that the effort made during the first two five-year plans was mainly one of setting up new production units, which mostly worked one rather than two or three shifts — which would have been a means of economizing investment resources — and manufactured a very limited range of products. This approach facilitates the training of manpower in the factory, but is in fact very expensive in capital. "The main effect of Soviet investment was not so much physical output, but much more the creation of an industrial labour force."[50]

Soviet economists themselves are not at all sure that investment costs in the Soviet Union are as low as they could be. During recent years, they have, for instance, deplored the fact that, despite the well-known lack of luxury building, building costs accounted for a far higher proportion of industrial investment than in the United States, while investment outlay on machinery was conversely much lower. Such a statement would scarcely bear out the argument that the capital coefficient is low. However, there is no doubt a greater emphasis in the USSR on the setting up of new factories, as opposed to modernization of existing ones, than there is in the United States, and this, together with under-evaluation of the cost of machinery, robs the above comparison of its validity.

In the absence of any conclusive statistical evidence, it can only be said here that there is no metaphysical reason why one country should continue to invest at a lower rate than another and still achieve the same results. Such a situation may be feasible in the short term, provided that those sectors where the capital rate is high, for example, building, agriculture or transport, can be temporarily neglected; for some years now the USSR has been endeavouring to make up for its relative backwardness

[50] D. GRANICK, Papers and Proceedings, *American Economic Review*, p. 156, May 1962.

in these sectors, and in addition, as T. Khachaturov points out, it also faces the task of developing the eastern regions and exploiting the poorer iron ore deposits, which requires a great deal of investment.

The low capital/output ratio might also be a consequence of the relative abundance of manpower, which meant that for a long time it was possible to disregard those auxiliary forms of equipment which would be considered essential in other countries, and to go in for the "extensive" type of investment which does not call for much scrapping of out-of-date equipment; but even if one does not subscribe to the view sometimes held that the USSR has now entered upon a period of relative manpower scarcity, the actual progress of the Soviet economy and the needs of "productivity" would themselves dictate a much more intensive approach. Or again, the situation might be explained as a result of the borrowing of techniques which have been perfected in other countries, which obviates the need for the appropriate research effort; but by very reason of the progress which the USSR has made, this way will be increasingly closed. Yet another explanation might lie in greater managerial efficiency, for example the creation of large-scale production units employing only the most advanced techniques, or in the individual quality of personnel and labour, and of the techniques used. But in the light of the many instances afforded us, it is clear that, although the USSR may in certain sectors have the advantage of scale, this advantage is outweighed by too many drawbacks of various kinds, and too many policy errors or organizational weaknesses, and Soviet industrial management cannot on balance be said to be superior, or even equal to that of other countries.

However, with the passage of time, and the general speeding up of technical progress, it may well be that the capital/output ratio will tend to decline in the USSR, as seems to be the case in other countries. As we have seen, most of the changes in progress in the Soviet economy would seem, in the course of the next few years, to be leading to an increase rather than to a fall in this ratio. Nevertheless, most of those with whom I discussed the matter stated that they did not foresee such an increase; the 1960–80 plan clearly makes the opposite assumption.

CONCLUSION

ALTHOUGH the purpose of this book is a study of the Soviet planning system, rather than an analysis of the country's economic situation and its problems, something should be said in conclusion about the present achievements of the Soviet economy and its future prospects. A planning system, like any other economic experiment, should after all be judged by its results.

WILL THE USSR OVERTAKE THE WEST?

It is a fact that, particularly since the XXIInd Party Congress in October 1961, there has been increasing emphasis in Soviet propaganda on economic competition with the developed countries. Paradoxically, as the "transition to communism" supposedly draws nearer, the doctrine seems to lose much of its original appeal; at present the promise of plenty, and of a standard of living for the people which will be "higher than that of any capitalist country", attract much more attention than the shape and nature of the future communist society. Since the Congress, there has perhaps from time to time been less insistence on this particular aspect, either because of economic difficulties, or for other reasons,[1] but for all that the question has lost none of its immediate interest. How much truth is there, then, in the statement that the USSR will soon have outdistanced all its "capitalist" rivals in output per head and in standard of living?

The brief indications which follow are based on comparisons drawn not so much from the United States, the principal target of the Soviet challenge, as from the countries of western Europe, and France in particular, which occupies a more or less middle

---

[1] This theme recurs frequently. Thus, Academician Arzumanyan referred to "the not too distant future when the Soviet Union will become the world's leading industrial power, with a standard of living second to none". *Pravda*, 24th February 1964.

position among these countries. Our estimates, like the Soviet estimates themselves, are based on extrapolation of recent trends and known plans.

As at 1st January 1963, the population of France was about 47·5 million (normal annual increase with immigration is approximately 1%) while the population of the USSR was over 223 million (annual increase 1·7%) which gives a ratio of roughly 4·7 to 1. Assuming that these rates of increase are constant in the two countries, the ratios should be 4·8 to 1 by the beginning of 1965, and 5 to 1 at the beginning of 1971.

For a start, let us take industrial output. In the present context, we shall confine ourselves to two main physical criteria for assessing a country's industrial output: those of steel and electricity; by so doing, we shall avoid for the moment the problems arising from comparisons of artificial indices. In 1963 both in steel (17·6 as against 80·2 million tons) and in electricity (80·2 as against 412 milliard kWh) French production was still appreciably ahead of production in the USSR, the ratios being 4·4 and 4·1.[1a]

In 1965, according to the original objectives of the seven-year plan, the USSR should produce between 86 and 91 million tons of steel, while France, according to the objectives of the fourth plan, should have a productive capacity of 24·5 and an average production of approximately 23 million tons; basing itself on past growth rates (8–9% per annum) the USSR was to

[1a] Allowance made for differences of definition in the case of electricity output. In France, as in most other countries, output is "measured as it comes out of the plant, after deduction has been made for electricity consumed by the plant's ancillary services and for losses incurred in transforming the electricity within the plant" whereas the figures usually published in the USSR do not deduct power-station consumption, as study of the official statistical yearbook will show; this is also confirmed by the report of the International Union of Electricity Producers. This point is also made by G. Grossman in his study on the validity of Soviet statistics, *Soviet Statistics of Physical Output*, 1959. It is confirmed by NOTKIN, Economic competition at its present stage, *Vopr. Ekon.*, No. 7, 1961: he reduces Soviet production of electricity by about 6% for purposes of comparison with output in Western countries. In 1957 power-station consumption in the USSR amounted to 6·3% of production.

The French fourth plan estimated an average annual increase of 9·6% for 1962–5, as against 8% for the period 1950–60. In 1962 there was an increase of 8·6%. The present Soviet rate of increase is 12%.

exceed its targets and produce some 96 million tons in 1965, but in 1962–63 steel output grew by only 5·1%, and the 1964–5 plan adopted at the beginning of 1964 fixed a target of 91 million tons only for 1965; and even if France does not achieve its original objectives (+7% per annum, against 6% in earlier years, with output stagnant in 1960–3) and actually achieves 21–22 million tons, output *per capita* would still be far higher in France (about 4·4 to 1). In respect of electricity, even if the USSR achieves its objectives in 1965 (500–510 milliard kWh), and at the present rate of growth it does not seem likely that they will be exceeded, and if France produces only 105 milliard kWh instead of the ambitious target of the fourth plan (109·5 milliard kWh), France will still have the advantage in production per head (output ratio of 4·5 to 1).

If one makes the possibly arbitrary but unavoidable assumption that the present growth rates will continue after 1965, it will be seen that the Soviet Union, which has the advantage of higher growth rates but has also a more rapidly expanding population, should reach the French level of production per head in steel and electricity between 1970 and 1975. By the end of the twenty-year plan (1980), the Soviet lead would be fairly modest.

The above calculation was not expressly designed to show an advantage in the case of France. Thus the French population figure made allowance for population returning from Algeria, and the estimated increase was based on the results of past years, and was slightly greater than the official estimate. Similarly, no account was taken of the more rapid growth rate shown by the fourth French plan, in comparison with the third plan. On the Soviet side, we took as our basis the actual output figures of the last few years, disregarding the annual growth rates laid down in the ten- and twenty-year plan (terminal years 1970 and 1980) which are higher than those of the seven-year plan 1959–65 up to 1970, but much lower from 1970 to 1980 (annual rates for steel 8·3% and 5·6%).

Moreover, it should be noted that a comparison based on steel and electricity (in which both western Germany and the UK are very appreciably ahead of France) on the whole favours the USSR: although the latter is clearly ahead of France in output *per capita* of fuel (coal, oil and gas) and probably also of machine-tools, armaments and certain scientific products, France still leads in all the consumer industries, the main agricultural products (with the exception of wheat and potatoes), chemicals, cement and even most types of equipment. A comparison between the two countries product by product showed that, in most sectors, France has during recent years maintained an appreciable lead.[2]

We turn now to the question of living standards. Despite the substantial progress which has been made in the Soviet Union in this respect, the French standard of living is still markedly superior. None of my colleagues at the Institute of Economics of the Soviet Academy of Sciences appeared to doubt this; in fact it was rather taken for granted. Nor, so far as I know, has any Western visitor to the USSR expressed any view to the contrary. The French are better fed than Soviet citizens, better dressed, and very much better housed — despite all the drawbacks which undoubtedly exist in France — they are able to acquire a much wider range of consumer goods, they enjoy longer holidays (it should be recalled that most Soviet citizens are still only entitled to a fortnight's holiday with pay per annum whereas in France 3 weeks' paid holiday is legal and 4 weeks has become standard practice in many collective contracts). In addition they are better catered for in respect of entertainment (Soviet "Palaces of Culture" and clubs, however interesting, do not appear adequate to the needs of the public and cinemas are relatively few in number). However, in the matter of medical care or social services, short of making a special survey of this question, there is nothing to indicate that France is better served than the USSR, where these things are virtually free; and the various educational facilities, which are available to all, are undoubtedly superior in the USSR. One must also take into account the fact that, since 1960–61, the actual working week seems to have been shorter in the USSR (41 hours) than it is in France, and is now closer to the American standard week (about 40 hours). It may well be, too, that social security payments and allowances are, on the whole, better in the USSR.

An analysis made by B. Apremont[3] showed that average real wages, for all socio-professional groups and all sectors of activity, in France in 1959 were about 50 % higher than average Soviet

[2] See, for example, J. MOCH, Le vrai combat Est-Ouest; la course au mieux-être, Revue de défense nationale, February 1961.

[3] Economie et Humanisme, January–February 1961.

wages. This analysis does not take into account indirect earnings (social services and family allowances) nor does it take into account, when comparing the relative purchasing power of money, the much more widespread use of private transport in France. The analysis also excludes, for the most part, the agricultural populations of both countries, and all non wage-earners in the case of France.

Some experts are of the opinion that the difference in favour of France may be even greater. The majority of foreigners who have spent a long time in the USSR are even convinced that the real difference in living standards is in fact much greater than that indicated by the above figures. It certainly would appear to be so if, as a means of comparison, one takes, for example, the *stock* of consumer goods owned by households in the two countries. The amount of clothing, furniture, linen and household articles, consumer durables (electrical household appliances, etc.) and private means of transport possessed by families, and also the amount of private savings, are, per head of the population, much greater in France than in the USSR, where there seems to be a paucity of private possessions of all kinds. The advantage on the side of the French is such that the real standard of living, which depends on the distribution of such stock as well as on the annual income, will manifestly continue to be superior to that of the USSR for a long time to come, whatever happens. Public works, particularly in the countryside (roads, wells and water supply, rural electrification, public buildings) are also of a much higher standard in France. We shall, however, leave aside this very important aspect, in order to confine the argument to the area actually covered by Soviet claims, and deal with the question of the annual income (either direct or indirect) of the population, or rather with the purchasing power of this income.

If allowance is made for all indirect (or social) benefits, it can be argued that the basis of the above comparison does on the whole favour the French. Let us assume that this is so, if only for the sake of argument, and let us say that in 1960 or 1961, the average income of wage-earners in France may have been as much as a third higher than that of Soviet workers (Soviet incomes are taken as being equal to three quarters of French incomes). It is also assumed that these figures are valid for the population as a whole.

I should like to quote here, without necessarily subscribing to them, some observations made on this subject by the officials whom I met at the Institute of Economics. One of these was to the effect that a comparison based on the wages of industrial workers alone, rather than the wages of workers in general, would be more favourable to the USSR: and indeed, whereas industrial workers in the West tend to be less well paid than other wage-earners, the position seems to be reversed in the USSR (my informants quoted in this connection a ratio of 0·75 in the United States as against 1·05 in the USSR).

Another point made was that in the USSR the incomes of persons employed in agriculture were, in relation to the incomes of the rest of the population, not so low as is usually assumed by Western observers; they were said to be about three-fifths or two-thirds of other incomes, a proportion which is fairly close to the French figure.

Thus, there might be some justification for regarding the figures given for wage-earners as valid for the population as a whole.

Soviet economists occasionally refer to studies carried out in the Soviet Union, which are said to be based on an average cross index (American consumption estimated in Soviet prices and Soviet consumption estimated in American prices). These studies are said to have shown that the Soviet standard of living was then 42–45% of the American standard of living. But so far neither France nor her neighbours can claim a standard of living which is more than half that of the Americans; and yet, as we have already said, our informants freely admitted that the Soviet standard of living was still appreciably lower than that of northwest Europe.[4]

On the basis of the figures quoted here, what likelihood is there that the USSR will either equal or surpass French living standards within the next few years?

In order to answer this question, let us examine the various plan objectives insofar as they relate to the standard of living.

---

[4] According to recent American figures, the level of individual incomes in the USA (including social services) in 1958 was exactly three times the Soviet level, viz. 1423 as against 475 dollars. (See J. C. CHAPMAN in *Economic trends in the Soviet Union*, by A. BERGSON and S. KUZNETS, Harvard University Press, 1963.)

The Soviet seven-year plan for 1959–65 provides for an average annual increase in the national income (or product) of 7·3 %; allowing for the increase in population, this would mean an increase in output *per capita* of about 5·5% per annum. This objective appears to take into account benefits in kind, which are to increase more rapidly than wages. However, let us assume that these are not entirely accounted for, and take a slightly higher figure. Moreover, the plan might be over-fulfilled, as is sometimes the case, although not to such a great extent as in industrial output, particularly because of backwardness in the agricultural sector. For the years 1959, 1960, 1961, 1962 and 1963, the increase in the Soviet national income was, respectively 8%, 8%, 7%, 6% and 4·5% (and 7% in 1964) which, up until 1963, corresponded almost exactly with plan objectives. However, during the four years 1958–62, the incomes of workers went up (according to official estimates) by only 18%, or an average of 4·3% per annum. In 1962 with the rise in retail prices, the increase was only 3%, and barely 2% in the case of incomes of workers and employees alone.[5] No figure is available at present for 1963 (according to what we are told by visitors to the USSR, there may even have been a drop in the standard of living in the months following the steep rise in food prices in June 1962). In respect of the ten years prior to 1961, we should note the observations made by Mikoyan, in his speech at the XXIInd Congress, to the effect that the real income of Soviet workers, peasants and employees had increased by 60% since 1950, which would mean an average annual increase of 4·4%, in the case of 1960, or 4·8% in the case of 1961.

However, the 1961–80 plan provides for a much greater increase in real incomes than is laid down in the seven-year plan; about 6·5% per annum for the period 1961–70, and about 6% overall for the period 1961–80. But there is no indication of how far this plan is in fact operational, or in other words linked with annual plans. At all events, an increase in real incomes of 6% per annum would be regarded as the maximum.

What are the corresponding French objectives? The fourth plan, (1962–5) allowed for an average annual increase in the na-

---

[5] Let us note that from the evidence of recent visitors, it is even necessary, since the sharp rise in the price of food products, to speak of a fall in the standard of living; but mishaps of this sort also happen elsewhere.

tional product of 5·5%, and for an increase of 5·3% in private consumption, which means an increase in the individual standard of living *(per capita)* of 4·5%. These are, as we know, very ambitious targets, being above the level of achievement of the past ten years (which was slightly less than 5% for the national product and 4% for the standard of living) and also above the objectives for the coming period recently adopted by OECD (an annual increase in production of 4·2%). However, results for the first two years would so far seem to have justified the more ambitious figures (an average annual increase, from 1961 to 1963, of 5·8% in the gross domestic product, and 6·4% in domestic consumption which, allowing for the exceptional rise in the population during this period, means an average increase in private consumption of about 4·4%).

Instead of an increase in the standard of living of 5 or 5·5% in the case of the USSR, and 4·5% in the case of France, which is based on the official figures for the respective current plans, we shall, in order to take account of the Soviet twenty-year plan, make the most favourable assumption from the Soviet point of view (although this is certainly over-optimistic, especially in view of the achievements of the past few years in the two countries) and assume an increase of 6% and 4% respectively.

At this rate, and assuming that the Soviet living standard was already three-quarters that of the French by 1961, it will be seen that the gap between the two countries may not be bridged by 1965, or even in ten years' time, that is by 1971. By the latter date, the Soviet standard of living would have increased from 75 to 91% of the French, having risen by 79%, while the rise in the French living standard would be 48%.

Thus, on the above assumptions, the Soviet living standard will not have overtaken that of the French within the next ten years. As for the future beyond this date, it would be unrealistic to make any prophecies at this stage. We can, however, add a few observations.

There is, for example, the complex question of housing. The Soviet authorities freely admit the desperate nature of the present situation — how indeed could they do otherwise in front of their fellow citizens? — but insist that it is in process of being put right. In his speech to his electors in Moscow, N. S. Khrushchev emphasized that, during the previous four years, a total of

315 million square metres of living space, or roughly 9 million properly equipped apartments, had been built in the industrial towns and cities.[6] On the same occasion, Demichev, first secretary of the Moscow Party Committee, stated that by 1967 "we will have cured the housing shortage. Those families who are now on waiting lists, and those at present living in barracks or cellars will have been rehoused in well-appointed houses."[7] According to other statements, the crowding of several families into one apartment would more or less be a thing of the past in a few years' time, and each family would have its own dwelling. According to statistics which were given world-wide circulation, and were, in particular, published by several international organizations, the USSR headed the list for all the countries of western Europe, and even the entire world, in the number of housing units built per head of the population (12·4 per 1000 in 1961, as against France 7). Impressive figures of the increase in the amount of housing available are published in the statistical yearbooks.

However, it should be noted that the total area of housing built in 1961, 1962 and 1963 (80, 81 and 77 million square metres respectively) falls short of the objectives of the seven-year plan (which called for almost 100 million square metres per annum), and seems to relate only to dwellings of an average area of 35 square metres. In France the number of houses built in those same years has remained static at around 310–320,000 (336,000 in 1963) but there has been an increase of 5% in their average size and the average floor space of each is 67 square metres, which represents a total of about 22 million square metres of living space. If in addition one takes into account the 500,000 dwellings put up in the Soviet countryside (only 400,000 in 1963), assuming that these are of the same size as the others, it will be seen that the ratio of house-building between the two countries more or less corresponds to the population ratio (1 to 4·7).

Furthermore, the increase in urban housing (22% from the end of 1958 to the end of 1961, or almost 7% per annum) is counteracted in the USSR by an increase of 3·5% per annum in the urban population. (In France the increase in the urban population was of the order of 1·8% per annum between 1954 and

[6] *Pravda*, 17th March 1962.
[7] *Pravda*, 3rd March 1962.

1962.) Assuming that the amount of space available per head of the population in the USSR, which was approximately 8 square metres in 1958, reached something like 9 square metres in 1962, it is clear that, at this rate, the figure could still only be about 12 square metres in ten years' time, which is certainly a very modest figure on which to lay claim to an advanced standard of living. It should be borne in mind that, in the United States, the amount of living space per head of the population is some 32 square metres.[8] In France the census figures give only the number of rooms per head of the population (approximately 1 per inhabitant), but the corresponding figure for living space must be in the region of 20 square metres per head, or even more; a report by a delegation from the Economic Council which visited the USSR some years ago even quoted a figure of 24 square metres for France.[9]

It is, of course, evident that there is a greater degree of inequality in the distribution of housing in Western countries than there is in the USSR: it should also be noted that in this respect — nor is it the only one — Soviet statistics are much more explicit than French ones. Be that as it may, the difference in the amount of housing available in the USSR as compared with other countries is such that the families of Soviet workers are clearly worse off in this respect than their counterparts elsewhere, and will obviously continue to be so for some time to come.

For an example drawn from outside France, we turn to west Germany. A comparative study of living standards in west Germany and the USSR has shown that by 1965, private consumption in the USSR, according to the objectives of the seven-year plan, will in certain sectors have come close to the German level of 1959 (for example, in the pattern of food consumption, and level of consumption of textiles and footwear) but in many other sectors (consumer durables) will still be far short of this level.[10] Since the west German economy is by no means static,

[8] L. TURGEON, US *Congress Reports (Comparison of US and Soviet economies)*, October 1959. It should be pointed out that, according to this author, consumption *per capita* in the USSR has risen by 5% per annum during the past few years.

[9] Quoted by G. GRIGOROFF, Population et logement en URSS, *Population*, June 1958.

[10] M. E. RUBAN, Private consumption in the USSR: changes in the assortment of goods, 1940–1959, *Soviet Studies*, Glasgow, January 1962.

it follows that it will be a long time yet before the Soviet standard of living catches up with the German one, if it does. German and French living standards are usually regarded as being roughly comparable (although French households are appreciably behind in the matter of domestic electrical appliances). However, the above study shows that, in volume of textile consumption and volume and composition of the food budget, the USSR is at present on a par with, or ahead of, countries such as Italy or Japan—countries which, it is true, have a much more temperate climate and which, moreover, have been showing a particularly rapid rate of growth in production; as we know, the Japanese rate of growth has for some years now been very markedly in advance of the Soviet rate.

Since neither France nor the other countries of western Europe have claimed that by 1972 they will have reached or surpassed the present American standard of living, to say nothing of the probable 1972 standard, there seems indeed to be little likelihood of the Soviet Union's doing so.

So far, we have not touched upon the question of the validity of Soviet statistics and indices.

This is a less controversial subject than it used to be. The indices of Soviet production and income calculated by Western statisticians at present differ only very slightly from the official Soviet figures; I met at least one Soviet statistician in Moscow who told me that "given the basis and the assumptions on which these exercises were undertaken", calculations by American statisticians for the pre-war or post-war period could be regarded as correct.

Many of the reservations made by Western economists have lost much of their validity since Soviet indices were given a more recent weighting (1955 at present); however, according to some authors, the fact that value of production is measured in terms of gross value (or turnover) instead of value added, as in the West, does still distort the growth figure by as much as 10 or 20%. On industrial production, the work of the American statisticians Kaplan and Moorsteen has produced a figure of 9·5% for the average annual rate of growth for the period 1950–55 (as against 13·2% according to the official index) and a figure of 8·6% for the period 1955–8 (official index 10·5%).[11] Soviet sources confirm

[11] However, the more recent index calculated by R. V. GREENSLADE and P. WALLACE gives a higher figure: 10·1% per annum between 1950 and 1955,

a corresponding divergence in recent years between the figures for gross value and value added. According to the studies carried out by Abram Bergson and the Harvard team, during the period 1950–5 the national income increased on an average by 7·3–8·3% per annum (as against 11·4% given in the official index), and by very slightly less in the three following years.[12]

In France calculations by J.–M. Collette showed an annual rate of growth in the Soviet national product of 8·8% for the period 1950–7 (as against an official index of 10·6%); this particular exercise was based on an original definition of national income, but the recalculation rests on a less complete product coverage than that used by American scholars, although this is not necessarily a disadvantage.[13]

It seems clear that the period 1952–8 was one of maximum growth for the Soviet national income. Whereas it would be true to say that, at the time of the first five-year plans, the only sector which showed any appreciable growth was heavy industry, with possibly in addition the activities of what Soviet statisticians describe as non-productive sectors such as education and the health service, while the consumer industries, housing and agriculture were in a state of semi-stagnation, or even recession, progress now is general. Since 1958, however, there has been a slowing down in the rate of progress. The growth in industrial production remains steady, but has slowed down (+8·5% in 1963, +4·1% in 1964), and growth in agriculture is at a standstill.

It should be made clear that the achievement by the USSR of what is undoubtedly a more rapid increase in production and living standards than that of many other countries has not been due to increased productivity alone. It may well be that in many sectors, and even for agriculture as a whole, or industry as a whole, the increase in productivity in recent years has been as rapid in France as it has been in the USSR (it should be borne in

and 8·7% per annum between 1955 and 1961 (an average of only 6·2% for 1960 and 1961). *Dimensions of Soviet Economic Power*, Joint Economic Committee, Congress of the United States, 10th–11th December 1962, 185–744 pp.

[12] A. BERGSON, *The real national income of Soviet Russia since 1928*, Harvard University Press, 1961, 472 pp.

[13] J. M. COLLETTE, Le taux de croissance du revenu national soviétique, *ISEA*, G, No. 12, November 1961.

mind that up until recent years the volume of the working population in France has either been static or slightly on the decrease). The overall increase in growth is also due to a transfer of the working population from low-productivity sectors (particularly agriculture) to other sectors. This gives the USSR an additional

TABLE VIII

Growth of Industrial Production in the USSR

INDICES	1913–28 (1913= 100)	1928–55 (1928 = 100)		1955–61 (1955= 100)	1961–62 (1961 = 100)	1962–63 (1962= 100)
Official index	132	2067		179	109	108
G. W. Nutter (National Bureau of Economic Research)	102	608		146		
Kaplan-Moorsteen (Rand)		583				
Greenslade-Wallace				165		
ANNUAL GROWTH RATES		1928–40	1950–55	1955–61	1961–62	1962–63
Official index		17%	13·2%	10·2%	9%	8%
Hodgman		13%	9·6%			
G. W. Nutter		8·9%	9·5%	6·5%		
Greenslade-Wallace			10·1%	8·7%		

advantage, since the amount of the population engaged in agriculture is still very considerable, but the advantage can only be a temporary one.

TABLE IX

Growth of Agricultural Production in the USSR

INDICES	1913–50 (1913=100)	1958	1959	1960 (1950=100)	1961	1962
Official index*	140	156	156	160	165	167
D. Gale Johnson**	97	166	166			
J. W. Willett***		157	148	154	162	

* *SSSR v tsyfrakh*, 1962, p. 29.
** A BERGSON and S. KUZNETS *op. cit.*
*** Joint Economic Committee, December, 1962, *op. cit.*

Thus, from 1958 to 1962, agricultural production increased by 7% (Official figures), whereas the seven-year plan provided for an increase of 70% from 1958 to 1965. And yet 1962 was a year of comparatively good harvests. No index for agricultural production in 1963 has been published, but production in 1963 was undoubtedly much lower than in 1962. Vegetable production, particularly grain, was very bad, and animal production also showed a drop.

The foregoing analysis is in no way intended to cast doubt on the validity and, above all, the extent of the Soviet achievement; when all is said and done, the present acceleration in the rate of economic growth in many of the non-socialist countries owes much to the Soviet example and to Soviet competition. Nor has it at any time been intended to argue that classification between countries is bound to remain more or less unchanged. But it must be emphasized that the rapid changes which are a feature of our time and which the Soviet plans, for their part, are intended to induce, are not a phenomenon confined to countries with one particular type of economic system. Evolution can work in many different ways and take unexpected turns. Expressed in the most moderate terms, the conclusion would seem to be that, whatever successes may be achieved by the Soviet Union and its system, these could never be such as to detract from the significance of other countries' experiences in this respect.

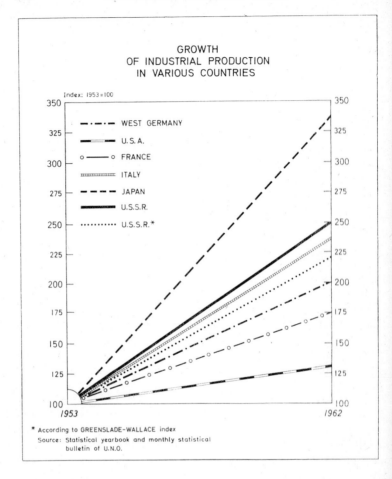

GROWTH
OF INDUSTRIAL PRODUCTION
IN VARIOUS COUNTRIES

Index: 1953 = 100

- – · – · WEST GERMANY
- ━━━━ U.S.A.
- o ━━━━ o FRANCE
- ▭▭▭▭ ITALY
- – – – JAPAN
- ━━━━ U.S.S.R.
- · · · · · · U.S.S.R.*

1953   1962

* According to GREENSLADE-WALLACE index
Source: Statistical yearbook and monthly statistical
       bulletin of U.N.O.

Furthermore, it should be noted that, in relation to the level of production which has been reached, the standard of living in the Soviet Union would still appear to be on the low side. Nor can this be entirely attributed to the speeding up in the rate of investment required to maintain the growth rate, or to the fact that the production effort is directed away from the consumer industries. The factors of climate and distance also represent a serious handicap. Thus, according to one unofficial source, the rigorous conditions of the Russian winter account for 6% of the national income (extra cost of house building, public works, transport and heating, which may well be as much as a third higher than similar costs in a more temperate climate). Yet another obstacle in the way of efficient organization of the economy is the geographical nature of this immense and sparsely populated country; its economically important regions are being increasingly extended lengthwise as the eastern territories are opened up, and it enjoys few advantages in the matter of sea communications; despite its wealth in natural resources and the potentialities of a vast market, there are many geographical factors which place it at a disadvantage.

But, at the risk of repeating ourselves, we must again emphasize that such comments as we have made about the economic situation in the USSR are in no way intended as a reflection upon the tremendous progress which has been achieved in the last fifty years. If we have said comparatively little about this progress, it is precisely because it is an indisputable fact. There is a world of difference between the Russia of Tsarist times, which had scarcely any modern industries, and was largely dependent on the outside world, and the great industrial power which is now the USSR. Those who have underestimated Russia or the Soviet Union in the past have always had reason to regret it; and it is significant that, with the passage of time, the findings of American statisticians on the USSR tend to become less and less patronizing in tone.[14]

ATTITUDES VIS-À-VIS THE SOVIET EXPERIENCE AND LESSONS OF THE LATTER

Is it good, is it bad? Whatever one's approach to the problem of the Soviet economy and the Soviet society, there comes a moment when Diderot's question is bound to arise, and one finds

[14] G. Warren Nutter estimated that Soviet industrial production in 1955 was little more than a fifth of American production (*The growth of industrial production in the Soviet Union*, Princeton University Press, 1962, pp. 249 *et seq.*). A. Tarn and R. W. Campbell recently suggested that by 1960 the proportion had risen to three-quarters, although it must be said that this estimate has been widely disputed. (A comparison of US and Soviet industrial output, *American Economic Review*, September 1962.) The Soviet central statistical office itself put the figure at 63% for 1962.

oneself in the position of having to make a value judgement. Indeed, insofar as Soviet society and the communist movement refuse to see themselves as a moment in human evolution, and to accept in their turn the historical and dialectical judgements which they apply to other societies, but persist in regarding themselves as the finished product of History, it is inevitable that attitudes towards them should be correspondingly clear cut.

If, then, we are to forsake factual appreciation for the value judgement, we should at least indicate the basis on which such judgements are to be made. Our standard is that of European thought, as it is defined for example in the following words by Paul Hazard: "What is Europe? Thought which is insatiable. Merciless towards itself, it unrelentingly pursues two ends: one is happiness; the other, dearer still to it, and more indispensable, is the quest for truth."[15]

Looking at Soviet society as depicted by its present-day spokesmen, one finds that it simultaneously fulfils this criterion, and fails to fulfil it. There is no doubt that it is striving, and striving unremittingly, for perfection. But this search has nothing in common with the quest for truth which we have just described. Self-criticism is the rule in the USSR, but it applies only in matters of detail; to question the superiority of Soviet society, and of its achievements and aspirations, is to run the risk of heresy. Even the content of the ideological key-words, in the economic or any other context, may not be questioned. Thus, whatever one's feelings may be about the efforts and the achievements of this society, whatever the admiration one feels for it, one cannot endorse a régime whose effort to build a new world has so far been characterized by such a wholesale and deliberate disregard for the rules of intellectual integrity which the West, for its part, prizes even above success itself.

In the light of the foregoing analysis, what lesson can be learned about the attitude which might best be adopted towards the USSR and its system? Matters of foreign policy certainly do not fall within the scope of the present work; but there are a certain number of economists or other specialists who do make contact

---

[15] P. HAZARD, *La pensée européenne au XVIIIe siècle*, vol. II, p. 261 (conclusion), Boivin, Paris, 1946.

with their opposite numbers in the East, and for them the problem of attitudes is a very practical one. If we can prove to our Soviet colleagues that we understand Soviet society and the Soviet economy, and our own economy, both in the way in which they understand them, and in our own way, without being overwhelmed in such a confrontation, it should in the long run be possible to exert some influence. It is in increasing understanding that our hope for playing a positive role mainly lies; indeed a great respect is paid by Russians or Soviet citizens precisely to intellectual activity and, of course, despite all the obstacles, frontiers now are no longer impenetrable.

It may be argued that the foregoing observations do not allow for the fact that the Soviet political and economic system is in a state of evolution, and that the days of Stalin are past; or that on every hand there is mounting evidence of conflict and dissension, so that it is increasingly unrealistic to think in terms of a monolithic socialist "bloc". Leaving aside the purely political aspects, and expressing the problem in its most general terms, what then is the likelihood of a convergence between the economic systems of East and West?

In support of the theory sometimes advanced[16] that a degree of convergence is taking place, certain authors point to the growing importance, in Western economies, of the area of supervision or State intervention, and the adoption of policies of economic development, occasionally in the form of national "plans"; in the Eastern economies, they instance the reintroduction, or the growing importance, of the role of money and prices, the use of economic calculation, interest or something akin to it, and much other evidence, already mentioned here, of a certain "Westernization" of the economy. It may well be that if both systems are pursuing the same aim of increasing production of material goods and raising the standard of living, and are at the same time engaged in a rational study of each other's methods, they will in the end come to resemble one another.

However, the question which we must answer is whether there is not some factor which would prevent the taking up of a posi-

[16] See particularly G. F. KENNAN, Disengagement revisited, *Foreign Affairs*, p. 191, January 1959, and J. TINBERGEN, Do communist and free economies show a converging pattern? *Soviet Studies*, April 1961.

tion halfway between the two systems, or would at least render such a course inadvisable. From the technical point of view, Professor Tinbergen tends to the belief that this is not so; in his view, there is no logical reason why some middle course between liberalism and planning should not be practicable.[17]

However, there is the further possibility that political or socio-political considerations may compel the maintenance of doctrinal purity. Clearly, the economic changes which are taking place in the Soviet Union cannot fail to influence the opinions of its citizens. There will be an ever-increasing number of people in the USSR who enjoy a comparatively satisfactory standard of living and who will be sufficiently well-informed to make judgements about the outside world which the latter will accept as being well-balanced. None the less, ideological obstacles will still persist. The ideological doctrine which equates the building of a better society with the fight against capitalism, and which is still widely accepted today, is a powerful bond in Soviet society. To admit the possibility of a convergence between the two systems would be to abandon this belief, and would amount to revisionism in the strict sense of the word, with all the risks it implies. It is therefore probable that any such tendency will continue to be opposed for a long time to come, unless events should take some at present unforeseeable turn.

Is it, however, possible that the developments of the last few years (the ideological dispute with China, the closer understanding with the USA) could constitute just such an event, which might precipitate a change? We can do little more than formulate the question, noting, however, that, open society or not (cf. on this point Chapter III) the effort to ensure that the content of ideological pronouncements remains unalloyed still goes on, and is as marked as ever.[18]

---

[17] *Op. cit.*

[18] It will, however, be noted that it is nowadays permissible for a Marxist to hold the view that "contradictions" may exist even in a socialist State between the state of productive forces and the institutional "superstructure". It is, of course, added that this is no more than a superficial divergence resulting from the errors of the comrades responsible or from other immediate causes which can subsequently be put right, whereas in a capitalist State the divergence is fundamental and ineradicable (for example, contradictions in the system of private property, etc.). Nevertheless, one wonders if this does not foreshadow a further change of attitude.

There is yet another dividing line between the two systems. It is possible to conceive of a planning system which would allow enterprises a greater degree of autonomy, and in which prices and resource allocations would be calculated in such a way as to take account of existing scarcities and pressures. But in the capitalist economies this equilibrium is achieved through the operation of the market, which affords organized financial interests a power which must for a long time to come be withheld by régimes for whom the planned economy is first and foremost a social, political (and moral) revolution. The age of the computer and of global models, and also changes in the concept of the enterprise and of the relationship between the public and the private sector, may bring about a convergence between our two systems. But who can say whether this time is imminent or not?

Leaving aside the question of attitudes *vis-à-vis* the Soviet Union, we turn now to the economic lessons which may be learned from the Soviet experience.

Firstly, there is a valuable lesson to be learned from the method of economic analysis by global quantities, the search for economic equilibrium, and the impetus given by State investment which is directed towards predetermined objectives. There is nothing new in all this: but it should be remembered that all these features of the Soviet economy, which may be found in various forms of planning today, and which, despite resistance, are being increasingly employed, have been a part of the Soviet planning system from the very beginning. Nor need anything more be said about the lessons to be learned from the policy of "investment in human beings" which is aimed at raising the standard of education and training.

Not all the lessons, of course, are of the positive kind. One of the most important and striking examples is the difficulty of operating a centralized system of economic control in which information and orders must be relayed throughout the chain of command. It is doubtless essential that, in a country of the size of the USSR, the system should operate both sectorally and territorially. But when it is used for the transmission not of directives and general policy statements but of detailed orders, which moreover are liable to constant revision and which even in the most routine context may provoke repercussions throughout the entire system, then its advantages are probably offset by its disadvantages. Likewise, as we have seen, the present organization of the Soviet economy makes it very difficult to determine which choices are the most profitable from an economic point of view.

It may be argued that the Soviet economic structure is in fact already adapted for the time when use can be made, at the macro-economic level, of the powerful techniques of economic analysis and calculation which have developed during recent years. But apart from the fact that little is to be gained from being in advance of one's time — after all, a proposal has just been mooted for the building of a complete mathematical model of the chemical reactions which take place inside a blast furnace, and this, one would have thought, is conceptually a much simpler task than the construction of a global economic model — there are grounds for doubt that the present Soviet structure is the best or the least ill-adapted to future needs. The ideal organization would appear to be one in which there were fewer command points to obstruct the flow of information, and more organs for the supervision and processing of information which would function outside the hierarchy, and would be able to communicate their findings to the appropriate authority with the minimum of delay. It may well be that this type of organization is more likely to take shape in a liberal society than in Soviet society.

Nevertheless, such developments as have so far taken place in the USSR along these lines are not without significance, particularly the sovnarkhoz experiment in territorial administration which was carried out in the period between 1957 and 1962. Something can also be learned from the Soviet experience on the important question of economic stimulus and initiative, particularly in relation to territorial units, and this is of particular relevance for those areas or regions which are classified as underdeveloped.

Another field in which, paradoxically, the USSR has produced few techniques worthy of imitation is that of forecasting. Something has already been said in these pages on this question, and a final word should be added about "norms" or standards, which are widely used in Soviet planning. Those which are most commonly used, and which are certainly worthy of study, are technical norms (for example, the relationship between the production of one article and the consumption of another) and also, occasionally, demographic or financial norms. But it would appear that very little attention is paid in the USSR, or less at any rate than in the USA, to what are sometimes known as "environmental control forms". These may be described as the size and the organization of a particular activity or service which will be optimal both from the point of view of investment cost, running costs, and the usefulness and efficiency of the service in question. One might give as an example the arrangement of work points in industry or offices, definition of the characteristics of residential areas, dwellings or commercial centres, the study of traffic problems, the organization of hospitals and schools.

These questions, which figure increasingly in the domain of planning, are certainly studied in the USSR. But, so far as we know, they do not up till now appear to have been studied in their totality, which requires that choices be made while taking into account a great number of different points of view. There is no indication that any large-scale research has been undertaken in the USSR into human needs and the environmental organization which is best adapted to satisfying them; the twenty-year plan (1960–80) certainly does not seem to have been conceived on the basis of such research, and it would appear that the authorities have done no more than draw up a production plan based on a few fairly superficial normative estimates of consumption needs (for example, data relating to food consumption, or the consumption of textiles, etc.).

But one of the most interesting aspects of the Soviet experience, and the one which will continue to excite interest, is their desire to influence the development of human society along certain well-defined lines. Under the general heading of the "transition to communism", this development will be characterized, in particular, by a certain number of so-called "social" benefits which will be conferred on the population, many of them free of charge: according to the twenty-year plan, these benefits will by 1980 constitute about 50 % of the total income of the population.

This trend is not without its parallel in other countries. There was, for example, the introduction of the health service in Great Britain by the post-war Labour government, this service being financed entirely out of the Budget. Similarly, in France, the fourth plan envisaged, between 1961 and 1965, an increase of

50% in the equipment for communal services—which as is known are seldom fully paid for by their users—against an increase of only 31% in total investments. In fact the text of the fourth plan expressly states that "this choice should be viewed as the beginnings of a shift in the structure of final consumption". Thus, if the criterion is not only ownership of the means of production but also State intervention in the domain of private consumption, it would seem that the economic systems of western Europe have been injected with a certain amount of socialism. The question is, how much farther should one go in this direction?

The provision of consumer goods or services for the population either free of charge, or at rates below their cost, which is merely a step in the same direction, can be regarded as State interference with the structure of private expenditure. By itself, it does not, of course, give rise to any increase in the volume of resources available for consumption. The advantage of such a policy is that it affords an opportunity for influencing consumption along what are considered to be socially desirable lines (such as, for example, giving priority to education at the expense of consumption of spirits). It might also be possible to economize in operational costs by providing the service in question free of charge (for instance, this proposal was made in connection with the Paris métro by Jules Moch when he was in office).

But there are many drawbacks in implementing a policy of this kind, which explains why such proposals are not taken very far:

(1) The elimination of charges means an increase in taxation, and in liberal societies, the maximum rate of taxation is soon reached;

(2) A system in which enterprises do not have their own revenues, and consequently have no direct incentive to increase them, but are dependent on the State Budget, would appear to be less conducive to rational management than a system in which enterprises, nationalized or otherwise, enjoy full financial autonomy;

(3) A move towards free distribution would be accompanied by an equalization of incomes, and a reduction or elimination of work incentives, which no economic system can at present afford to dispense with.

(4) Lastly, an attempt to influence the structure of consumption in a way which may not accord with the choice of the consumers may be regarded as undemocratic, at least if it is carried too far.

These arguments, especially the last one, are frequently used in the United States, where there is a deep distrust of anything resembling "creeping socialism". But it may well be that in the USSR too they deter the authorities from carrying this policy as far as they might wish.

In western Europe the same considerations are also relevant. However, it should be noted—and this is a point in which Europe differs from the United States—that the desire to exert some influence on the structure of expenditure and on social behaviour is shared, especially in France, by many intellectuals, administrators and politicians of the most widely differing viewpoints. In this sense it is true to say that, for a great many Frenchmen, the whole concept of the plan goes far beyond the mere idea of material progress. However, it should be added that since, for the most part, the French share a common liberal outlook, it would not seem to them either practicable or desirable to persist in any policy which ran counter to the natural tendencies of the population.

It may be that the contradiction between these two statements is more apparent than real. And indeed, it ceases to exist if one assumes that, by influencing the pattern of consumption in a particular way, one is doing no more than anticipating the course of future demand; in many cases, such as for example education and culture, for which there is a growing and more widespread need everywhere, this would seem to be a very reasonable assumption.

There is one final question, which in the present context we can do no more than touch upon very briefly: from the point of view of one of those countries which were formerly described as backward or under-developed, and which are nowadays referred to as the developing countries, what lessons can or should be learned from the Soviet example? They are increasingly inclined towards the idea of planning and like to regard themselves as socialist, but also show a growing determination to steer clear of any political alignment. In fact they are prepared to borrow ideas and models simultaneously from the right or the left, from Moscow, Paris or anywhere else.

The striking thing is the amount of necessary correctives which one must apply, even when one is making every effort to avoid any suggestion of anti-Soviet propaganda. Firstly, it should be noted that, according to Soviet statements, there can be no middle course. "No proper planning is possible without nationalization of the means of production," as, for instance, the Soviet delegates to the United Nations committee for industrial development said in New York in May 1963. But in the case of a small country which has few resources of its own, and cannot, as most frequently happens, count on much co-operation from its neighbours, unless an attempt is made at some form of federal union, nationalization must almost infallibly lead to a flight of foreign capital and enterprise which can ill be spared; if this is not to happen, two things are necessary, and these are seldom found together: sound financial organization and reliable State technical bodies. Even leaving aside this particular problem, the fact of isolation from world markets, which results from an authoritarian system of planning which is not based on profitability and prices, makes it almost impossible to carry out any reliable calculations on the benefits of external trade; and this is a matter of prime importance for any small and relatively under-developed country whose national product, or income, unlike that of the USSR, is very largely dependent on external trade. It should further be noted that Soviet practice has no particular formula to offer for determining optimal resource allocation as between different sectors and enterprises, or for making forecasts on which such allocation is based; at least the techniques which are at present being perfected in Western economies would seem to be better adapted to solving this particular problem, whether they are employed within the framework of a planning system or otherwise.

Soviet propagandists frequently quote Marxist analysis in support of the affirmation that no industrialization or economic development is possible unless priority is given to the building of industries which produce the means of production (or, to use a less committed phrase, producer goods). This statement is, admittedly, very largely true, and the principle is applied now even in the most advanced countries, in respect of their more backward industrial regions. But although the principle is sound, the idea is usually expressed in a misleading way, and countries which seek to put it into practice in their planning may find that the attendant difficulties outweigh the advantages. To say that, in practice, all economically developed countries have a producer goods industry is to state the obvious; but to declare that a country which, in economic terms, is only just learning to walk must first, in order to progress, set up its own producer goods industry, is quite a different proposition. This would be to assume a causal link (as of one factor giving rise to another) in place of what may simply be a link between two concomitant factors (since the two factors in question are both dependent on a third factor). In practical terms it must be said that the building up of heavy industry, regardless of cost, may in certain cases prove a dangerous strain on limited financial and human resources, and jeopardize promising developments in other fields without necessarily providing the goods which the country really needs. (The principle underlying the demand for a producer goods industry is based on the *interdependence* between the various branches of the economy which is to be found in well-balanced economies. The industries to which it is important to give priority are those which, because of their natural advantages and the privileged position which they occupy as suppliers or eventual customers of other branches, can act as *growth industries* or basic industries in the economic development of the country as a whole; often, though not necessarily always, these happen to be producer goods industries.)

For a long time, this argument had such powerful support that those who were reluctant to endorse it wholeheartedly were liable to be accused of putting obstacles in the way of underdeveloped countries who were anxious to become industrialized. And it must be admitted that these accusations were not always ill-founded. But it appears that the Soviet doctrine that any country which is bent on industrialization must first build up its heavy industry is undergoing some change, certainly insofar as concerns the East European COMECON countries, over which the USSR continues to exercise *de facto* authority. Indeed, what has happened is that the USSR, possibly in an effort to match the success of the West European Common Market, but no doubt also to further its own efforts at enterprise specialization, has demanded increased specialization within the COMECON countries, with the result that at least one country, Rumania, which had been trying to build up its heavy industry, protested against a change in policy which would unfairly penalize it. Whatever the outcome of this episode, it may well mean that one of the features of the Soviet formula is less permanent (or less genuine) than had hitherto been supposed.

Moreover, this problem seems to have figured in the Sino–Soviet dispute in May 1963. The Soviet demand for increased economic specialization at international level was denounced by the Chinese as evidence of self-centred nationalism. The maintenance of a state of economic inequality among the socialist countries also calls forth accusations of "embourgeoisement", to which the Soviet reply is a mocking reference to the idea that "if a nation walks in birch-bark shoes and eats cabbage soup out of the same bowl, that is communism", while living well is capitalism. It sounds like Danton, faced with Robespierre, calling for a Republic of Cockaigne.

And yet, on the positive side, there is undoubtedly something to be learned from the Soviet experience so far as the developing countries are concerned. The first lesson (and what an important one it is) is the affirmation and the proof, that when conditions allow (but is this not, so to speak, always the case?) and when a country's efforts are concentrated on the task, rapid economic progress is possible. In this connection, it would be hard to overestimate the influence which the Soviet example has had on the rest of the world. To take a specific instance, there is the great attention which has been paid to the utilization of natural resources, despite the fact that this cannot be claimed as an original feature of the Soviet economic system. The individual responsibility which is placed on local cadres is in effect a means of stimulating local initiative, and it is this initiative which is so often lacking in many parts of the world, and which is nevertheless one of the essential prerequisites for sustained economic development. The importance attached to education and technical training is another feature of the Soviet system which is very conducive to economic growth, so much so that it has been said that even the errors and failures of the USSR have served a useful purpose by involving the training and employment of large numbers of technical cadres.

There is one last feature of the Soviet formula whose virtues are less immediately apparent, and that is the circumstances in which, as we know, the funds essential for the country's economic development were obtained by putting pressure on the peasants; a few countries whose economic development came at a later stage seem to have achieved the same results at less cost, although conditions in the Soviet Union, in terms of resources and population, were by no means unfavourable; however, there is no simple answer to this particular problem, as present-day examples abundantly illustrate.

POSTSCRIPT*

In September–October 1965 a major overhaul of the Soviet planning system again took place. This was announced in a speech by A. N. Kosygin, Chairman of the Council of Ministers, at the central committee (*Pravda*, 28th September) and was finalized in a series of laws of 2nd October (*Pravda*, 3rd October). The most important single piece of news in this reform is the suppression of the sovnarkhozy and the re-establishment of the industrial ministries, thus bringing to an end the experiment begun in 1957. However, the situation of the enterprise is also abundantly dealt with.

Since the middle of 1964 it is indeed on this topic, the degree of autonomy of the enterprise, the tasks it has to perform and the indicators employed to measure its success, that attention continues, as previously, to be focused.

One of the ways to interpret the current of discussion which followed Prof. E. Liberman's much-talked of proposal of September 1962 is that it was leading away from command planning towards some form of what is known elsewhere as "planification souple" (of which "indicative planning" is not exactly the right equivalent), in which influence is exerted indirectly on the enterprise through such instruments as prices, subsidies, credit and fiscal policy. If indeed, as was proposed by Liberman, the compulsory Plan indices coming down to the enterprise are to be very much reduced in number, if the enterprise is to take its decisions according to its own interest and seek as large a profit as possible and if, as a rule, the enterprise is to enjoy as much autonomy as the system will allow, then it is clear that the planning system will have undergone a complete change in character.

Of course the selection of profit as the only criterion was strongly opposed by Soviet economic officials from the start, as it was felt that this would lead to doing away with the whole administrative system of planning. This attitude continued in the follow-

* This note was added in proof by the author.

ing period. The selection of profit as a unique or overall index was opposed by the majority of economists assembled by the USSR Academy of Sciences on 25–26th September 1962 and 7–8th January 1963, and was not endorsed by the Party conference of November 1962. In *Pravda* of 17th August 1964, Academician Trapeznikov gave his approval to those in favour of the use of profit. But in November 1964, as previously, a joint meeting of two committees of the Academy of Sciences, those for economic calculation and stimulation of production and for the improvement of planning methods and of plan indices, attended by some 300 Soviet economists, did not approve the selection of profit as the basic index:

> The majority of speakers held the view that it is not yet possible to express in an objective way in a unique index all the multifarious economic process and the peculiarities of the various sectors of production. A "universal index", as practice shows, cannot lead to the results looked for. It is indispensable to have a system of indicators which would reflect accurately the basic results of the productive activity of the enterprises and stimulate their work.[1]

When analysing some 600 letters received in answer to the Trapeznikov theses, *Pravda* published only a few which openly approved of profit as a unique index.[2]

Nevertheless, this did not prevent the major Soviet economists from presenting numerous proposals for reform of the planning set-up. Reference has already been made to the late Academician Nemchinov's suggestions.[3] These were that the system of administrative orders ought to be replaced by regulation of an economic character, and that central planning should be made compatible with some form of self-direction of the enterprise. Delivery orders passed by the planning organization to the enterprise would ensure the necessary links, while a system of state trading organizations would replace the inefficient material and technical supply system. The sum of these orders would replace the annual plans. The enterprises would be linked together, and to the plan-

---

[1] *Vopr. Ekon.*, No. 3, 1965. See E. Zaleski, *Les tendances réformistes dans la planification soviétique*, Mont Pelerin Society, 15th general meeting, Stresa, 3–8 September 1965, and forthcoming revised manuscript on the same subject (to be published by the Thomas Jefferson Center, University of Virginia).

[2] *Pravda*, 17th February 1965.

[3] *Kommunist*, No. 5, 1964.

ning organizations, through a network of contractual obligations. In the same way, L. Kantorovich spoke in favour of the replacement of administrative orders by the use of economic instruments: "the economic assessment obtained during the preparation of the centralized plan, with the help of mathematical optimization, will allow really decentralized economic decisions and the identification of the profitability of the enterprise with the global economic profitability."[1] V. Novozhilov thought similarly that an optimum organization of the economy could be obtained only through the co-operation of a strong centre and self-managed basic units.[2] E. Liberman himself again entered the discussion by stating that what is important is in fact much more the autonomy of the enterprise in the establishing of its plan than the number of indices it has to deal with,[3] while L. A. Vaag advocated the establishment of the plan of all enterprises, including quantity, product mix and delivery dates, on the basis of contracts between clients and suppliers.[4]

It probably appeared that the discussion about the plan indices was to some extent unrealistic, since the number of forms of all kinds that the enterprise had to fill in and pass on up, and the information required, was in any case clearly on the increase and not on the decrease, as is shown by all the available information. Whatever the use made of these data at a higher level, the desire to present a favourable picture on as many counts as possible cannot but influence the managers' behaviour. But the important problem, as all authors involved in the discussion agreed, is the degree to which the enterprise may take decisions and make direct arrangements with other firms or organizations, and whether or not it depends on the supply of materials and equipment organization.

To test these ideas, a very important experiment was that of "direct links" *(priamye svyazi)*, which was initiated on 1st July 1964 in the clothing enterprises *Bolshevichka* and *Mayak*. The production plans of these enterprises and the prices of their products were to be established on the basis of the contracts

---

[1] *Vopr. Ekon.*, No. 9,1964.

[2] *Ekonomicheskaya Gazeta*, 20th June 1964.

[3] *Pravda*, 20th September 1964.

[4] L. Vaag. *Sovershenstvovat ekonomicheskie metody upravleniya narodnym khozyaistvom*, Moscow, 1964

made with department stores and shops. The enterprises were free to choose their suppliers and could themselves determine all other elements of their plan (but not, apparently, their investments).

Although it was later subject to several limitations (reduction of the number of stores which could enter into contracts with the pilot-enterprises), the experiment was declared positive. For instance, it was reported that, whereas unsold inventories piled up in other enterprises of the clothing industry, this did not happen in the pilot enterprises, where the profit position improved and it was possible to increase the wages.[1] The experiment was not stopped by the fall of N. S. Khrushchev in October 1964. In early 1965 the sovnarkhoz of the USSR adopted a programme of extension of the "direct links" policy.[2] As from 1st April 1965 this was to be applied to 128 enterprises in the fields of textiles, clothing, leather and fur, and to the corresponding retailers. As from 1st July 1965 a further extension was to take place so that, in the four sectors involved, from 18 to 30% of the enterprises were to be covered. From press reports it would seem that this programme was implemented. At the same time, several authors were pressing for a generalization of the experiment in the field of consumer goods and some of them in the field of producer goods also.

However, in Kosygin's report of 27th September, reference to the "direct links" is made in two lines only, which could mean, if not a negative decision on this policy, at any rate, for the moment at least, a slow-down in its extension.

As already mentioned, in so far as they are of immediate application, the reforms of September–October 1965 deal mainly with the administration of planning. This may be interpreted as a sign that, for the Soviet leaders, there is no trend towards a reduction of the planning apparatus. This interpretation finds support in a leader which appeared in *Ekonomicheskaya Gazeta* only two weeks before the central committee meeting and which stated that it was wrong to suppose that, with a higher degree of development, administrative planning would be superseded, provided, of course, that the latter respected the economic laws.

The reforms include the suppression of the Supreme Council for the National Economy (which in fact never seems to have

[1] See Henri Pierre, *Le Monde*, 20-21st June 1965.
[2] *Ekonomicheskaya Gazeta*, 20th January 1965.

played a really important role in its two years of existence) and the Sovnarkhoz of the USSR. Gosplan remains in charge of current and long-term plans. Most of the industrial state committees are promoted to the rank of ministries (of which 22 are of federal rank and 25 of union republican rank). Their powers, much increased, include "implementing plans, directing production and solving the problems of technological policy, of material and technical supplies, of financing, of employment and wages"[1].

The planning of supplies is placed under the authority of Gosplan. However, after the suppression of the Sovnarkhoz of the USSR, the general directorates for inter-republican supplies are now subordinated to the State committee for material and technical supply *(Gossnab)*, of which V. Dymshits, former chairman of the sovnarkhoz of the USSR, becomes chairman. This committee is nominally in charge only of the execution of the supply plans, which are prepared by Gosplan, but in this field experience has been that organization and current management are more important than plan elaboration.

Whereas the suppression of the sovnarkhoz of the USSR takes place immediately, that of the regional and of the republican sovnarkhozy is to come into force only at the beginning of 1966. The 1966 plan is still being prepared on the basis of the sovnarkhozy. This suppression does not, of course, come as a complete surprise. Many criticisms had been heard of the sovnarkhozy when their number was reduced by more than half in 1962, and the fall of N. S. Khrushchev — whose personal creation they were to such an extent — must have given a new impetus to those who had never completely approved of the institution. A. Kosygin states that it has been proved that the territorial principle was wrong, as it was interfering with the principle of specialization by sector, which is seen as a necessity of modern technology. The powers of the sovnarkhozy are transferred to the industrial ministries. It is claimed that this suppression does not mean that the pre-1957 situation is re-established as it was.

A. Kosygin stresses that the republican Gosplans are to have wide powers but the definition of these given in the new laws is not very clear. In November 1962 they were expressly given

Pravda, 28th September 1965.

power to plan and control the execution of the plans for the whole economy of their republic. For that part of industry which is at present under the supervision of union ministries, their power will now be limited to the putting forward of suggestions, which looks like a curtailment of their authority; however, it may be that, prior to the present reforms, their power of control over some of the industries existing in their republic was more formal than real. Mention has since been made of the necessity of maintaining strong local (i.e. at the oblast level) committees having a view on all the economic activity of their territory. At another level, what is to happen to the co-ordination councils of the great economic regions appears uncertain.

Outside of the reorganization of the planning set-up, the September–October reforms contain few decisions for immediate application, but include numerous declarations of intentions. All of these point to a further liberalization of the economy.

The most important single change decided by the central committee is the adoption of the principle of payment for the capital put at the disposal of the enterprise. At present, as has been seen, most of the funds for investment are given by the Budget as subsidies, i.e. free of charge. The assessment levied on the enterprises' profit in favour of the Budget bears in fact no relation to the amount of capital provided. It has now been announced that these subsidies will be replaced by long-term credits, first for existing enterprises and investment, and then for new investment having a fast recoupment period (which means that it is recognized as necessary to maintain subsidies to finance for heavy investment). As regards working funds, a great part of these is already provided in the form of interest-bearing credits, but these will be generalized. The assessment on the credits (i.e. the interest paid) will be made according to norms fixed for several years ahead.

This change, which affects one of the fundamental characteristics of the Soviet economy, is intended to induce enterprises to make a better use of the funds put at their disposal. However, it appears that, because of the imperfection of the wholesale prices, an immediate application of this new policy is possible only in the sectors where a turnover tax is levied at present. A reform of wholesale prices is promised by A. Kosygin, but not before 1967–8. In fact this means that another reform of the price system has been postponed, as has been continuously the case since 1962. Previously, the definitive date for the adoption of a new set of prices had been given as 1st January, 1966. When the price reforms become effective and the above-mentioned change is in force, most of the Budget resources will come from payments on investment or working capital and from assessments on profits.[1]

Another reform announced by A. Kosygin, this one to be made effective in 1966, is the generalization in all enterprises of a "fund to provide material incentives for workers" and a "fund for social and cultural activity and for housing". These would receive a fraction of the profits of the enterprises. This fraction would be determined in relation to the amount and rate of profit and the level of output. It seems that, in the assessment of enterprise efficiency, value of sales might have precedence over the output[2] — a measure which could be far-reaching. Polish sources commenting on these reforms indicate also that realized (i.e. sold) production is to replace gross output as index of the enterprise's achievement. Another possibility which must be noted in this connection would be the replacement of the gross output index by the "normed processing value" (i. e. more or less "value added") index, which has already been mentioned,[3] and which, according to the same source, is already in force at an experimental stage.[4]

A change which would also be of importance if confirmed, concerns depreciation. Previously depreciation funds were paid to the State (or more exactly to the sovnarkhozy). Information is given that these, together with part of the profits, would now be retained by the enterprise and placed in a fund for the development of production.[5]

Other points of importance in A. Kosygin's report, either as declarations of intentions or actual reforms, include:

A reduction of the number of indicès which are imposed on the enterprises. The greatest changes are in the field

---

[1] V. Garbuzov, *Ekonomicheskaya Gazeta*, 13th October 1965.
[2] *Pravda*, 10th October 1965
[3] See above, p. 170.
[4] Z. Lewandowicz in *Zycie gospodarcze* (Economic life), Warsaw, 24th October 1965.
[5] *Ibid.*

of labour, where the only index retained is the total wages fund. The indices for labour productivity, employment in the main groups and total employment, and average wage in each group, will no longer be in force. This will mean a much freer management for the enterprise.

A reduction in the classification of products included in the plans: in that field, however, it may be, as experience has shown, that this is not much more than a wish, as control organizations, when working on an enterprise plan and evaluating its results, have a built-in tendency to take account also of non-compulsory indices.

An increase in the importance of economic contracts (together with an extension of the "direct links" experiment) and in the legal guarantees enjoyed by the enterprises. The gradual replacement of administrative distribution of resources by wholesale trade.

It is also mentioned that plans ought to be stable, that unnecessary regulations ought to be abolished, etc. Other information adds that what was said at the September plenum concerns agriculture as well as industry and that pilot sovkhozy could be created, which would have complete autonomy in fixing their production targets as well as in their financial management.[1]

All these reforms or proposed reforms are moving in the direction of a greater liberalization of the economy. Some of these affect characteristics of the Soviet economy which, especially in our analysis of the conditions of equilibrium, have appeared to have strategic importance.

The picture is not completely clear, however. In one sense, the suppression of the close supervision of the sovnarkhozy and the reestablishment of the strong but distant control of the industrial ministries might be a necessary requisite for giving greater autonomy to the enterprise. The new system, it is repeatedly stressed, is not a return to the pre-1957 system. However, what is also striking is first, the slowness with which the reforms that affect the enterprise are to be implemented; this certainly could be a sign of seriousness more than of anything else, and the present leaders probably want to guard against the semi-impro-

[1] Pr. Obolenski, director of the Central Research Institute on rural economy, quoted in *Le Monde*, 3rd November 1965.

visation of their predecessors. But what is also striking is the limiting effect that the controls which have been retained may have on the new reforms. Let us look only at the list of the indices which, according to A. Kosygin's speech, are still to be imposed on the enterprise: amount of realized production, main classification of production, wages fund, profits and profitability per rouble of productive fund, payments to the Budget and receipts from this source, amount of centralized investments and new capacities to be developed, new techniques to be adopted, material and technical supply indicators. The payment for capital, or the stimulation of the enterprise by its retentio of profit, were conceived by such men as Nemchinov or Vaag as instruments for an efficient management of a really autonomous enterprise. If these reforms are introduced at the same time as a strong administrative planning apparatus is kept, they may in fact not be of much help for the enterprise management (and may even at times appear as no more than an additional burden).

BIBLIOGRAPHY

(French and English works only)

BOOKS

BARANSKI, *Géographie économique de l'URSS* (Ed. en langues étrangères), Moscou, 1956, 390 pp.

BERGSON, A., *The Real National Income of Soviet Russia since 1928*, Harvard University Press, 1961, 472 pp.

BERGSON, A. and KUZNETS, S., *Economic Trends in Soviet Union*, Harvard University Press, 1963.

BERLINER, J. S., *Factory and Manager in the USSR*, Harvard University Press, 1957.

BETTELHEIM, Ch., *Problèmes théoriques et pratiques de la planification*, Presses Universitaires de France, 1946.

BETTELHEIM, Ch. *L'économie soviétique*, Sirey, 1950, 472 pp.

BOBROWSKI, C., *Formation du système soviétique de planification*, Mouton, The Hague, Paris, 1956.

BORDAZ, R., *La nouvelle économie soviétique*, Grasset, 1960.

BRUHAT, J., *Histoire de l'URSS*, collection "Que sais-je?" Presses Universitaires de France, Paris, 1958.

CAMPBELL, R. W., *Accounting in Soviet Planning and Management*, Harvard University Press, 1963.

CHAMBRE, H., *Le marxisme en Union soviétique* (ed. DU SEUIL), Paris, 1955.

CHAMBRE, H., *L'aménagement du territoire en URSS*, Mouton, The Hague, Paris, 1959.

CHOMBART DE LAUWE, J., *Les paysans soviétiques* (ed. DU SEUIL), Paris, 1961.

COLLETTE, J. M., *Le taux de croissance du revenu national soviétique*, Cahiers de l'ISEA, suppl. No. 119, November 1961, série G, No. 12.

DOBB, M., *Soviet Economic Development since 1917*, Routledge & Kegan Paul, London, 1948.

DUMONT, RENÉ, *Kolkhoz, Sovkhoz et le problématique communisme*, Editions du Seuil, Paris, 1963.

FAINSOD, M., *How Russia is Ruled*, Harvard University Press, 1953.

GRANICK, D., *The Red Executive*, Doubleday, New York, 1960.

GREYFIE DE BELLECOMBE, L., *Les conventions collectives de travail en Union soviétique*, Mouton, The Hague, Paris, 1958.

GROSSMAN, G., *Soviet Statistics of Physical Output of Industrial Commodities: their Computation and Quality*, National Bureau of Economic Research, 1959.

HUNTER, H., *Transports in the USSR*, Harvard University Press, 1957.

JASNY, N., *Soviet Industrialization 1928-1952*, The University of Chicago Press, 1961.

KAPLAN, I. M. and MOORSTEEN, H., *Indexes of Soviet Industrial Output*, Rand R. M 2 495, and *American Economic Review*, June 1960.

LAVIGNE, M. L., *Le capital dans l'économie soviétique* (ed. SEDES), Paris, 1961.

MARCUSE, H., *Soviet Marxism, A Critical Analysis*, Columbia University Press, New York, 1958.

NOVE, A., *The Soviet Economy, An Introduction*, Allen & Unwin, London, 1961.

NUTTER, G. W., *Growth of Industrial Production in the Soviet Union*, Princeton University Press, 1962.

PROKOPOVICZ, S. N., *Histoire économique de l'URSS* Paris, 1952.

SHABAD, T., *Geography of the USSR, A regional survey*, Columbia University Press, New York, 1951.

SPULBER, N., *The Soviet Economy, Structure, Principles, Problems*, Norton, 1962.

STRUMILIN, *La Planification en URSS*, Editions sociales, Paris, 1947.

VOLPER, I., *L'industrie de l'abondance* (Ed. en langues étrangères), Moscou, 1958.

DE WITT, N., *Education and Professional Employment in the USSR*, National Science Foundation, US Government Printing Office, Washington, 1961, 856 pp.

WRONSKI, H., *Le troudoden* (ed. SEDES), Paris, 1956.

ZALESKI, E., *Planification de la croissance et fluctuations économiques en URSS* (ed. SEDES), Paris, 1962.

L'économie soviétique en 1957. Exposés faits à la Semaine d'Etudes sur l'Economie soviétique (Octobre 1957), Institut de Sociologie Solvay, Bruxelles.

Comparisons of US and Soviet Economies, Joint Economic Committee US Congress, 2 vol., October–November 1959.

Dimensions of Soviet Economic Power, Joint Economic Committee, US Congress, December 1962, 185+744 pp.

Les méthodes actuelles de la planification soviétique. Rapport d'une mission d'économistes français. Cahiers de l'Institut de Science économique appliquée, série G, No. 7,

L'édification culturelle en URSS, Recueil statistique (Ed. en langues étrangères), Moscou, 1958.

L'économie nationale de l'URSS, Recueil statistique (Ed. en langues étrangères), Moscou, 1957.

Les progrès du pouvoir soviétique depuis quarante ans (Ed. en langues étrangères), Moscou, 1958.

The Soviet Seven-year Plan, with an introduction by Alec Nove, Phoenix House Ltd., London, 1960.

Soviet Economic Growth, Conditions and Perspectives (ed. A. BERGSON), Row & Petersen, Evanston, Illinois, White Plains, New York, 1953.

Value and Plan, Economic Calculation and Organization in Eastern Europe (ed. G. Grossman), University of California Press, 1960.

MAIN PERIODICALS

Problems of Economics. Full translations of articles in Soviet periodicals, International Arts and Science Press, New York.

Current Digest of Soviet Press (weekly).

Soviet Studies, Glasgow.

Survey, A Journal of Soviet and East European Studies, London.

The Russian Review, Hanover, New Hampshire.

Slavic Review, Seattle, Washington.

Cahiers du monde russe et soviétique, Ecole pratique des Hautes Etudes, Paris.

Cahiers de l'Institut de Science économique appliquée (ISEA), Série G, Paris.

Bulletin du centre d'études des pays de l'Est, Institut Solvay, Université Libre de Bruxelles.

L'URSS et les Pays de L'Est. Revue des Revues, Centre de recherches sur l'URSS et les pays de l'Est, Strasbourg.

La Documentation française, chroniques étrangères: USSR (monthly).

United Nations Organization. Economic Commission for Europe. Quarterly bulletin and annual report.

INDEX

Academy of Sciences 31, 255, 258
Agriculture
  administration of xxii, 22–25, 40, 43, 51, 123, 130–1, 194–5; *see also* Kolkhoz
  population engaged in 41, 193 ff.
  production 276
ALAMPIEV, P. M. 33, 36, 84, 121, 175
ALEXANDER I. 18
Allocation, *see* Supply
Amortization, *see* Depreciation
ANTONOV, O. 163–6
APREMONT, B. 267
Artels (co-operatives) 21, 127
Autonomous Soviet Socialist Republic (ASSR) 31, 86

Balances 57, 59, 75, 80–83, 101–4, 223, 257.
BARONE, E. 234
BERGSON, A. 62, 269, 275, 277
BERLINER, J. S. 149, 160, 161
BERNARD, J. 261
BERNARD, Ph. 84
BETTELHEIM, Ch. 60
Birth-rate 44, 202, 206
Blat 161
BLOK, Alexander 50
BOBROVSKI, C. 55
Bonuses, *see* Indicators, success.
BOYARSKI, A. 52, 246, 253
BORDAZ, R. 78, 276
BRUHAT, J. 61

CAMPBELL, R. W. 104, 238, 279
Capital co-efficient 261–3

Capitalism, Western capitalist economies, free enterprise, or market xxi, 13, 46, 58, 63, 165, 221–3, 229–31, 239, 258, 281–3; *see also* Economy, Western; Planning, French; Planning, regional.
CARRÈRE D'ENCAUSSE, H. 39
Cement works, location of 186, 194
Central Asia 39, 204–13; *see also* Regions, eastern
Centralism, democratic, Leninist principle of 20, 38, 69
Centralization xxii, 111–12, 134, 140; *see also* Decentralization
CHAMBRE, H. 31, 35, 46, 70, 74, 181
Choice, freedom of 15; *see also* Demand, role of
Choice of objectives 65, 78, 95–101, 106, 247 ff., *see also* Criteria
CHOMBART DE LAUWE, J. 22
Coal production 99, 228; *see also* Power
Co-existence xxiv, *see also* Competition, peaceful; Ideology
Collective agreements 117
Collective farms, *see* Kolkhoz
Collectivization 57, 64, 109; *see also* Socialist ownership
Collegial principle 39
COLLETTE, J. M. 275
Colonialism 214–16
Combines 177, 181
Comecon 289
COMEY, D. 48
Commissariats, people's 109
Committees, State 29–30
Communism, building of, transition to, 20, 27, 28, 47, 51, 53, 61–62, 100, 264

Communist Party of the Soviet Union (CPSU) 8, 20, 21, 22, 47, 48, 53, 61 ff., 66, 79, 86, 93, 128, 141, 157, 203, 215, 248, 264, 270
Programme 27, 28, 47, 55, 61–62, 194, 217
Role and organization 36–41, 49, 66, 67, 78, 111, 130, 160, 213
Competition, peaceful 14
Complexes, regional 179–86, 210; see also Combines
Computers, use of 93; see also Mathematics; Econometrics.
Concentration of Industry, 42–44
Construction 3–4, 129–30, 200, 204, 211, 271–3
Contracts, commercial 77, 158
Contradictions 282; see also Ideology
Control figures 70, 75, 78
Co-operation, enterprise 146–59.
Co-ordination 85, 87–92, 106, 130, 139 ff., see also Co-operation.
Council, technico-economic, attached to the sovnarkhoz 117–18
Criteria
investment 247–53
location of industry, see Location of Industry
Culture, level of 2–4, 18, 192, 203–4, 213

Decentralization 40, 69, 117, 201 ff., 218.
DELAMOTTE, Y. 113
Demand, role of 96, 99–101, 162, 242, 286
DEMICHEV, P. N. 86, 272
DENIS, H. 60
Demographic factors, see Emigration; Employment; Birth-rate; Urban population.
Depreciation, 51, 52, 238, 239, 262
DIDEROT, D. 279
DIETERLEN, P. 231
Directorates, industrial, by sector 112, 116 ff., 124, 153

Directors of enterprises, 116, 160, 161, 164
Distribution, see Supply
Dnieper commission 145
DOBB, M. 43, 51, 197
DOSTOEVSKI, F. 9
DUDINTSEV, V. 237
DYMSHITS, V. 157, 296

Economic Commission of the Soviet of Nationalities 29, 39, 185
Economic fluctuations 221, 232
Economic regions, large 34–36, 83–86, 145, 158, 177, 202
Econometrics 51, 253–5, 258
Economy, market, see Capitalism
Economy, Western 152, 173
EFIMOV, A. 28, 52, 67, 97, 98, 105, 241, 248
Electricity production 265–6; see also Power
Emigration-Immigration 187, 199–202, 206, 209
Employment,
problems of 41–45, 174, 176, 186–9, 192–5, 199–203, 207–9, 262–3, 276
of women 8, 44, 192
Emulation, socialist 200
Energy, see Power
ENGELS, F. 47, 48, 55, 195
Enterprises, see Co-operation; Directors; Khozrashchot.
Enterprises, satellite 153 ff.
Equality of opportunity 10, 16
Ethnic groups, see Nationalities

FASSIER, R. 74, 76, 81, 82, 96, 101 ff., 106, 122, 137
FEIGIN, I. G. 179, 183, 197
Firms, see Combines
Fluctuations, economic 221, 233; see also Economic
Freedom of choice 13; see also Choice
FURTSEVA, E. A. 203

GALBRAITH, J. K. 62
Gas, natural, use of 177–85, 209, 238, 252
GATOVSKI, L. 58, 59, 237, 247
Goelro Plan 56
GONCHAROV I. A., 11
Gorkom (town committee) 37
Gorsoviet (municipality) 33, 127
Gosbank (State Bank) 30, 145, 223, 226
Gosekonomsoviet (State scientific economic council) 30, 67, 79, 84, 90, 98, 100, 166, 168, 175
Gosplan, republican 31, 71 ff., 82 ff., 92, 93, 114, 122, 128, 132, 138, 141, 142, 158, 188, 189, 256
Gosplan (State planning committee) 30, 35, 39, 67, 69–85, 90–93, 98, 102, 104, 114, 139, 141, 142, 145, 147, 157, 177, 182, 211, 255
Gosstroi 144
GRANICK, D. 42, 65, 262
GROMAN, V. G. 57
GROSSMAN, G. 27, 181, 243, 265
Gubernii, see Provinces

Handicrafts 21; see also Artels
HARDT, J. P. 181
HARROD, R. F. 222
HAZARD, P. 280
History of the Communist Party of the U.S.S.R. 48, 49
HOEFFDING, O. 1113
Housing, see Construction
HUNTER, H. 253

Ideology 16, 27, 46 ff., 96, 111, 280 ff.; see also Marxism–Leninism
ILYICHEV, L. F. 48, 58
Incentive, material, principle of 7, 20, 28, 162 ff
Indicators, success 143, 159 ff., 236
Indices, planning 79–83, 161, 166
Industry
chemical 66, 97, 191, 142
heavy 60, 96, 275
small-scale, administration of 42,

43, 113, 125 ff
Input-output tables 257
Institutes
project-making 144, 177
research 203
Interest, rate of 226, 227, 239, 250, 251
Investments
choice of 50–51, 96, 247–52
financing of 117, 123, 143–5, 211, 224–32
rate of 260–1, 276 ff
Iteration, method of 105

JASNY, N. 57

KAPLAN, N. 261, 274
KASER, M. 40, 71
KENNAN, G. F. 281
KERBLAY, B. 81, 96
KEYNES, J. M. 220, 222
KHACHATUROV, T. 248, 261, 263
Khozrashchot 28
KHRUSHCHEV, N. S. 22, 44, 51, 67, 78, 79, 111–12, 130, 147, 182, 241, 252, 271
KLEIN, L. I. 221
Kolkhoz (markets) 20, 21–24, 37, 43, 130, 193–4, 210–11
KOSYGIN, A. N. 94, 141
KOZLOV, F. 37, 39
Krai (province) 31, 32, 34
KRONROD, YA. 60
KUZNETSOV, A. 10

LANGE, Oskar 167, 227, 234
Large economic regions, see Economic regions, large
LAVIGNE, M. L. 148
Leading links, 105
LENIN, V. I. 47, 48, 55
Leninism, 11; see also Marxism-Leninism; Centralization
LEONTIEF, W. 57, 254
LERNER, A. P. 234
LEVINE, H. S. 74, 78
LIENCOURT, F. de 17

Localism 121 ff., 128, 129
Location of industry, principles of 63 ff., 216–18, 234
LOMAKO, P. 36, 85, 120, 151

Machine-building enterprises, 183, 189
MALENKOV, G. 60
MARCUSE, H. 46
MARCZEWSKI, J. 225
Market economy, see Capitalism
Markets (kolkhoz), see Kolkhoz (markets).
MARX, K. 27, 46–48, 52, 55, 59, 245
Marxism (analysis, dialectics, Marxist doctrine), see Marxism-Leninism
Marxism–Leninism 8, 20–21, 46 ff., 194–5, 217, 222, 233, 244 5, 282, 288; see also Ideology.
MASSÉ, P. 232, 249
Mathematics, use of mathematical techniques in economics 82, 202, 253–260; see also Econometrics; Computers
MERLEAU–PONTY, M. xvii
Ministers, Council of, 29–30, 37, 60, 67, 72–74, 76, 78, 113, 117, 144
Ministries 29, 108–13, 119, 130–1, 142, 144, 147, 164
MISES, L. VON 235
MOCH, J. 267, 286
MOLOTOV, V. 61
Money, role of 20, 27–28
Moscow, growth of 201–2
Motor-cars, production of, 100, 147, 151
MOUSHKELY, M. 118
MSTISLAVSKI, P. 235, 249

NACOU 51
Narkomat, see Commissariat, peoples
Nationalities, questions relating to, 2, 5, 15, 30–32, 39, 192, 196, 204–6, 211–14, 218
Needs of population 99–101, 128, 186; see also Demand
NEKRASSOV, PR. 86
NEMCHINOV, V. 59, 82, 106, 176, 178, 180, 199, 246, 255, 258–9
NEP (New Economic Policy) 27, 56
NIKOLAYEVA, GALINA 237
Nomenklatura, see Product classification
Norms 71, 76, 100, 101–3, 241 ff., 284–5
NOTKIN 265
NOVE, A. 124, 243, 244
NOVIKOV, V. I. 79, 182
NOVOZHILOV, V. 246, 255
NUTTER, G. W. 276, 279

Obkom, (oblast party committee) 37, 86, 92, 177
Oblast
    autonomous 31–32
    provinces 22, 29, 31–32, 33, 86, 125–7, 132, 155, 177, 190–1, 198
Oblispolkom (oblast executive committee) 21, 126
Obsolescence 52, 240
Oil and oil products 97, 239, 252
Okrug (national territories) 31–32
Over-fulfillment of plan objectives 159, 167, 265–6

Parasites, struggle against 199
Party, see Communist Party of the Soviet Union
People's Commissariats, see Commissariats, people's
Plan
    five-year; first, 57, 90–91, 145; fifth: 97, 253; sixth: 66, 97
    seven-year: 66, 78 ff., 90, 194, 265 ff
    1960–80: 66, 79, 99, 266, 270–1
Plans
    current 66
    function of 65
    investment 74, 92, 143–5

Plans *(cont.)*
  long-term 66
  production 74, 92, 104, 141, 160
  supply of materials and equipment,
    see Supply
Planning
  aims of 64, 65; *see also* Criteria
  continuous or uninterrupted 67,
    90, 91
  criteria 64, 104, 259, 260; *see
    also* Priorities
  French, Western, or indicative
    18, 95, 98, 99, 223, 231, 264 ff.,
    285, 286; *see also* Planning,
    regional
  regional (or complex) 83–88,
    106, 107, 172 ff., 216 ff
Plenum, *see* Communist Party of the
  Soviet Union
POLYANSKI, D. 128
Population, urban and rural 41,
  189, 190, 201
Power, problems relating to 99,
  179, 180, 238–9, 252
PRESSAT, R. 97
Prices, role of 20, 27, 101, 169, 170,
  173, 174, 228 ff., 241 ff., 260
Priorities, system of 64, 96 ff., 104,
  122, 141, 232, 252
Product classification 74, 79 ff
Product mix 160, 168
Productivity 4, 208, 275; *see also*
  Technical progress
Profit 20, 28, 161, 225, 226, 235
Programme, *see* Communist Party
  of the Soviet Union
Property, private 20, 22, 25, 26
Provinces 31

Quality of production 161, 164,
  165, 243

Racial groups, *see* Nationalities
Raikom (Raion committee) 37,
  131
Raion (district) 33, 130
Rationality, economic 65, 235, *see
  also* Criteria *and* Choice of
  objectives

Region
  economic 182 ff., *see also* Econo-
    mic regions, large; Raion; Ob-
    last; Krai
  economic administrative, *see* Sov-
    narkhoz
Regions, eastern 1, 3, 5, 22, 120,
  175, 184, 195 ff., 263; *see also*
  Central Asia
Regional policy, *see* Planning, regio-
  nal
Reproduction, expanded 222
Republic
  Russian (RSFSR) 30, 31
  Union 30 ff
Republics, autonomous, *see* Auto-
  nomous Soviet Socialist Repub-
  lic
Reserves 76, 93, 103, 104
RICARDO, D. 245
ROBERT, PH. 257
ROBINSON, JOAN. 60, 223

SHEPILOV, D. 60
SHOLOKHOV, M. 204
Siberia, *see* Regions, eastern
Small-scale industry 42, 113, 125–7;
  see also Industry
Socialism
  laws of 57–60, 235
  nineteenth century 55, 61
Socialist ownership 20
SOPS (Council for the Study of
  Productive Forces) 84, 189
Soviet, Supreme 20, 28, 29
Soviets, local 114, 125–8
Sovkhoz 22, 23, 43, 109, 130, 211
Sovnarkhoz (Council for the nation-
  al economy) 33–35, 37, 70 ff.,
  80, 85 ff., 91 ff., 108–128, 138,
  145 ff
Sovnarkhozy, republican (supersov-
  narkhozy) 85, 92, 125–6, 144,
  158
Specialization in industry 120, 143,
  146–59, 239
SPIRIDONOV, V. J. 93, 158, 177
SPULBER, N. 235

STALIN, J. V. 13, 18, 43, 53, 57, 60, 96, 194, 244, 281
Standard of Living, see Wages
Steel production 184, 195–7, 265–6
Steelworks, location 141, 155, 180–1, 195–7
STOETZEL, J. 113
STRUMILIN, S. 49, 52, 58, 59, 197
Sub-contracting, see Co-operation enterprise
Success indicators, see Indicators, success.
Supply of materials and equipment 74–76, 92–93, 137–43
SUSLOV, A. 47

Tables
  input-output 257
  regional 257–8
TALLEYRAND, Prince DE, 18
Technical progress, effects of 224 ff.; see also Techniques, new
Techniques, new, adoption of 237–8
Tekhpromfinplan (technical-indust-rial-financial plan) 70
Territorial principle 40, 112, 172, 175
Territory, national, see Okrug
TINBERGEN, J. 281
Transformation of nature 218
Transport problems 106, 118–20, 139–40, 163–4, 216, 252–3, 256

Trudoden (work-day unit) 6, 24
Trusts 127, 129, 153

Ukraine, economic problems of 184 ff., 189 ff
Upravlenie, see Directorates
Urals, see Regions, eastern
Urban installations 129–30, 193
Urban population

Valovaya Produktsia (global or gross output) 114, 148, 160, 161, 274
Value, law of 51, 59, 235, 241–7
VEDICHEV, A. 84, 119
VORONOV, G. I. 130

Wages and Standard of Living, 3, 9, 44, 45, 159, 188, 200, 211, 215, 267 ff
WATINE, M. 113, 118
WETTER, G. 46, 52
WITT N. DE 5
Wood, industries 185
WRONSKI, H. 24, 82

ZALESKI, E. 21, 55, 57, 64, 90, 101, 121, 225, 226